Plagiarism

Plagiarism

Alchemy and Remedy
in Higher Education

Bill Marsh

State University of New York Press

Published by
State University of New York Press, Albany

For information, address State University of New York Press,
194 Washington Avenue, Suite 305, Albany, NY 12210-2384

Production by Kelli Williams
Marketing by Michael Campochiaro

Library of Congress Cataloging-in-Publication Data

Marsh, Bill, 1964–
  Plagiarism : alchemy and remedy in higher education / Bill Marsh.
      p. cm.
  Includes bibliographical references and index.
  ISBN-13: 978-0-7914-7037-4 (hardcover : alk. paper)
  ISBN-13: 978-0-7914-7038-1 (pbk. : alk. paper) 1. Plagiarism. I. Title.

PN167.M285   2007
808—dc22

2006021548

10 9 8 7 6 5 4 3 2 1

Contents

Preface

IT IS CUSTOMARY in books about plagiarism to begin with an apology and an immediate retraction. The apology usually goes like this: plagiarism is an old topic, treated to exhaustion elsewhere, and this book cannot, and perhaps dares not, offer anything new. The subsequent retraction, as one might expect, is grounded in the corollary claim that the subject of plagiarism, while certainly well traveled, is nonetheless worthy of further study if only because it continues to nag, plague, and inspire those who take even the slightest peek at its history.

As an author of a book about plagiarism, I hereby issue that apology and its companion retraction. To be sure, *Plagiarism: Alchemy and Remedy in Higher Education* owes much to works that have come before. Even so (and this is the essence of my retraction), I have elected in this book to focus not only on plagiarism per se but also on the ways in which teachers, policy makers, and entrepreneurs have endeavored to manage and remedy the plagiarism problem via an assortment of creative solutions. This emphasis on solutions, I propose, is what makes this book, if not entirely original, at least different from other books about plagiarism.

I approach the topic as both a writer and a teacher of writing. In both domains, I have held an abiding interest in plagiarism—and the related issues of piracy, pastiche, sampling, and intertextuality in artistic practice—throughout my career. I can remember wrestling with these issues as a graduate student teaching composition for the first time. When I first encountered student plagiarism, in an introductory writing course at a large state university, I found myself instantly propelled into unfamiliar territory. In this particular case, the evidence was glaring, the student culpable and contrite, and the punishment uncomplicated: in accordance with university policy, the student received an "F" on the assignment and was denied the option of a rewrite. Future infractions— of which there were none, to my knowledge—would have resulted in stiffer penalties, such as failure in the course and possible expulsion or suspension from the university. At each turn in this process—and I remember this vividly almost twenty years later—I felt remarkably ill-equipped and unprepared. Positioned as I was on the front line in this particular battle between literary propriety and the literary sin known as plagiarism, I had few tools at my disposal, and little knowledge in my storehouse, with which to negotiate those tricky issues—of guilt and innocence, success and failure, right and wrong—which quickly surfaced when I sat down with this student and announced, "There's a problem with your paper."

Since those early teaching experiences, I have continued to explore plagiarism wearing at least two different hats. As a teacher, I have sought to understand not only why students plagiarize and via what methods, but also how those on the receiving end of plagiarized texts go about both recognizing and then managing these particular infractions. As a writer, editor, and small-press publisher I also hold a keen interest in plagiarism as a kind of literary experimentation akin to collage, assemblage, cut-up, and other forms of material repurposing or remediation. In both domains, I have found plagiarism to be a vexing, inspiring, and amusing topic, and one rich with legal, aesthetic, ethical, pedagogical, and even religious implications. This book, then, is in some ways an attempt to reconcile these multiple concerns. In the end, however, I am primarily concerned with plagiarism—and plagiarism detection—in today's institutions of higher learning and particularly in the realm of student writing. In that sense, I return in this book to that moment when I first spotted plagiarism in my student's essay and understood, in a flash, that my job as a writing teacher would be more complicated than I had first imagined.

My aim in writing this book is to add historical and theoretical context to the plagiarism debate, building on the recent work of Howard, Buranen and Roy, Randall, Kewes, and Lunsford. I hope to provide a modified framework for studying the uses to which plagiarism-related rules and conventions are put, particularly in the age of the Internet and computer-mediated communication. In this work I cannot go deeply enough into questions of individual practice— for example, the application of Turnitin.com as an instructional and administrative tool in specific colleges and universities. I opt instead to provide a largely analytical account of plagiarism and plagiarism detection systems and the several techniques arising at different moments in answer to the plagiarism problem. I hope that future research (of my own and others) will test the claims made below against more specific sets of questions centering on writing and research practices, particularly in the composition classroom. In the last chapter, I offer my own understanding of how such projects might proceed and, in addition, suggest alternative methods and modes for teaching research writing in today's institutions of higher learning.

I should add, finally, that this book is the culmination of research that began five years ago at the University of California at San Diego. For its support of this research, I would like to thank the university and the Department of Communication, and in particular the many people whose inspiration, encouragement, and loving kindness helped sustain my efforts. I would like to extend a special thanks to my adviser and mentor, Valerie Hartouni, as well as all others who helped along the way, especially Robert Horwitz, Brian Goldfarb, Linda Brodkey, Bud Mehan, and Susan Leigh Star. I would also like to thank Gayle Aruta, Bea Velasco, Jamie Lloyd, and Judy Wertin for their vivifying good humor and generous help in times of need. I thank as well my friends and colleagues, in particular Ricardo Guthrie and J. R. Osborn, whose focused critiques and artful suggestions kept me honest and on track throughout. And I thank my daughters, Maya and Zazil, for their love, their laughter, and their well-placed notes and reminders.

Finally, I would like to thank Octavia Davis, my partner in literary crime. This book, first and foremost, is dedicated to you.

Acknowledgments

AN EARLIER VERSION of "Turnitin.com and the Scriptural Enterprise of Plagiarism Detection" (in chapter 7) was published in *Computers and Composition* 21:4 (2004): 427–38. Reprinted with permission from Elsevier.

Introduction

Understanding Plagiarism

THIS BOOK EXAMINES an old problem—plagiarism—as well as a range of techniques and technologies introduced over the years in an effort to solve it. I should begin by pointing out that what I have termed the "problem" of plagiarism tends to arise, and thus tends to be treated (identified, punished, cured, even encouraged), differently in different domains. Plagiarism infractions in most U.S. colleges and universities, for example, will likely elicit different reactions than related crimes perpetrated by, say, top-selling popular historians or avant-garde novelists. Nonetheless, the terms of the debate, and even the treatment of the perpetrator, may at times turn out to be the same. I begin, then, by suggesting that plagiarism continues to draw the attention of scholars and educators in part because the problem, while often dismissed as a simple matter of textual misuse, betrays a range of complexities not easily managed via simple, straightforward solutions.

Plagiarism often shows up under different names: misappropriation, faulty citation, copyright infringement, literary theft, imitation, cheating, cribbing, and stealing, to name a few. Sometimes described as an affront to traditional values of authorship—and a threat to long-standing economic values attached to authors—plagiarism poses a perennial problem for some because it raises a host of questions about ownership, property, convention, law, education, technology, and more broadly the social and ethical codes in defiance of which the plagiarist, as the story usually goes, plagiarizes. Out of respect for these and other complexities, I work from the premise that plagiarism cannot be understood—as either historical construct or local practice—without addressing the many concerns (legal, ethical, aesthetic, and pedagogical, in particular) informing institutional efforts to define, detect, prevent, and punish this particular brand of literary malfeasance.

1

In this study I take postsecondary education in the United States as my general field of inquiry. While I have a keen interest in plagiarism as a particular kind of writing practice, and plagiarism detection and prevention as recurring administrative and pedagogical concerns, I travel a somewhat circuitous route in order to chart a historical and theoretical approach to plagiarism that both extends and departs from other works on the subject (see, for example, Lindey [1952], Mallon [1989], Howard [*Standing* 1999], Buranen and Roy [1999], Randall [2001], and Kewes [2003]). Kewes has warned against the kind of long, transhistorical view of plagiarism that this book in many ways takes. This approach, while convenient for supporting particular claims on behalf of today's practitioners (see Randall's defense of "guerrilla plagiarism," for example, discussed in chapter 2), may overlook the ways in which plagiarism meets with differing public reactions in different local contexts (Kewes 14). While I grant this important caveat, I nonetheless take the long view in studying plagiarism in order to identify a set of thematic concerns that have informed and continue to inform debates on the topic, particularly in higher education. I hope to demonstrate that such themes—e.g., the equation of plagiarism with false alchemy or with social or personal disease—are not only relevant to today's plagiarism debate but also essential to the growing business of plagiarism detection at the turn of the twenty-first century. My aim, then, is not so much to trace the evolution of a particular, perhaps favored, thematic lineage but rather to show how themes historically relevant to the plagiarism problem materialize in various ways in the service of larger aesthetic, political, economic, and pedagogical agendas.

To that end, I begin the book by recounting the 2002 plagiarism scandals involving historians Stephen Ambrose and Doris Kearns Goodwin. I focus specifically on how mainstream press coverage of the Ambrose and Goodwin cases included corollary subnarratives targeting college and university students, who functioned as ciphers in a broader debate about professional and academic ethics. Through a critical retelling of this story, I lay the groundwork for a more thorough analysis of plagiarism and antiplagiarism discourse in higher education.

Chapter 2 investigates several definitions of plagiarism rooted in notions of failed authorship and intellectual property violation. I argue in this chapter that recent solutions to the plagiarism problem, including Web-based plagiarism detection services, enact a particular kind of societal control unique to postindustrial technologies of information exchange and processing. Building on these arguments, chapter 3 addresses early-twentieth-century plagiarism policies and assignment protocols, including the "research paper" model that emerged in the 1920s in partial response to administrative concerns about student misuse of library materials. I argue here that plagiarism detection has functioned and continues to function within a broad educational regime that emphasizes the management of student writing practices and the enforcement of protective or preemptive measures to regulate potential authoring errors.

In chapter 4, I address one prevailing notion of plagiarism as a kind of failed transformation of literary content, considering in particular the historically popular association of plagiarism with false or fraudulent alchemical transmutation. I demonstrate the ways in which this figurative equation of alchemical and literary change appears in modified form in late Renaissance notions of literary imitation, digestion, and incorporation. I then argue that the Renaissance pursuit of literary transmutation informs later modern approaches to reading, research, and the rightful and wrongful use of text materials in academic writing.

In chapter 5, I consider a range of research writing conventions often associated with plagiarism. Using the tools of critical discourse analysis, I show, for example, how common handbook rules for avoiding plagiarism tend to occlude, albeit in the language of clear and concise technique, what remain largely inexplicable processes of textual transformation. To teach the prevailing conventions of quotation, paraphrase, and summary, I propose, is to teach a pseudo-alchemical lesson whose secrets require a level of genre (or insider) knowledge not usually accessible to beginning writing students.

In general, these first five chapters serve to foreground late-twentieth and early-twenty-first-century attitudes about, and approaches to, the plagiarism problem. As mentioned above, plagiarism takes on different cultural meanings in relation to a set of contingent, local variables—available technologies, genre, social and economic arrangements, cultural and political climate (Kewes 17)—emerging at different historical moments. My aim, therefore, is to avoid a kind of "moral absolutism" (Hammond 46) in my study of plagiarism and plagiarism detection. I take issue, for example, with Christopher Ricks's insistence on a historically stable definition of plagiarism, arguing instead that difficulties in adjudicating plagiarism often arise due to inherent difficulties in defining the term (Ricks 23). In fact, most definitions of plagiarism—in handbooks, dictionaries, and university plagiarism policies, for example—suggest a confluence of "semantic inflections and resonances" (Kewes 1) that in turn echo the many moments at which plagiarism has changed or hardened as a categorical imprint. In the first half of this book, then, I consider various definitional patterns in an effort not to further destabilize or relativize plagiarism, but rather to establish what I believe is a necessarily flexible historical framework within which to consider recent approaches to plagiarism and plagiarism detection.

Chapter 6 links the alchemical and intellectual property traditions discussed above to late-twentieth-century progressive writing pedagogy. I look at particular examples of research writing assignments, policy revisions, and craft recommendations designed to remedy the problem of student plagiarism. I argue that a particular emphasis on the "spirit of inquiry" in research writing instruction, as well as corollary concerns about the arguably unspirited writing activity known as plagiarism, draw much of their inspiration from a nineteenth-century American Protestant interest in the management of human minds and souls through fundamentalist indoctrination.

In the seventh chapter, I analyze four popular antiplagiarism services: Glatt Plagiarism Services, Essay Verification Engine (EVE2), Plagiarism-Finder, and Turnitin.com. I argue that these and other plagiarism detection services, under the aegis of pedagogical reform and the promise of technological progress, serve to regulate student writing and reading practices in ways reminiscent of precomputer, even preindustrial, solutions and remedies. I also show how each service prioritizes notions of originality, uniqueness, and textual purity derived in turn from rhetorical, legal, and alchemical traditions. In my concluding chapter I consider plagiarism and plagiarism detection in light of recent debates about research writing practices in the age of networked computers. I offer provisional suggestions for future research on the plagiarism topic and offer my own recommendations for how to teach and remedy the plagiarism problem in accordance with conclusions drawn from this study. In part, then, this book tells at least one version of the story of how Web-based plagiarism detection services—with the four mentioned above serving as major examples—emerged at the turn of the twenty-first century to solve the perennial problem of student plagiarism. As "administrative therapies" (Illich, *Tools* 46) designed to manage this problem, plagiarism detection services promise more generally to correct, or right, errant information flows while also teaching the prevailing lessons of modern authorship and intellectual property in the digital age.

A few questions surface at this point that I will treat in different ways throughout this book: First, if computer-based plagiarism detection services represent, as I suggest here, a conservationist project on behalf of modern authoring techniques, then what values—i.e., conventions and laws pertaining to authorship and copyright in particular—underwrite the development of such services? Second, what can a study such as this one, focused on antiplagiarism remedies, teach us about authorship and, more broadly, written communication in the age of networked computers? Third, as new solutions to the age-old problem of plagiarism, how do Turnitin, Glatt, and other services function in relation to solutions implemented in the past? Fourth, what can we learn generally about plagiarism—in today's institutions of higher learning especially—by studying the forms and functions of antiplagiarism remedies? Fifth, if plagiarism has a history and, arguably, is as old as authorship itself (a claim taken up in the early chapters), then why are so many so eager to call it a problem (a disease, a *diablo*) in the first place—as opposed to, say, a solution by another name? And finally, who benefits, if anyone, and how, from sustained attacks on plagiarism as a perennial problem for institutions of higher learning?

Before offering my own provisional answers to these questions, I will address some of the theoretical and methodological assumptions informing my analysis. I should note first that in any foray into the plagiarism debate there is always the temptation to take sides by either condemning plagiarism as a de facto wrong or defending versions of the practice as evidence of alternative, perhaps subversive, authoring activities. In what follows I do my best to avoid that temptation, taking to heart Harold Love's judicious remark that in studying plagiarism, "one will learn more by observing the debate than entering it" (151). Any claim to nonpartial observation, of course, belies what historians of ideas might refer to as the inherently normative bias of any purportedly objective observing. Thus, I grant that I may lean at times toward particular points of view (in my first and concluding chapters especially), but I endeavor throughout to focus less on competing views in the plagiarism debate than on the ways such views have tended to reproduce, "through theory and action," particular assumptions about plagiarism and plagiarists (Love 151).

To make my case for studying plagiarism and plagiarism detection as particular kinds of communication activity, I begin with George Herbert Mead's well-rehearsed definition of communication as "significant symbols" shared between and among individuals who, by using such symbols, enter into subjective and objective relation with both self and others (203). In assuming a symbolic interactionist approach to communication, I focus specifically on the ways in which individuals, in general accordance with Mead's formula, interact over communicative objects of a decidedly textual nature. Such interactions take place, for example, in and through the techniques and technologies of reading and writing specific to modern literate societies and, in particular, to modern institutions of higher learning. The modern writer, to adapt Mead, stands in symbolic relation to the modern reader, and vice versa, with both becoming, via applied techniques of reading and writing, mutually "directed" in the exchange of significant symbols (203).

To offer just one hypothetical example, a student writer conducting research for a college assignment may make use of available sources, such as textbooks, handbooks, libraries, databases, the Internet, professors and other students, to complete the assignment in accordance with general academic, local institutional, and course-specific conventions. At each turn in this hypothetical research writing process—interpreting the assignment, asking and answering research questions, performing searches, compiling data, composing drafts, negotiating conventions, and so on—the student writer is also a reader of information sources pursued for purposes of assembling a document worthy of submission and course credit. The process of research writing conceived here, therefore, involves a series of communicative exchanges between and among human beings, textual objects, and relevant technologies of reading and writing.

Such exchanges assume a particular value and valence in modern textual economies that capitalize in specific ways on the communicative interaction of readers and writers. As Rosemary Coombe has argued, discussing intellectual property law, the current "paradigm" for communicative production and reception places "an individual intentional author" in relation to "a rationally deliberating reader" (258). This author-reader paradigm guides a particular reader or writer's technical approach to the forms shared or exchanged across communication networks. Thus, to study plagiarism and plagiarism detection as communication activities is to pay particular attention to the techniques and technologies of production and reception that mediate symbolic interactions of this sort. Today's networked computer, for example, suggests for some a new communication apparatus inviting new strategies for dealing with the particular "grammars" inherent to computer operations (Hawisher and Selfe 11). Where these grammars (pertaining, for example, to keyboard and screen use, word processing, and online networking) intersect with the techniques and technologies of computer production, new questions, such as those asked above, arise for critical communication studies.

For some, the recent proliferation of computers as communication tools marks a significant transformative moment in the history of human activity. Ivan Illich, among others,[1] has defined this moment as particularly relevant to historians of technology concerned with "the symbolic rather than the intended instrumental effect of technique" (*Vineyard* 115). The historian who studies alphabetic techniques and technologies, for example, must distinguish between early "manual techniques" of reading and writing (in Illich's case, twelfth-century monastic reading practices) and the "mechanical techniques" that emerge later to reify the object (alphabetic text) in some material form. In formulating this distinction, Illich's ideal historian may come to recognize the fifteenth-century European print revolution as an instance of "manual" technique reified in "mechanical" technologies of textual production and reproduction. One could argue that a similar process of reification applies to the late-twentieth-century move from print-based, mechanical production to the digital production of new media objects.

Following Illich, I aim in this book to study the techniques and technologies, as well as the manual, mechanical, and digital modes and procedures, surrounding plagiarism and plagiarism detection. At different moments, therefore, I will address plagiarism as an individual communication activity (in the sense understood by Mead) both reflective and productive of particular techniques, in this case of reading and writing. I will also address plagiarism as a production activity inhering, for example, in structural or institutional responses to the plagiarism problem, among them the recent use of plagiarism detection software to identify and regulate instances of presumed plagiarism.

In this latter case, I take as my object of study the "cultural production process" of plagiarism detection in relation to the relevant social arrangements emerging at particular historical moments (Jameson 408). Where I pursue a "mode-of-production analysis" (Jameson 408) of plagiarism and plagiarism detection, I operate in general alignment with Marxist cultural theory as described, for example, by Raymond Williams and Stuart Hall. Specifically, to study plagiarism as a legal, ethical, and/or pedagogical problem and plagiarism detection as a structural solution to that problem is to address, via this particular example, the "real social process" on which "an effective and dominant culture" depends (Williams 414). For Williams, this real social process underwrites an emphasis on "certain meanings and practices" at the expense of others (414). Moreover, this general process of selective tradition operates in tandem with, at times supports, all "organized forms of social thinking" (Hall 27). Where today's educators and administrators, for example, select and reject (pass and fail) on the basis of particular epistemological forms, such selections reflect an ideological "transmission of an effective dominant culture" (Williams 414).

Ideology, for Hall, can be understood as a set of "categories and discourses" (Hall 27) that facilitate interaction in social networks. Ideological forms also intersect with the specific apparatuses, mechanisms, or techniques of human communication. For example, both the individual accused of plagiarism and the individual who accuses assume an identity in relation to that accusation. Thus, in examining the related discourses of both plagiarists and plagiarism hunters, I will emphasize the ways in which producers and consumers of textual commodities participate in discursive practices that, in turn, serve to define authors and readers in relation to given social categories.

This book, then, is on one level an investigation of disciplinary power focused specifically on plagiarism and plagiarism detection mechanisms in higher education. In adopting Foucault's theory of power, however, I want to emphasize the ways in which the rules of plagiarism detection materialize in the structures and institutions, as well as the techniques and tactics, of antiplagiarism remedies. In other words, I approach the plagiarism problem as an instance of social and political contestation made real in the micromechanisms of composition pedagogy, intellectual property law, and, more recently, computer technology. Each of these mechanisms, as Foucault urges, has its own history and trajectory, and, as I hope to show, the discursive practices of plagiarism and plagiarism detection remain tethered to those trajectories (Foucault, *Power/Knowledge* 99).

Plagiarism can be understood, finally, as a perennial threat to modern values of educational progress and merit. Lester Faigley, discussing the history of composition instruction in the United States, describes what he sees as the current functionalist, merit-centered bias in higher education. In a meritocracy,

Faigley writes, society "is reinterpreted as neutral space where individuals are set against each other in competitive relations and rise and fall according to their abilities and motivation . . ." (49). These "competitive relations," according to Faigley, have the dual function of promising each individual "a great deal of power" and also freeing the individual "from a sense of social responsibility" (49). To be sure, the structures, techniques, and technologies of plagiarism detection—some of the built-in apparatuses, that is, for guarding the meritocracy—go far to reinforce social interpretations such as those described by Faigley. More specifically, plagiarism detection services offer their own kind of "neutral space" for the adjudication of individual successes and failures, setting the plagiarist and the nonplagiarist against each other in communicative, competitive relation.

The "rise and fall" of plagiarism in the supposedly neutral space of plagiarism detection is my chief concern in this book. Throughout, I will address the specific ideas and institutions that, over time, have produced and reproduced plagiarism as a problem to be taken seriously—for some, to be feared—in modern educational systems. As ideological form or discursive technique, plagiarism continues to signify in ways that have real effects on student writers and others trying to understand the rules and codes of social life at the turn of the twenty-first century. In what follows, I contribute my own sense of what plagiarism means in today's institutions of higher learning, considering as well what plagiarism detection can and does mean to today's readers and writers.

1

"A Flurry of Fascination"

The (Anti)Plagiarism Cases of Stephen Ambrose and Doris Kearns Goodwin

IN THE FIRST week of January 2002, a crime was committed. For some, the crime had actually taken place many months, even years, before the *New York Times* published the first of many reports on the topic. For others, the offense came later as scattered details coalesced and the several participants (perpetrators and victims alike) stated positions for the record. And yet, for many the crime never happened at all, but rather those accused had been falsely charged by an envious, resentful few. In the end, it would not be clear as to who did what, when, where, to whom, and why.

Nevertheless, something did happen in early 2002, and the goal of this retelling is to consider how the many players involved managed to articulate both the nature of the crime and its relevance to education, scholarship, and American culture at large. These players would include a handful of state universities, several college professors and students, one major publishing house, a slew of journalists, a few concerned citizens, three spokespersons, a staff of research assistants, and a series of experts prepared to wax eloquent on topics ranging from the proper use of punctuation marks to the diabolical repercussions of selling one's soul. The issues at stake would be biggies: integrity, truth, honesty, discipline, courage, tradition. New and old technologies—computers, word-processing software, and the Internet, but also plain old paper, pencil, and handwriting—would factor in as evidence, and even accessories to the crime.

The story begins on January 5, 2002, when the *New York Times* posted the following headline: "2 Say Stephen Ambrose, Popular Historian, Copied Passages." The headline alone reveals the complexity of the issue at hand: Who is Stephen Ambrose? Who are these mysterious "2," and why are they interested in this particular "Popular Historian"? In what sense is a popular historian different (or not) from a historian per se? Finally, why is it important that Ambrose

"Copied Passages," an activity I can imagine many historians, like most writers and scholars, engaged in readily and often? My recounting here will attempt to answer these questions. I conclude by addressing two related questions that set the stage for the remainder of this book: What can we learn—in particular, about writing, reading, and scholarship in higher education—by examining the ways in which the *Times* and other mainstream press vendors handled the Ambrose and Goodwin stories? Furthermore, in what ways do popular understandings of the issues and concerns surrounding these cases either support or belie those perspectives commonly found in the academy?[2]

ANATOMY OF A LITERARY CRIME

The crime under discussion here is literary theft, or plagiarism. To answer at least one of the questions posed above, Stephen Ambrose, Popular Historian, did something wrong not in copying passages but in copying, in his book, passages later traced to a book written by someone else. More specifically, Ambrose erred in failing to credit—via the rules and conventions of academic writing—the passages he purportedly chose to copy. The two books affected in this case are Ambrose's *The Wild Blue* and Thomas Childers's *Wings of Morning*, and as David Kirkpatrick reported in the January 5 *New York Times*, Ambrose's error was essentially one of punctuation: while he did acknowledge Childers as a source, he did not acknowledge "quoting from the book or borrowing phrases or wording."

At issue, then, is a discovered similarity between two works of history: Ambrose's book makes use of several phrases that can be found, word for word, in Childers's book. Ultimately it would be argued that this unacknowledged similarity marked a certain degree of "sloppiness" or "carelessness" on Ambrose's part. This carelessness—failing to mark off borrowed text with marks conventionally used to indicate such borrowings—amounts to what most scholars of literary convention would call *plagiarism*.

Considering the nature of the act itself—a punctuation lapse—one might wonder what all the fuss was about. But much indeed was at stake when Professor Ambrose neglected or chose not to use " " in the text of his book. As one of many who would chime in on the topic, *Times* reporter David Kirkpatrick helps to articulate just what is involved, and at stake, in acts of plagiarism. There is something particularly vexing, he suggests, about finding similar passages in two otherwise distinct historical works. The situation gets even more troubling when "several sentences and paragraphs" in one text "closely echo words" in another, and when footnotes and other credit markers do not go far enough to "acknowledge quoting from the book or borrowing phrases or wording." In other words, acts of innocuous quoting and borrowing become criminal, or at least unethical, when the debt of one author to another is not properly paid via credit evidently due the receiver ("2 Say").

As Kirpatrick goes on to explain, such breaches of literary etiquette—and copyright law, no doubt—can be verified by the time-honored technique of "side-by-side" comparison. In the case of Ambrose, text comparisons did reveal that some of his wordings, in these and other passages, were identical to wordings found in Childers. This act of overt imitation, sans quotation marks, sufficed as proof positive that Ambrose, knowingly or not, plagiarized. And as Thomas Mallon states often in his scintillating history of plagiarism, originality in literary authorship is all about how one manages "the infinitely varied molecular matter of the words" (108). Or as Mallon claims elsewhere: "[T]he words are all" (123).

But are the words—and the quotation marks that go around them—really the "all" of this story? The answer, in a word, is yes. In "Sanctioning Voice: Quotation Marks, the Abolition of Torture, and the Fifth Amendment," Margreta de Grazia tells us that over time quotation marks have come to "privilege and protect" an author's utterances, reminding us whenever we see them that the words of another can be borrowed but "only on certain conditions" (289). Evidently, Ambrose failed to honor these "conditions," and in so doing, broke a literary (and civil) law. For as de Grazia argues convincingly, these "grammatical ciphers" do legal work as well, protecting the individual (in this case, Childers) via "protective warranties" that guarantee an author's rights to textual ownership (291).

Thus, to recap, Ambrose has been accused, quite simply, of violating Childers's right to protected property. He (Ambrose) has stolen—or kidnapped (for that is what plagiarism originally meant)—Childers's "children," his words. Meanwhile, Ambrose has allegedly committed the related and equally egregious crime of being unoriginal, of failing to use his own children, if you will, in writing his history.[3] So indeed "the words are all," but only insofar as words coded as belonging to one writer (without quotation marks) in fact belong to another. In violating this time-honored code of quotation, Ambrose has undermined the sanctity of protected stuff. More specifically, Ambrose has compromised—we might say stolen—Childers's very originality as a writer, and, by default, Ambrose has called into question his own originality as well.

As one might expect, then, the first response issued on behalf of Professor Ambrose came as a direct defense of his authorial originality. Adam Rothberg, spokesperson for Ambrose's publisher Simon & Schuster, was quick to claim that Ambrose's *The Wild Blue* "is an original and important work of World War II history. All research garnered from previously published material is appropriately footnoted" (Kirkpatrick, "2 Say"). Another spokesperson will later reverse this claim, but for now note that Rothberg's defense of Ambrose mentions originality and footnotes almost in the same breath. There is obviously a larger issue of *techne*, or craftwork, at play here that is hard to separate from issues of authorial integrity and honesty. In brief, to make a technical error of the sort Ambrose evidently made is to mess quite profoundly with deeply embedded codes of decency and propriety. Indeed, just as quotation marks code sanctioned voice, the accusation of technical sloppiness in this story codes a legal and moral violation that we, as deputies and witnesses, would be loath to ignore.

And what of our accused plagiarist, who has so far chosen to remain silent? Ambrose was "unavailable for comment" on January 5, but David Kirkpatrick did track down the putative victim in all of this, Thomas Childers. Initially, Childers's response was generous and forgiving. Admitting that he felt "sort of disappointed," he could not bring himself to attribute any "malice" to Stephen Ambrose: "[H]e did it with the left hand," Childers commented, translating a German expression meaning that Ambrose was "focused on something else." The next day, on January 6, Ambrose supported Childers's account when, according to Kirpatrick, he "apologized and said the repetition had been inadvertent" ("Author Admits"). This apology, along with a promise to correct all future editions, seemed to satisfy Childers, who referred to Ambrose's response as a "gracious gesture" and "a classy thing" for a "fellow scholar" to do.

The story does not end here, however. Kirkpatrick assures the reader that the Ambrose incident is likely to "further debate among historians about the kind of blockbuster history that Mr. Ambrose writes" ("Author Admits"). This subtle change of topic is significant. Up to now, the debate has turned primarily on questions about words, quotation marks, originality, and similarity, but here the issue on the table is not just Ambrose the historian but that class of literary objects known as blockbuster histories—those histories, in other words, produced quickly, in large quantity, and for a vast reading public. Ambrose now stands in, as cipher, for a genre now under review as well.

Ambrose himself may have prompted this focus shift. By January 10, according to the *Los Angeles Times*, his single-book infraction had grown to a total of four books then "under question." While Ambrose's son and agent, Hugh Ambrose, declined to comment on this development, a new spokesperson for Simon & Schuster, Victoria Meyer, assured the public that all errors would be remedied in subsequent editions. When finally reached for comment, Ambrose remarked only that he was "unsure" about his other books. . . . "'I don't know. It's a lot of books,' said Ambrose, author of more than 20 historical works . . ." ("More Questions").

Speed and quantity of production, in particular, were issues central to both the prosecution and the defense in this case. Was Ambrose "sloppy"—did he make mistakes with quotation marks (did he plagiarize)—because his governing mode (blockbuster history) led to the production of too much too fast? The January 10 *Los Angeles Times* would answer in the affirmative, and over time these related issues of production speed and quantity would be used, at turns, to both justify and vilify Ambrose and the trade publishing industry supporting him.

By way of justification, the *Los Angeles Times* theorized that Ambrose had absorbed (memorized, incorporated) the material he had read so thoroughly "that he unconsciously replicated it, or . . . the problem originates with his team of research assistants; Ambrose is also highly prolific, increasing the chance of error" ("More Questions"). In short, Ambrose may have plagiarized for one or more of three equally viable reasons: (1) After years of practice in the art of literary transmutation, his occasional repetitions became unconscious and thus, we can assume, uncontrollable. (2) His research assistants actually made the mistakes, which again poses a challenge to Ambrose's mode of production, while likewise compromising the authenticity of his authorship in the first place. (3) The "chance for error" is inherently increased with such a "highly prolific" author, who by his own admission produces "a lot of books" whose repetitions he cannot track with terrific accuracy.

The goal here, in trying to understand the nature of Ambrose's alleged crime, is not to settle on any one of these explanations but instead to situate the act (and the activity of plagiarism in general) in a web of related issues whose collective import must be taken into account. To construct an accurate anatomy of plagiarism, we must understand what body—or species of body—is under review. We may conclude from what we have seen thus far, for example, that plagiarism infractions turn on issues of originality, similarity, acknowledgment, borrowing, debt paying, wording, and the use (or lack) of quotation marks. Still, in looking at the Ambrose case specifically, it remains unclear where to locate the crime scene. Did the offending act take place in the pages of Ambrose's *The Wild Blue*, or perhaps somewhere between this one book and the other—*Wings of Morning*—from which he appears to have lifted material? Did Ambrose commit the crime in his mind or, to be more precise, in his "unconscious" mind, where immersed in a solution of "source material" he found himself honestly "unsure" about which material was his? Or was the crime distributed across several books—the four, in fact, that were at this point "in question"—or, more radically, across several minds and persons, including Ambrose's son Hugh and the team of research assistants who may, in the end, prove culpable? Or should we look beyond these materially bounded corporealities (human being, book) and consider the larger corporations, even the literary corpi, as potential targets? In other words, is Simon & Schuster holding the smoking gun? Or is the industry of trade publishing itself, run amok with its blockbuster production pace, to blame?

For answers to these and related questions, read on.

A Strange Mix of Contempt and Sympathy

In a climate of general confusion, there is often a tendency to seek higher ground. Indeed, many involved in the Ambrose case demonstrated this tendency in the weeks following the initial disclosure of wrongdoing. Stuart P. Green's January 13 commentary in the *Los Angeles Times* promises, from the start, to be a staunch apology for Stephen Ambrose. Green begins by reminding us that plagiarism can be a "fluid and murky concept" that, once again, is difficult to define. "In all likelihood," writes Green,

> Ambrose did not intend to deceive his readers into believing that the words were his own. Rather, this prolific, bestselling and widely celebrated author of 30 history books seems to have been guilty of more instances of sloppy note-taking than would be tolerated even from a college freshman.

Note, first of all, the invocation of the student writer (here, the "college freshman") as a suitable point of comparison. More will be said on this move later, but for now note as well that Green goes on in the article to cite sloppy "note-taking" (an artifact, one might say, of an older technology, handwriting), the Internet (particularly online paper mills), and cut-and-paste editing features as major "temptations" facing the hurried writer. Ambrose, as well, has stated on one occasion that the computer did in fact help him produce—and produce quickly—his blockbuster histories, thus facilitating the hyperactive writing pace that would later, according to some, cause trouble.

In citing the computer (Web sites, cut-and-paste) as an agent of plagiaristic "temptation," Green touches on a classic connection between literary originality and original sin further elaborated by Nick Groom in *The Forger's Shadow*. As Groom explains, the word *original* was originally "tainted" by the notion of original sin (18) but over time would shed this meaning and come to signify "secular idealism, or the archetypal" (20). It is this meaning that we commonly invoke today in using the word *original*. Groom proceeds to argue that the concept of plagiarism, in contrast, has come to represent "a perversion of theories of origin" (25), "a threat, a fear, a panic, a plague . . . contagious, sickening, unnatural, and terminal . . ." (27). Groom then makes the astute point that "[in] its demonization, plagiarism has perhaps inhabited some of the space vacated by the word original" (27). In other words, in committing the sin of plagiarism (crime against originality), plagiarists commit an equally egregious sin of "original" betrayal (crime against humanity). New technologies, for some, hasten this descent into the realm of the diabolical. Or as Green intones, computers are "temptations" because they provide opportunities for writers such as Ambrose to cut-and-paste too much too fast and for students to go online and buy term papers.

Meanwhile, returning to the "fluid and murky" waters of plagiarism itself, Green's apology of January 13 continues with a brief aside in which he chronicles his experience with a student plagiarist. I quote his story at length for reasons that will become clear toward the end of this chapter:

> Recently, I sat on a university disciplinary committee hearing charges of plagiarism against a student who had copied long passages from various sources, often without quotation marks or footnotes. As I listened to his rambling explanation of how he had gotten himself into such a predicament, I felt a strange mix of contempt and sympathy for what he had done.

The comparison of Ambrose to the hypothetical student writer, first mentioned above, bears out here in a particularly poignant way, for now it is a real student whose charges are meant to parallel those leveled against Ambrose. Green goes on to cite the case of Jacob Epstein, who in the early eighties took "plot elements and descriptive passages from a novel by Martin Amis." He also mentions Susan Sontag, who allegedly "lifted various phrases from mostly dead authors for her novel 'In America.'" And, finally, Green includes in his informal list of plagiarists the university student who sat before him at the disciplinary committee. Green summarizes the punishments issued to all three as follows:

> Epstein was skewered by Amis in a scathing rebuttal that essentially ended his novel-writing career. Sontag was given a national book prize. Meanwhile, the hapless student plagiarist on whose disciplinary committee I sat was denied his degree and asked to leave the university.

Of course, we have yet to learn what punishment—or prize—awaits Stephen Ambrose, but Green is clear on the related points that while Sontag faired quite well in the end, Epstein was "skewered" and "the hapless student plagiarist" banned from the university. Which is not to say—playing the devil's advocate here—that this particular student did not deserve expulsion. My question at this point, rather, is, What does Stephen Ambrose deserve and how might his punishment differ from that which befell the student plagiarist?

Green's proposed answer to that question begins with some rather bold invective: "[Ambrose] did a great disservice to the writers on whose work he improperly relied, and his practices cast serious doubt on his integrity as a scholar." For these reasons, according to Green, Ambrose's community of "fellow historians" is by all means authorized to "censure him" for this impropriety. But—and this is the core of Green's defense:

> Ambrose is a beloved figure whose numerous books have brought history alive to many thousands of ordinary readers. No one has claimed that his books are inaccurate or that they cannot still be a source of pleasure and edification. He did, after all, apologize.

A loaded, but I think reasonable, question presents itself here: If it is enough for Ambrose to apologize for wrongful copying, then why is it not enough for our hapless student? It will be proven by story's end that not one or four but *six* of Ambrose's histories contained copied, unquoted passages. Even if the student's "rambling explanation" somehow trumped, in Green's mind, the several public declarations Ambrose made in his own defense, are we being asked to believe that whatever crime this university student committed in the end was, somehow, more serious than that committed by a popular historian who plagiarized in half a dozen of his published books?

Aside from announcing the committee's sentence, Green has nothing to say concerning the fate of the student after expulsion. Regarding Ambrose, however, he concludes his article as follows: "In the future, Ambrose will certainly be more conscientious in his research and writing. And, in a few months, I suspect, whatever it is exactly that he did wrong will be all but forgotten." In short: time heals all wounds, a wrist slap is enough, and apologies go a long way—if you are, as Ambrose evidently is within Green's community, a "beloved figure." If you are a "hapless student," however, making roughly the same mistake, there might be less to forget in the days and weeks following your experience with Green's committee.

TEMPTATIONS AND THEIR CONSEQUENCES

In mid-January 2002, standing before his well-attended history class, Thomas Childers announced that "he would cease using [Ambrose's] books" in his classes (Schemo). For some, the decision made sense. Others (such as Green, perhaps) would wonder if it was fair, to readers and author alike, to censure the beloved historian via outright censorship. As it turns out, the debate over Ambrose was now situated within a larger academic debate about "whether universities should continue to assign works by scholars who have been accused of appropriating someone else's work" (Schemo). Students at the University of Pennsylvania, for example, took issue with the potential problem of a double standard:

"They're telling us not to plagiarize," Sumit Walia, a sophomore majoring in economics, said on his way to class this morning. "But what kind of message does it send if they accept it at the very highest levels?" (Schemo)

Ray Groller, another student at U. Penn., agreed with Childers's decision to ban Ambrose from the classroom: "Teachers are supposed to be role models in students lives," Mr. Groller opined. "They should try to lead by example" (qtd. in Schemo).

This seems like a fair request, especially since students, broadly speaking, are often faced with the same temptations to which Ambrose evidently succumbed. In fact, as U. Penn. student Groller confessed, he had been tempted "lots of times" to lift material, but "the thought of the consequences kept [him] from doing it" (qtd. in Schemo). In other words, where professors in this story might see a debate over whether or not to include Ambrose in the curriculum, college students (Walia and Groller, at least) see a clear-cut case in which the acceptance of wrongdoing "at the very highest levels" would send a contradictory message to those residing (reading, writing) at the lower levels. Some professors also recognized the danger of a double standard: "What Ambrose did is something I could haul students before the honor council for," admitted Professor Carlton of Vanderbilt University. "And I actually have students who have trouble understanding why they should be hauled before the honor council for doing something like that" (qtd. in Schemo).

For professors, and academic historians in particular, the Ambrose case also raised some troubling questions about the role of traditional, serious scholarship in an age of blockbuster histories. *New York Times* reporter Diana Jean Schemo reported the following:

> Among academics, Mr. Ambrose's popularity . . . provoked soul searching and no small measure of envy. History professors on Internet chat groups wondered what the success of Mr. Ambrose and other popular historians said about their own failure to write readable books.

A second kind of failing, then, informs this story: The agents of scholarly good—the ones at the highest levels who follow the rules—fail nonetheless to garner the readership that those such as Ambrose, whose example is less than stellar, enjoy. Once again, the question arises: Who, or what, is on trial here? For now it appears that some academics, in the wake of the Ambrose case, felt as bad about themselves as they did about Ambrose.

Indeed, blockbuster envy might explain why Thomas Childers would later decide to sing a different tune with regard to the Ambrose infraction. While initially praising Ambrose's "swift apology," Childers changed his mind when he read an account in which Ambrose described his purportedly sloppy method for taking notes and writing histories. "It was not just a matter of using quotation marks," Schemo reported on behalf of Childers, "but of toiling to write a good passage rather than appropriating one." In the words of Childers himself, he just could not "conceive of that. . . . It doesn't take so much effort. Find the words. Write it yourself" (qtd. in Schemo).

On the block again is Ambrose's method. As Childers's testimony suggests, plagiarism for some is not just about placing quotes around borrowed materials but also the kind of "toiling" that goes into the act of writing. The message is clear: To write requires "effort" but not "much." Just "[f]ind the words. Write it yourself." Thomas Mallon's insistence that plagiarism invariably comes down to "the words" and nothing else is here echoed in reprimands laid down by the victim himself. And he (Childers) should know, for he seemed quite capable of finding "the words" and writing his book himself. What lapse of conscience—or, perhaps, consciousness—prevented Ambrose from doing the same, from putting forth the same effort? Was he just lazy, as many claimed? Did he lose sight of his words and give in to the temptation to steal another's? Did his blockbuster pace interfere with his otherwise sound judgment? Did the "popular" historian err in forgetting his "professional" obligations before the sacredness of protected voice?

Where before the carelessness of a fellow scholar's "left hand" seemed an adequate explanation, this week the excuse will not do. A sin of omission, in short, has now been recast as a moral sin—to be precise, a sin against authorship. The "soul searching" that Schemo reported among academics can thus be read not only as possible envy before Ambrose's popularity but also as a kind of publicly acknowledged disgust at a soul (that is, Ambrose's) tainted and mired by the muck of plagiarism.

Letters to the editor in the January 17 issue of the *Los Angeles Times* lend support to this point. David J. Oliphant of Granada Hills reminds us, for example, that when historians plagiarize, readers "are denied the honesty of original research. If the first writer makes an error, the second one repeats it and less conscientious writers continue to repeat it until it is installed as the common view" (Oliphant). In other words, Oliphant is less concerned about the "honesty" of the research than its accuracy. He is worried, as he goes on to write, that when the "common view" gets tainted with erroneous or felonious research, "teachers, opinion writers, editors and others who form public opinion base their views on it." In brief, literary sin spoils the empirical evidence conveyed through "public opinion" by perpetuating a string of inaccuracies. Truth, in other words, is at risk when "original research" meets the original sin of plagiarism.

OF ECHOES, SETTLEMENTS, AND
SURVEILLANCE MACHINES

When David D. Kirkpatrick resurfaced on January 23 to write yet another story on plagiarism ("Historian Says Publisher Quickly Settled Copying Dispute"), his subject was not Stephen Ambrose but equally popular popular historian Doris Kearns Goodwin. Admitting that her 1987 book *The Fitzgeralds and the Kennedys* "closely echoed" sentences from other books, Goodwin announced that her publisher—Simon & Schuster—had decided to settle with one of the authors, Lynne McTaggart. The "repetitions were accidental," Goodwin is on record as saying, and all future editions would reflect Goodwin's debt to McTaggart's book, *Kathleen Kennedy: Her Life and Times*. Goodwin's plagiarism, I should add, "surfaced as part of a flurry of fascination with literary theft" in the wake of Ambrose's earlier admissions (Kirkpatrick, "Historian Says").

Thus, the Ambrose debate has echoed on under the aegis of a strikingly similar offense committed by Goodwin. To conclude this chapter, I follow that echo all the way to Brit Hume's *Fox Special Report Roundtable*, which aired on January 23, 2002. Hume's interview that day with Fred Barnes (executive editor, *The Weekly Standard*), Mort Kondracke (from *Roll Call*), and Mara Liasson (of National Public Radio) led to some important comparisons between Ambrose and Goodwin that intersect with other concerns taken up throughout this book. It will be useful, therefore, to review that conversation in light of the questions asked at the beginning of this chapter.

We learn from the roundtable, for example, that the Ambrose story reported by David Kirkpatrick back on January 5 can be traced to Fred Barnes and *The Weekly Standard*, the Web journal that had first covered the story a few days prior. When Barnes got a call from the *Times* just after completing a first draft, he did not realize at the time just how valuable his story was. "It hadn't been edited, hadn't been proofread," Barnes says, but nevertheless "everybody was interested in it." Equal interest materialized when, nearly three weeks later, the *Boston Globe* released a story about Goodwin that Barnes (and later Kirkpatrick) would write up in their respective publications.

At issue here is the discussion that ensues between Barnes, Liasson, and Kondracke over the amount of news coverage allotted thus far to Goodwin and Ambrose respectively. Ambrose, a "giant" in popular history (according to Liasson), had also received the giant's share of coverage. Hume asks Liasson to comment on that disparity:

LIASSON: You know, Steven Ambrose was the first. He's bigger. I would hope that Doris Kearns Goodwin gets as much scrutiny as Steven Ambrose.

KONDRACKE: I think it was an old news-new news story.

BARNES: I don't think that. And *The New York Times*, you know, there was another story recently about a scholar who made up a bunch of stuff about guns in America and said there weren't many in the early days. *The Times* ignored it for months. But when Steven Ambrose came along, they couldn't wait to run it. (*Fox Special*)

In brief, Liasson hopes that Goodwin will ultimately suffer the same "scrutiny" heaped on Ambrose because, I presume, she (Goodwin) committed a similar crime and thus deserves similar attention. Barnes insists that the *Times* played favorites to Ambrose because, to use Liasson's term, he is the "giant" they were anxious to topple. In other words, Ambrose was better news while Goodwin, as Kondracke implies, was "old news" and therefore not worth targeting.

Unlike Ambrose, Goodwin settled with the one author evidently most wronged by Goodwin's pilfering. As Fred Barnes points out, Lynne McTaggart was evidently not willing to accept a simple apology from Goodwin. "She didn't care about the footnotes," Barnes said. "She wanted her stuff in quotes. It was the lack of attribution in quotes that angered her, and of course, she says, a substantial sum of money changed hands." Evidently, this sum was "substantial" enough to appease McTaggart, who found the end result "satisfactory" ("Historian Paid").

One other difference in the Goodwin case is worth mentioning. In her list of excuses, Goodwin offers one that, to her mind, stands out above all others. In writing her book she took a lot of "handwritten notes" and then made the error of mistaking quotes in her notes "for her own words." The defense, I must say, is fascinating. With Ambrose, a new technology (the computer) contributed to the "blockbuster pace" that would eventually lead to his errors; here, conversely, an old technology (handwriting) serves as a partial excuse for misrecognizing the difference between one's own words and someone else's. Goodwin admitted that "she should have used directly attributed quotes." The method is "so simple and so right," she said, "and you learn as you do these things over time" (Kirkpatrick, "Historian Says").

We heard similar language when Green cited Ambrose's "sloppy notetaking" as a possible explanation for his "beloved" author's momentary lapse. But Ambrose, at least in the literature reviewed here, never ventured that excuse himself. For Goodwin, however, it would become the central feature of her defense. In late January, for example, in a PBS *NewsHour* feature discussed further below, Goodwin made the case that her "technique of citation [for the 1987 book in question] proved not to be foolproof in the end" because her materials ("running commentary" and "passages" found in books) got mixed together into one indistinguishable stockpile of "notes." In conducting her research, she "would recheck every one of those 300 books to make sure the quotes were accurate and make sure the citation was right," but "[s]omehow, in that process, a few of those 300 books did not fully get rechecked." This mistake, however, of mixing up longhand notes is no longer a problem for Goodwin, for as Margaret Warner would later report, Goodwin "now does her research on computer, keeping quotes from sources and her own comments in separate files."

Several issues intersect here. For one, we have been asked to believe that not Goodwin but Goodwin's outdated "technique" (we might also call it a technology) of longhand note taking is really to blame for her plagiarism. The implications are somewhat daunting. The technology of handwriting—as old, we could say, as writing itself—is here invoked to excuse a crime against writing. Secondly, a newer writing technology—the computer—marks the transition from a mistake-ridden past to a well-organized present in which "quotes" and "comments" can be kept in "separate files," thus helping reproduce the age-old epistemological distinction between one's own words and someone else's. Furthermore, as Emily Eakin will show in her January 26 article "Stop, Historians! Don't Copy That Passage! Computers are Watching," the networked computer now factors in as a powerful weapon in the battle against plagiarism. "Over the last decade," Eakin reports, "plagiarism detection has gone high-tech." The several software solutions Eakin describes, including Turnitin.com, are interesting in their own right (see chapter 7 for a closer analysis). Important to note is simply that Green's "temptation" device proves relevant to a wide variety of related activities and not just paper downloading and cut-and-paste shortcuts. For Ambrose, the computer, in particular the spell-check function, helped increase his creative "pace" but also may have induced a particular kind of editorial sloppiness. For Goodwin, the computer facilitated a move from primitive hand-based note taking to the more sophisticated (and safer) world of quotes rendered "separate" from their related comments. Finally, for outfits like Turnitin.com, "which uses a software program to check the content of student work against millions of sites around the Web and a database of papers from online term-paper mills," the computer functions as the definitive surveillance device, poised and ready at a moment's notice to separate not just the "quote" from the "comment" but also the "honest" from the "dishonest" literary document (Eakin).

Doris Kearns Goodwin's plagiarism infraction would also be a topic of conversation on the January 28, 2002, edition of the PBS *NewsHour*, hosted by Margaret Warner. Warner begins the conversation with an ostensibly clear and distinct definition of plagiarism, borrowed from Merriam-Webster: To plagiarize, she says, is "to steal and pass off (the ideas or words of another) as one's own." Whether or not Ambrose and Goodwin committed such acts of literary theft would be the subject, in part, of the ensuing discussion, but first we are treated to Goodwin's own defense (recorded earlier) of her literary behavior. Much of that defense—turning on errors of "technique"—has been treated above. Worth noting now is Goodwin's eagerness to situate her infraction within the larger debate still raging over the "double standard" invoked by our U. Penn. students back on January 15. "I absolutely believe," says Goodwin, "professional standards for historians need never be sacrificed in popular history . . . and it's critical to credit the people who have plowed the fields before." Regarding her own "professional standards," Goodwin assures the viewing audience that she is plowing her own literary territory: "There is absolutely no intent to appropriate anyone's words as my own, which is what plagiarism is."

Merriam-Webster's definition of "steal" suggests that Goodwin is correct, or at least justified, in amending the given definition of "plagiarize" to include this matter of intent. She did not intend to steal or appropriate, so despite her error of technique, she did not plagiarize. Not everyone, however, would accept Goodwin's gloss, most notably Timothy Noah, one of three guests on the *NewsHour* that night and staff writer for the online magazine, *Slate*. Noah rejects Goodwin's excuse and insists that what we have here is a case "where two academic historians or at least former academic historians [Ambrose as well as Goodwin] are distorting the definition of plagiarism. Plagiarism does not have to be deliberate. It can be inadvertent." Noah is "surprised," in fact, that Goodwin would make that claim given the fact that she "sits on the board of directors . . . at Harvard University where this is stated quite clearly in a handbook given to freshmen."

Noah has returned to the source, if you will, of the problem by invoking the Harvard freshman handbook as the definitive authority on issues of text appropriation. With the reader's permission, we will accept this introduction of new evidence because, in fact, the rules in the Harvard handbook, as explained by Noah, seem remarkably consistent with the rules we have accrued, willynilly, so far (not to mention those discussed in chapter 5). The handbook

> says clearly if you borrow . . . [i]t doesn't have to be an entire sentence. If you borrow a lengthy phrase and you do not put quotation marks around it, that's plagiarism whether you did it on purpose or not and whether you included a footnote or not. The quotation marks are the key thing that defines plagiarism.

If "the words are all" (Mallon) and "quotation marks are the key thing" (Noah), then indeed the case should be closed, especially if errors of this sort are considered plagiarism "whether you did it on purpose or not." Ambrose and Goodwin, despite their protestations, are guilty.

But Jerah Johnson, history professor at the University of New Orleans and also a guest on *NewsHour*, vehemently disagrees. "No. No. No. No. Absolutely not. Simply errors. Simply errors." Johnson then clarifies his point: This case, he says, is just a prime example of how easy it is for any of us to make these kinds of errors. I agree with her definition of plagiarism, that it's a conscious act, a deliberate act, a calculating act to simply steal someone else's work.

Like Stuart Green, Johnson wants to position this kind of error making within a community of "us" for whom it is "easy" to make such mistakes.

Margaret Warner then asks her third panel participant, Eric Foner of Columbia University, to weigh in on the topic of authorial intent. At first glance it appears that Foner casts the deciding vote in favor of Noah's view that intention is not the "all" of plagiarism. It "doesn't depend," he argues, "on the motivation. It depends on the evidence that we have before us." Reiterating that Ambrose's initial denial was "rather more damaging in a way," Foner praises Goodwin for at least admitting her mistake. What Foner finds damaging, however, in Ambrose's explanation is that it violates his definition of good writing. Ambrose's "explanation that when he finds a good story he just plugs it into his own writing, that's not what most of us consider writing to be." Furthermore,

> writing is putting these things into your own words, creating your own argument, not just sort of scavenging other people's books and taking their good writing and putting it out as your own words.

Thus, to write, according to Foner, is to create your "own argument"; to plagiarize is to scavenge another's creation. Hence, the double sin of literary theft: in failing to credit another's creation, you fail to create yourself and thus become, by extension, both unlawful and illegitimate.

Warner turns back to Johnson: "[W]hat do you say to the point Tim Noah raised about what students are told and I think disciplined for in this area?" Johnson responds:

> Certainly. A student should be. They have to be taught and they should be taught. It takes a long time. It's not just freshmen. Our beginning graduate students have a terrible time understanding when to footnote and where to footnote and how to use quotations. It takes a very long time to get people trained.

As Berkenkotter and Huckin have pointed out, there is for any discourse community a given "genre knowledge" that novices within the community must learn in order to "perform effectively" (2). Johnson makes the same point with regard to the academic community, broadly conceived. Both graduates and undergraduates—any, in fact, who seek certification within this community—

must be taught or "trained" in the conventions of source citation. Warner clarifies her question: "But I mean do you think there should be a double standard or a different standard for college students than Professors—or historians?"

"No," replies Johnson, "it's all the same standard but again I go back to what I said originally. We all make errors, students and professional historians alike." So, contra Warner's leading question, Johnson insists that students and "professional historians" are similar in making mistakes of this kind. It is "all the same standard," and that standard should make allowances for simple human error. Tim Noah, however, disagrees. Referring again to the Harvard rule set, Noah insists:

> [I]f you make such an error as an undergraduate . . . they have very stern sanctions against it. You are typically asked to leave the university for two semesters. You're not even allowed within the [c]ity of Cambridge, Massachusetts. You'll lose all of the credit hours that you've accumulated until then, which means a lot of lost money. And you have something put permanently on your record that states that you did something dishonest when you were an undergraduate.

In response, Johnson wonders out loud whether Noah is "saying that Harvard students are not allowed to make errors?" Noah is ready with a quick reply: "They're not allowed to make this error apparently."

Once again, Warner turns to Foner for help, and it is here in Foner's testimony that the "flurry," I believe, reaches its fascinating climax. Warner asks him to state, for the record, his view on the question of plagiarism "standards" in academia, and Foner replies:

> Well, obviously, if a student turned up, if a freshman turned up with a paper with these errors I would probably give him *[sic]* a stern warning, send him back and have him rewrite it. If it were someone a little further advanced, the penalty would be more severe. But, you know, I think that there's . . . [t]he problem here goes beyond these two individuals. You have the publishers who refuse to acknowledge these infractions and refuse to withdraw the books from publication. (ellipsis in original)

The ellipsis here—marking an abrupt change of subject—is important for reasons I will go into below. For now I focus on Foner's apparent admission that there is, indeed, a double standard. First of all, we have our typical (male) student—a freshman—turning up in Foner's office and getting a "stern warning" for making citation errors. No problem, Foner might say, just "rewrite it," only this time be sure to "write" it—i.e., put "things into your own words"; create "your own argument"; don't just go "scavenging other people's books." But there is another student waiting in the hall who swallows his fear and shuffles into Foner's office. If this student, suggests Foner, is "someone a little further advanced, the penalty would be more severe."

Foner believes, in short, that there should be a certain amount of play (slack, maneuvering room) in adjudicating problems of this sort. The final decision is a judgment call—in the most literal sense—issued by a responsible member of a discourse community. The "freshman," in other words, stands in symbolically for the amateur to whom any well-reasoned university expert should show a little mercy. But even the most reasonable of experts will not forget that there is also a respected community whose traditions must be upheld, as well as a particular "genre knowledge" whose rudiments, as Johnson said so well, "should be taught." Therefore, both during and after learning those rudiments, students will be held to a higher standard, and penalties for infractions will be more "severe." The logic makes perfect sense for an educational system, stretching from Columbia to New Orleans and beyond, that stresses the importance of moving up through progressive stages of development and joining the ranks of the "further advanced."

Moreover, by suggesting rather coyly that severe penalties should be meted out to those a little higher up on the academic ladder, Foner implies that Ambrose and Goodwin are just as culpable as any student who has moved beyond the first year. To summarize, if there is a double standard (Noah's argument), then students obviously get the short end of the stick. But if there is just one standard (Johnson's apparent belief, Foner's veiled argument), then clearly Ambrose and Goodwin should be subject to "more severe" sanctions than perhaps they have so far endured. The debate about double standards in education ends there, however, since as noted, Foner jumps rather abruptly to a new topic: negligence on the part of publishers. This leap, marked in the text with an ellipsis (. . .), is significant, and I will conclude my discussion of the Ambrose/Goodwin cases by ending where I began—in the realm of punctuation.

An ellipsis in grammar shows the omission of one or more words that are obviously understood but that must be supplied to make a construction grammatically complete. For example, "The text that she copied" may be changed, by ellipsis, to "The text she copied." Clearly the ellipsis in the *NewsHour* transcription of Foner's response is meant to indicate not an omission of this order but a sudden leap, as definitions of "ellipsis" suggest, without logical connectives from one topic to another. Still, it could be argued that in pausing between subjects, Foner both leaps toward a new topic and omits (removes from the debate) the very issue under review. "The problem," he says after the pause, "goes beyond these two individuals." And indeed, the issue on the table now goes beyond not only Ambrose and Goodwin but also beyond the other individuals— I will call them students and professionals—for whom Ambrose and Goodwin have so far served as specially coded surrogates. In brief, Foner has replaced the student with the figure of the publisher. The problem of a double standard in academic life has been erased, bypassed, left behind, omitted from the discussion, and Margaret Warner anchors the transition: "So I take then *[sic]*, Professor Foner, that you don't think there should be a different standard for so-called popular history."

Obviously, the leap makes sense in context. After all, Goodwin opens this segment with the ardent claim that "professional standards" need not be sacrificed for popular success. As might be expected, Foner and now Warner have simply moved on to this part of the debate. Still, we have lost even the question of whether or not students and professionals (professors) do, indeed, occupy separate domains where plagiarism is concerned. Have students, in other words, now been surreptitiously moved over into the camp of the "professional" in order to better frame this now-revised debate concerning "so-called popular history" and its potentially "different standard"? At the very least the debate has shifted noticeably from one in which students are pitted against professors to one in which academic professionals (which may or not include students) face popular historians in the battle over literary terrain.

This battle plays out in the ensuing dialog, wherein Warner proposes a subtle distinction between "serious" academic scholarship and blockbuster-paced writing: referring to Stephen Ambrose, she asks, "Is it really possible to do serious research and original thinking and write a book of history in a year?" Surfacing again, we see, is the issue of blocks and their associated busters. Warner's question to Johnson is leading, to say the least, and Johnson takes issue with the implied critique of Ambrose's "original thinking": yes, he replies, it is possible if you happen to be Stephen Ambrose, who is "simply a phenomenally hard-working historian. . . . That's all Steve knows how to do is work."

Taking issue with Johnson's remark, Foner acknowledges that Ambrose may be a "very hard-working person," but "there are many other historians who are also equally hard working." In other words, hard work is not the province of popular or blockbuster historians alone. Those who do scholarly history are "hard-working" as well. But Foner, at the same time, wants to emphasize the difference between "other historians" and Ambrose:

> They don't produce a book a year. It's humanly impossible to produce as many books so fast as Professor Ambrose has and give each one the care and the originality that is required by professional standards.

Foner then assures the viewing public that Ambrose and Goodwin are "unfortunate" but "isolated instances." In brief, the world of historical scholarship is for the most part safe, as long as Ambrose and those like him are suitably dealt with: "The largest sanction against a scholar is really what has happened here: Publicity and simply some diminution of their reputation." Moreover, in claiming that it is "humanly impossible" to produce so prodigiously, Foner makes the point that I made less elegantly earlier: Ambrose could not have acted alone, simply because the amount of work done in the time it took to do it is not possible for a single human being. In other words, in ferreting out weakness, we must look not to "Ambrose" but, perhaps, to "Ambrose and Ambrose, Inc." and then to the blockbuster publishing racket which underwrites the kind of super- or inhuman feats that Foner finds "impossible."

Nonetheless, the damage to the man himself—via diminution—has indeed been done, in part by critics such as Foner. To put it briefly, without "care" and "originality" and the blessing of "professional standards," Ambrose stands before other historians as someone who has nothing to show for himself— besides the millions in his bank account, that is. In performing the "humanly impossible," Ambrose has been stripped of his humanity, which for our purposes means that, in the end, he is profoundly and irredeemably unoriginal.

CONCLUSION: FASCINATION REVISITED

Where has plagiarism gone in all this? It has gone where it often goes— absorbed into a larger, murkier realm in which debates turn less on individual (human) actors and more on institutional battles over contested terrain. In this case, a potentially envious professional sector cordons off a kind of careful, original, slow, and honest work and builds a barricade against the careless, false, too fast, and dishonest activities of the popular. A "flurry of fascination" builds up around the ensuing drama, and we, as participants and observers, play our respective parts in either damning or defending.

My goal in telling this story has been to reconstruct that flurry and, along the way, to note what remains murky in such tales of literary malfeasance, particularly where issues of education and student writing are concerned. I have tried to avoid taking sides—or at least have endeavored to define and temporarily occupy the several sides represented—but the alert reader will surely have guessed by now that while I am curious about Ambrose and Goodwin and their related fates, I find my affinities drifting ever farther away from those who have enjoyed over time the most attention and closer to those whose voices were seldom if ever heard in the debates captured here.

I am more concerned, that is, about the "hapless student" who, without the kind of publicity heaped on our infamous historians, has been left somewhere hidden—anonymous and mute—in the folds of this story. As Geoff Nunberg would say in late February, 2002, on NPR's *Fresh Air*, the "striking thing about plagiarism is how rarely anybody has anything original to say about it." Echoing Thomas Mallon, Nunberg goes on to point out that there is

> a remarkable sameness about these literary scandals going back to the eighteenth century. The indignant accusations, the protestations of innocent error and above all the puzzling gratuitousness of the crime. I'm not talking now about a student who goes on the Internet to buy a term paper for a course he hasn't attended all semester. That may be reprehensible, but it isn't mysterious.

Indeed, we are not "talking now about a student"—neither Nunberg's hypothetical-reprehensible nor the hapless-voiceless one introduced above. And, to be sure, wherever student infractions are discussed, there is often a "remarkable sameness" about the ways in which the student plagiarist is cast as criminally minded at worst, ignorant or careless at best—like an "Ambrose," in other words, but without recourse to research teams and bankrolls. To sum up, finally, on the issue of standards and their potential doubling, I propose that there is only one, but the repercussions are radically different depending on where you happen to do business and just where you sit on the scale of least to most "advanced."

So, at the risk of having something original to say about this age-old topic, I think we have barely begun to understand—as students, teachers, scholars, professors, historians, reporters, publishers, and letter writers from Granada Hills—precisely what is going on when a student, or anyone for that matter, engages in the kinds of literary activities lumped together under the murky catchall of plagiarism. Thus, to confront all such incidents as crimes of either theft or negligence—and the basic tenor of the reporting in this case reinforced just that reduction—is, to my mind, the true crime that goes largely unreported. Not that acts of theft and negligence do not take place. My concern, rather, is that there appears to be little interest—in popular or professional culture, to hold onto that troubled binary just a bit longer—in considering possible causes and explanations (and even solutions) other than those serving to replicate and reinforce the common idea that what is not correct in literary practice is by nature deviant and evil. The story told in these pages seems to make that point rather well.

In general, then, the Harvard handbook—like others addressed in chapter 5—would have us believe that the issue of correct appropriation is closed, the problems easy to define, and the various cases of literary transgression so obvious (for an Ambrose, a Goodwin, or a student) that everyone would likely agree on both the nature of the crime and the need for adequate punishments. I hope this retelling of the Ambrose and Goodwin stories has shown, however, that the issue is far from closed, the problems not at all easy to define, and our system of punishment so skewed that even a group of three professionally and academically minded experts cannot, before a national audience, either agree on what plagiarism is or keep the conversation focused long enough to isolate the source of disagreement. The only sense common to all of this is that professors, publishers, blockbuster and professional historians, universities, newspapers, radio and TV stations, and hapless students are all caught up in the "flurry" of plagiarism, and too often it is not clear who ends up paying, in the end, for whose crime.

2

The Plagiarism Debate
History and Contexts

PLAGIARISM DEFINED

BY MOST ACCOUNTS, plagiarism is a dirty word, and one reserved for particularly vile, dangerous, and disruptive forms of literary activity. Dictionary definitions suggest that if one plagiarizes one violates a major rule pertaining to the use and incorporation of textual sources. Plagiarists commit acts of petty larceny, trying to "steal" or "pass off" the words or ideas of another as if they were their own. Most handbooks, defining plagiarism in the broader context of research writing and the rules of source incorporation, invoke an economy of "credit" to suggest that users or borrowers of another's work typically pay dividends—via footnotes, citations, and other scholarly paraphernalia—to the material source used or borrowed. To take credit for work done by another, or to neglect or choose not to give credit, is to plagiarize—in particular, to present the derivative (in some cases, the copy) as if it were in fact original.

The 2003 Modern Language Association (MLA) *Handbook for Writers of Research Papers* recalls the Latin *plagiarius* in defining plagiarism as a "form of cheating" involving the wrongful usurpation of another's intellectual property (Gibaldi 66). Lindey defers to the Roman legal definition of *plagium* as "the stealing of a slave" or the "stealing of a freeman with intent to keep him or sell him as a slave" (95)—in other words, as a form of kidnapping. Most sources agree, as well, that the first-century poet Marcus Valerius Martialis (Martial) was the first to use the Latin *plagiarius* to mean "literary theft." In sum: as user, thief, or borrower, the plagiarist steals, takes credit for, and/or kidnaps literary content or material belonging ostensibly to someone else.

Ancient records reveal both frequent instances of plagiarism and scholarly concern over the practice as a moral or ethical wrong. The ancient Roman architect Vitruvius (first century BC) condemned plagiarism and even warned

31

against critical attacks on the work of dead authors, which under certain circumstances could warrant the death penalty (Long 34). Plagiarism may certainly have involved the wrongful use (or stealing) of someone else's creative output, but for ancient practitioners and authors of late antiquity, the violation offended more for its inherent affront to authorial honor and piety. The Renaissance revival of classical aesthetics carried with it this classical understanding of plagiarism. As Hammond notes, drawing on White's 1935 *Plagiarism and Imitation During the English Renaissance*, Renaissance authors acknowledged their borrowings both "as an act of *pietas*" and in an effort to position and protect themselves within "a glorious literary tradition" (47).

As impious insult, plagiarism undermines cultural valuations of authorship and does so via the same technologies of production and distribution used for more accepted creative practices. Thus, as Groom intones, plagiarism in modern times has come to represent a "plague," an "illness," even a "madness"—in short, a kind of "social abnormality" (*Forger's Shadow* 27). Moreover, as Howard Becker points out with regard to modern art practices, plagiarism inspires negative responses because, in addition to stealing property, the plagiarist steals an artist's "reputation" (23). For literary artists, as Ricks and others have suggested, the author's loss to the plagiarist might not be quite so grave. Plagiarizing a poem, for example, does not necessarily deprive the poet of her status. Still, in taking credit for original authorship, the plagiarist seeks the same status and protection as the originator and thus intrudes on sheltered spaces normally reserved for reputed authors.

A stable and reliable definition of plagiarism continues to elude scholars and practitioners across the disciplines. As compositionist Margaret Price has suggested, definitions of plagiarism and their related injunctions—in academia in particular—often shift in accordance with cultural, professional, and disciplinary assumptions and prejudices. Most sources agree, however, that plagiarism does not align strictly with copyright infringement or intellectual property theft more broadly. The MLA *Handbook*, for one, insists on the one hand that plagiarism suggests "two kinds of wrongs"—"intellectual theft" and "fraud"—but grants on the other that plagiarism is "sometimes a moral and ethical offense rather than a legal one" (Gibaldi 66). To clarify, "intellectual property" in its modern sense refers to the monopoly right granted to individual authors for the transformative work performed in the production of literary and other textual materials (Boyle xii). This work of textual transformation, as Boyle suggests, is "more often assumed than proved" but nonetheless earns the author a "limited right of private property" in exchange for the gift of innovative ideas "to society at large" (xii).

In general, then, this assumed right of original authorship—reified under late-seventeenth- and early-eighteenth-century European and U.S. copyright law—converts the textual products of authors into commodities both "partial" and "deliberately restricted" in their availability (Boyle 35). Plagiarism, in this context, may certainly threaten or undermine claims to both originality and authorial right, but intellectual property or copyright claims invariably target the latter as the main avenue of dispute. Therefore, as Ricks and others have argued, plagiarism reflects more the taking of credit (for origin) than the stealing of property, despite the frequent equation of plagiarism with literary theft.

One might conclude, then, that plagiarism constitutes the "stealing" of someone's else's creative work but only metaphorically. However, the frequent equation of plagiarism with literary theft suggests a sense of illicit transfer in a manner consistent with the discourse of property rights. Therefore, the important point should be made that in "modern legal systems" plagiarism and intellectual property are not "distinct entities" at all but rather "overlapping [if] not entirely synonymous categories" (Long 10). The MLA caveat with regard to "some instances of plagiarism" reinforces that conclusion. Likewise, repeated conflations of the expressions "copyright claim" and "plagiarism litigation" suggest a tacit willingness—within modern legal systems and elsewhere—to overlay and even interchange these otherwise distinct categories. Plagiarism may not be an actual crime, as Hammond and others suggest, but it often gets treated—talked about, punished—as if it were. Groom puts it this way: "[P]roper crimes [such as copyright infringement, piracy] lurk in the wings when plagiarism is on stage because they are replete with legal authority" ("Forgery" 74).

In an effort to avoid confusing plagiarism with rights violation, some have pushed the point that plagiarism and intellectual property/copyright do indeed represent distinct categories but that the law is slow to honor, or perhaps incapable of honoring, that distinction. As Debora Halbert argues, plagiarism "is about personal feelings, not profits," and copyright law is not equipped to manage the "personal issues" of plagiarism (117). Laurie Stearns makes the related point that plagiarism tends to be seen as a matter of "creative process" whereas copyright infringement concerns the "creative result" (9). Thus, plagiarism is not a criminal infraction so much as a "failure" on the author's part either to acknowledge the source or to alter, or transform, the material borrowed (Stearns 7).

Here and below, I concentrate on this conventional understanding of plagiarism as a failure of the creative process. Like Stearns, however, I use the term *failure* to mark a historically contingent and context dependent assessment of practice which is itself dependent on particular assumptions about the nature of authorship, ownership, and, in this case, literary production. The plagiarist may often defy the law's exact letter in usurping the original creations of someone else, but this defiance nonetheless marks the plagiarist as one who fails to conform to at least two sets of rules: those pertaining to traditional ideas of authorship and those more recent inventions designed to protect the rights and privileges of authors. The creative failure to produce an original work—through either overt theft or the inability to warrant claims to textual transformation—

creates the plagiarist as a subject controlled by law. As Coombe points out, "By creating objects of property, the law simultaneously creates subjects of politics" (50). The author who does not fail but succeeds in making claims to "limited right" also claims subjective authenticity and originality in relation to a social space made better by the introduction of fresh ideas. The politics of authorship thus begin and end in the creation and authentication of authoring subjects set against a social body exchanging rights for beneficial knowledge.

The plagiarist, conversely, in compromising authorial right, compromises (in most cases forfeits) all claims to authentic subjectivity. Thus, the plagiarist as inauthentic subject assumes an alternative identity, as false, fraudulent, or anti-author, in relation to a society threatened by the wrongful use of words and/or ideas. The legal stronghold known as intellectual property serves as a "locus for the control and dissemination of those signifying forms with which identities and difference are made and remade" (Coombe 29). Here and throughout this book, I stress the "signifying forms" of authorship and plagiarism as articulated not only in copyright and intellectual property law but also in education in general and the discourses of writing instruction in particular. Where the law distinguishes discrete objects in order to defend intellectual property claims, literary conventions and writing pedagogies create plagiarists and plagiarism in accordance with strict aesthetic and ethical codes of conduct. Plagiarism must be understood, then, not solely as an individual failure to comply but rather as a socially meaningful activity calibrated—as is authentic authorship itself—against very specific signifying forms.

As Marilyn Randall argues, plagiarism can therefore be read as a "pragmatic category" whose "existence depends on an act of reception" (vi). Feminist critiques of authorship—Randall's among them—have stressed in various ways this pragmatic approach to literary *plagiarius*. As discussed above, plagiarism in a modern context implies the intentional (albeit figurative) stealing of intellectual property, granting again that copyright law does not necessarily distinguish between intentional and unintentional theft. Composition scholar Rebecca Moore Howard goes farther in pointing out that discussions of plagiarism often involve "metaphors of gender, weakness, collaboration, disease, adultery, [and] rape" as well as "property" ("Sexuality" 474). Echoing Groom, Howard contends that most accounts of plagiarism treat it as a "disease" and "transgressive variant" ("Sexuality" 479) of masculine authorship, threatening to contaminate—and feminize—anyone who might "come into contact with the offender" ("Sexuality" 481). These gendered metaphors, Howard argues, are more than just coincidence or analogy: they are "the *meaning* of plagiarism" ("Sexuality" 486). More broadly, plagiarism and plagiarism injunctions, as sites of cultural and political meaning, recast identity in strict relation to middle-class, masculinist, and primarily white European understandings of authorship. In short, to copy or take credit for the original work of another is to pretend to be an author (creative, original); once caught, however, the plagiarist assumes the position of a feminized other (aberrant, destructive, even pathological).

As a kind of "authorship run amok" (Howard, "Sexuality" 486), plagiarism for some provides an opportunity to challenge the legal, aesthetic, and ethical assumptions pertaining to authorship addressed so far. Indeed, it could be argued that where a writer intentionally copies for the sake of art, the typical charge of plagiarism does not apply (Randall 127). In the case of novelist Kathy Acker, for example, intentional copying provides a "positive antidote to the evils of cultural imperialism" via the focused and deliberate critique of power and property values (Randall 217). Groom suggests more generally that plagiarism, as an aesthetic activity, can function to subvert a dominant work ethic that defines value as "the expenditure of labour and capital in production" ("Forgery" 84). Citing Stewart Home's claim that plagiarism is "the negative point of a culture that finds its ideological justification in the 'unique,'" Groom traces Home's and others' interest in the cultural subversion of plagiarism to an earlier "Situationist stratagem" ("Forgery" 85). In a similar vein, Randall posits plagiarism as "a guerrilla tactic" for postmodern, particularly feminist, authorship (228).

To take just one example of this kind of plagiarism, the Web-based, collaborative arts group Critical Art Ensemble employs "guerrilla" tactics in the domain of what they call the "techno-infrastructure" (106). Given the modes of production in this domain—e.g., with the advent of personal computers, the Internet, and widely available digital editing technologies—plagiarism, they suggest, is not only likely but necessary as a means of furthering cultural output. Practicing various forms of "recombinant methodologies"—such as mixing and repurposing digital content—today's self-styled plagiarists do not "stop invention" but rather participate in invention without thwarting the prevailing "economy of representation" (Critical Art Ensemble 109). In an apparent effort to clean up plagiarism's bad reputation (as characterized, for example, by Groom), the Ensemble proposes a "productive" plagiarism to promote innovation; with today's media systems, they contend, productive plagiarism is not only "acceptable" but "inevitable" (Critical Art Ensemble 106). Important to note here is Coombe's cautionary critique of "[r]omantic celebrations of insurrectionary alterity"—in particular, those moments of guerrilla plagiarism where "the very resources with which people express difference are the properties of others" (10). In brief, convenient dichotomies pitting the dominant against a resistant subculture might oversimplify the power structures within which guerrilla plagiarists choose to intervene for purposes of upsetting traditional modes of knowing.

Furthermore, Groom wonders whether the kinds of guerrilla, productive, or activist plagiarisms described here can even count as actual plagiarism, which "is first (and by definition) a covert activity"; where a plagiarist "cheerfully admits to plagiarizing, the act stops being plagiarism and becomes something else entirely" ("Forgery" 85). Groom's point is well taken but may not apply, for example, in the case of student plagiarism. One can imagine, for example, a student "cheerfully" admitting to plagiarizing but for whom the plagiarism nonetheless does not become "something else" before a writing instructor or academic review board. In fact, a student may want to believe that what he or she is doing is a form of productive sedition, but once the act—or its artifact, its trace, its admission—gets read in a particular way, it might at that point "stop being" something else and become plagiarism per se. Of course, this simple hypothetical account stretches the larger point argued above. For every act of plagiarism—whether mounted as a "guerrilla" tactic or performed covertly in pursuit of a higher grade—a range of prevailing contexts (historical, institutional, legal, cultural, and pedagogical) inform local assessments of whether or not a given act can be defined as "something else entirely" or the real thing itself.

For these and other reasons, I disagree with Groom's conclusion that plagiarism is a "purely textual transaction" ("Forgery" 88). Likewise, I take issue with his broader indictment of the "current tendency in English studies" to stress "miscellaneous contexts" (e.g., historical, material, moral, legal, etc.) over the "immediacy and proximity of the *literary* context" ("Forgery" 89). To begin with, Groom's insistence on the immediacy of the literary requires recourse to rather limited, if well-established, academic hierarchies. "Writers," Groom proposes, "need to be considered as an entirely different kettle of fish than cheating students, who are so many more red herrings" ("Forgery" 88). Groom's defense of absolutist "literary values," in other words, requires the overt dismissal of student writing as categorically insignificant to the question of literary plagiarism:

> What we are really talking about in university cases is students cheating, and we should call it precisely that, *cheating*, not plagiarism—with all its rich and subtle variations and insinuations. A student submitting fraudulent term papers is not at all like a writer plagiarizing phrases or sentences, poems or stories. . . . ("Forgery" 87)

I concede Groom's point that plagiarism often amounts to plain old "cheating" and, likewise, that cheating should be handled accordingly ("Forgery" 87). However, the argument hinges on the somewhat rash assumption that student writers, even "students cheating," do not engage in the "subtle variations and insinuations" of plagiarism. Much depends, of course, on what Groom means here by "fraudulent term papers," a category which seems to cover a lot of ground in the service of Groom's larger point. But even where student cheating presents a simple case of fraud (downloading and submitting a paper purchased on the Internet, for example), the fact remains that student writers (like all writers) can and often do plagiarize "phrases" and "sentences," "poems" and "stories," as well as essays, reports, and term papers. Furthermore, they do so in potentially subtle ways that defy Groom's reduction of student cheating to simple cases of fraud (see Howard and Price for more on this point).

In short, Groom offers up the university cheater as the scapegoat—the bad fish, as it were—in his larger attack on English studies and its misguided interest in "miscellaneous contexts" at the expense of the literary. Oddly, though, his reliance on categorical distinctions of this sort—pitting writers "plagiarizing" against university "students cheating"—lends support to the countervailing claim that attention to a wide set of contextual variables is not only preferable but necessary to any study of plagiarism and its associated remedies. If writers and frauds in a "university" context should be treated differently than writers and frauds in another (a point based on the premise that student writers do in fact *write*), then clearly the "literary" is only one among several equally important contexts to consider when looking at specific acts of plagiarism. In his apparent move to discourage continued attention to "academic" and other contexts so as to encourage greater attention to the literary, Groom nonetheless makes a context-specific argument in order to bolster a rather important distinction. Speaking of the academy, Groom writes that "[i]t is clear within this context what is right and what is wrong," but in "literature . . . the same rules do not apply" in part because "writers are not governed as members of a formal institution" ("Forgery" 87). This is an arguable point but one that obviously treats of differing contexts in order to argue on behalf of the one that is ostensibly more "literary."

Clearly several factors or concerns—ethical, moral, religious, legal, pedagogical, and literary—complicate efforts not only to punish but also to define plagiarism. Thus I agree with Rebecca Howard that to know what plagiarism means (as word, as policy, as signifying form) is to delve into a wide range of metaphorical constructions informing both conventions and current critical-theoretical approaches to the topic. Moreover, if plagiarism really cannot be defined, let alone critiqued, outside of its availing contexts, then as Randall rightly suggests, plagiarism should be read as a pragmatic category, and thus all forays into the concept—as property violation, as fraudulent writing activity, as dishonest and deceitful conduct, as guerrilla activism—must operate from the start in acknowledgment of historical and practical contingencies. Therefore, in order to understand plagiarism and antiplagiarism remedies, the critical historian must look beyond not only dictionary and handbook definitions but also critical approaches that place emphasis on individual practice—student writers and writing, for example—as the only valuable unit of analysis.

Plagiarism does not necessarily materialize, or materialize solely, in the products of textual assembly—be they student essays, research papers, popular histories, experimental novels, or Web sites. Rather, as Becker, Groom,

Howard, Kewes, Randall, and many others have suggested in different ways, plagiarism exists where it is recognized—or *mediated*—by readers offering up the specific charge of plagiarism in a particular time and place. Moreover, I should stress that today's "readers" are not just teachers, editors, publishers, lawyers, artists, scholars, journalists, and other writers, but also the formalized rule sets, administrative policies, course assignments, and software services used to substantiate accusations of plagiarism. In other words, the plagiarist, the plagiarized text, and institutional definitions of and responses to plagiarism are always mutually productive moments or "mechanisms," in Foucault's sense, within the same disciplinary network. To treat any one in isolation is to force an analytical distinction that, in the end, serves up a false categorical stability.

AUTHORSHIP, OWNERSHIP, AND WRITING

The author and the plagiarist have long worked side by side, each depending on the other to substantiate related, if contradictory, claims to authorial identity. Modern understandings of authorship—in particular the notion that the author is a "solitary and originary" inventor of discretely embodied texts (Lunsford, "Refiguring" 68)—bespeak a corollary understanding of creation bounded on all sides by potential threats to origin. To author, to create, to invent, to originate, and to do so independently of others: these are the embedded imperatives informing the "Romantic ideology of creativity," an ideology resonating with nineteenth-century, particularly Hegelian, notions of "personality" (Coombe 220). As discussed above, such notions can be set against a wide array of signifying forms emerging in the seventeenth and eighteenth centuries in part to justify claims to authorial right and textual ownership. Hammond notes the special use of the word *author* in Queen Anne's 1709 Act for the Encouragement of Learning which, setting the tone for copyright statutes throughout eighteenth-century Europe, established "a framework whereby authors could claim infringement" not just for "wholesale copying" but also "where a few elements had been lifted rather than wholesale piracy" (51). This distinction—between all-out piracy and at least one kind of plagiarism via the lifting of "elements"—is an important one, since it points to an emerging legal context in which acts of metaphorical literary theft become punishable under modern copyright law. In short, as the notion of literary property "thickens up," modern "attitudes towards plagiarism also harden" (Hammond 49).

Some have questioned the recent move in plagiarism studies to advance historical arguments "in terms of the evolution of print culture and the rise of the author" (Kewes 16). Ricks in particular challenges the "prelapsarian revisionism" that posits the "invention of the author" as the defining moment for an emergent and decidedly pejorative understanding of plagiarism (28). Kewes makes the more specific point that transhistorical approaches to plagiarism, while not necessarily "incorrect," can nonetheless be "seriously incomplete" in their failure, for example, to account for "short-term variation and local change," particularly across genres (14). Hammond, as one proponent of a largely transhistorical study of plagiarism, defends his position by conceding that plagiarism certainly predates the seventeenth-century "invention" of the author. However, he insists that in the English Restoration period "the degree of cultural salience and penetration of plagiarism is new" (51). More specifically, plagiarism at this time comes to be seen as "a species of moral crime against authorship because it threatens literary livelihoods" (Hammond 52). In a similar fashion, Coombe points out that the plagiarist—long since known to engage in dishonorable literary activities—becomes roughly synonymous by the end of the seventeenth century with the "piratical" thief (49) whose persistence alone warrants ever more stringent protectionist regimes. Kewes's point is nonetheless well taken: a thorough understanding of plagiarism—in the seventeenth century and elsewhere—requires a more comprehensive treatment of the several variables at work at any given historical moment. Plagiarism may have posed a threat to literary livelihoods in the seventeenth century and beyond, but the degree and seriousness of that threat hinged on a set of local contingencies, such as the "economic status" of both the author and the plagiarist and the "commercial viability" of the product in question (Kewes 17).

With these caveats in mind, I nonetheless adopt Hammond's position that modern distinctions between authors and plagiarists operate in close proximity with progressively hardened intellectual property laws—in particular laws regarding text production and ownership emerging in the late seventeenth and early eighteenth centuries. I grant, however, that this historical interpretation, outlined broadly here, makes it difficult to discuss authorship, and by extension plagiarism, as anything but an issue pertaining to property and ownership rights. Thus, Hammond's and to some degree my own narrative of authorial "evolution" may serve to reify the kinds of definitional quandaries described at the beginning of this chapter. That is, plagiarists may continue to invite the arguably dual distinction of false creator and property thief in part because both narratives together serve a larger progressivist bias in critical studies of writing and authorship.

With regard to today's antiplagiarism remedies, however, I would argue that one of the key issues in understanding plagiarism detection at the turn of the twenty-first century is the degree to which favored historical positions—at times implied, at times stated openly—support institutional efforts to solve this particular problem. In the realm of plagiarism detection software, the prototypically original, proprietary author figures largely in the assumed rules of correct textual use and citation. Likewise, the dual logics of proprietary ownership and Romantic creativity, taken for granted as fundamental mainstays in the world of writing and literary production, serve widely to legitimize efforts to eradicate or remedy cases of creative failure and property infringement. The dressed up, commercially viable figure of the stable original author, along with the transhistoric myth of emergent originality, serve as the chief signifying forms against which today's plagiarists are often measured and tested.

Moreover, the notion that textual materials—words, phrases, sentences (not to mention images, codes, sounds, performances, designs, scripts, etc.)—can be owned by their producers assumes a metaphorical valence supporting related notions of authorship (writing or composing) as a solitary and exclusive creative process. At the very least, the signifying forms of intellectual property and copyright law have clearly made their way firmly into other disciplinary domains and discourses. A telling example from the early twentieth century is Mikhail Bakhtin's now famous discussion of "ventriloquation" and, in particular, his claim that "[t]he word in language is half someone else's" (293). I cite Bakhtin in this context not to rehearse his well-documented influence on mid- and late-century poetics but rather to highlight the ways in which his language assumes the contours of intellectual property law but to a decidedly different end. The word is always "half someone else's," but Bakhtin is most concerned not with property rights per se but rather the process by which the language comes to be owned through a semantic reworking of content:

> [The word] becomes "one's own" only when the speaker populates it with his own intention, his own accent, when he appropriates the word, adapting it to his own semantic and expressive intention. (Bakhtin 293)

Here we see how one might own language in a manner that differs somewhat from explicitly legal intellectual property claims. Still, even where Bakhtin challenges the notion that one can own the "whole" word outright—for half always belongs to someone else, perhaps to language itself—the process of assuming ownership positions a (male) speaker in relation to a word which he then "populates" with "intention" and "accent." Where the law makes and unmakes identities through well-entrenched "signifying forms" (Coombe 29), here the language of literary appropriation—another key concept in Bakhtin's theory—posits literary identity via the conversion of difference into "one's own." The stamp of "expressive intention," in other words, codifies for aesthetic purposes the exclusive use of language. Indeed, this language of conversion, adaptation, or transmutation (discussed further in chapter 4) departs only slightly from what one might find in intellectual property claims.

Bakhtin's model is clearly more nuanced than I have presented it here, but I aim to highlight, first, the extent to which tropes of property ownership inform discussions of literary activity and, second, to point out for future refer-

ence at least one way in which claims to authorial "personality" speak likewise
to a parallel tradition of scriptural transformation in the arts. For now I will
note only that Bakhtin's act of appropriation is also an act of adaptation, a direct manipulation of material borrowed or taken. The word, according to
Bakhtin, becomes one's own when the speaker appropriates it, adapting it to
one's "own semantic and expressive intention." The circularity here—that language becomes one's own when one makes it one's own—marks a logical bind
that carries through into other places and moments where discussions of authorship, and of course plagiarism, rely on similar tropes of authorial appropriation or incorporation. As a kind of literary or pedagogical law, the ritual
conversion by which a word becomes one's own often marks the chief signifying form underwriting distinctions between authors and plagiarists.

Throughout this book, I will consider authorship in terms of a very particular kind of authoring activity: *writing*. I use the word in the sense offered by
Michel de Certeau, who in *The Practice of Everyday Life* designates writing as
"the concrete activity that consists in constructing, on its own, blank space (*un
espace propre*)—the page—a text that has power over the exteriority from which
it has first been isolated" (134). De Certeau's definition is notable first for its
own subtle invocation of the discourse of property and enclosure. By his account, writing is a constructionist activity that turns a blank space ("the page")
into a text that in turn "has power over" its own outside—its "exteriority"—
from which the writing is "isolated." De Certeau thus describes writing as a
kind of exclusion, a working of text out of an unmarked territory. And yet, the
blank space on which writing materializes is, in language now familiar, "its
own." While I only cautiously adopt (and adapt) this model for my own analysis of plagiarism and antiplagiarism remedies, I do so because the language of
"power" and "exteriority" so crucial to de Certeau's definition bears out in particular ways below—in those forms of writing, for example, that turn text pages
into Web pages, assuming in the process a kind of power over related spaces,
blank and otherwise.

De Certeau's vision of writing carries with it a related sense of textual
transformation that both echoes Bakhtin and suggests a compelling framework
for studying literary activity—including plagiarism—in the so-called digital
age. "The island of the page," he writes, "is a transitional place in which an industrial inversion is made: what comes in is something 'received,' what comes
out is a 'product'" (135). Mixed metaphors aside, this particular "island" of writing is home to an "industrial inversion" that can be likened to Bakhtin's notion
of semantic adaptation. In using language, de Certeau's idealized writer performs a kind of reworking or refiguring of "received" content into something
redefined as, perhaps, one's own, one's intention, one's "product." In stark contrast to the "ideology of creativity" informing Romantic views of authorship, de
Certeau proposes a decidedly postindustrial formula for the making of texts out

of preexisting materials. Writing thus conceived suggests a transitory "activity" resembling something closer to factory production than the spontaneous generation of authorial genius.

At the very least, de Certeau offers a compelling theoretical framework for understanding the kind of writing taken up in this and later chapters. Resisting an overly literal interpretation, I nonetheless take up the industrial model for purposes of studying the ways in which pages, texts, and other material artifacts function within an economy in which pages of student writing, for example, serve as raw material for a special kind of productive inversion. Chapter 7 addresses this issue in greater detail, but for now I point out that a plagiarized text by definition thrives on the fodder of received pages. More generally, plagiarism detection systems—whether formal institutional injunctions or Web-based services—recast received content in terms of very specific distinctions separating the original from the copy. In some cases, the end result of that process is indeed a literal product bearing the explicit marks of industrial inversion.

In language combining the literary and the industrial, as well as the aesthetic and the economic, de Certeau further defines writing as a "scriptural enterprise" that "transforms or retains within itself what it receives from its outside . . ." (135). Boldly reminiscent of Lockean property theory, de Certeau's choice of metaphors goes far to reify legal notions of textual ownership and even to encourage proactive colonization of external spaces: the scriptural enterprise also "stocks up what it sifts out and gives itself the means to expand" (135). Committed to "making the alterity of the universe *conform* to its models," the scriptural enterprise is, finally, "capitalist and conquering" (135). In the ensuing analysis I borrow this admittedly knotty definition of writing as "scriptural enterprise" in order to argue that antiplagiarism remedies, of the sort described in this book, are themselves—along with plagiarism and not in contradistinction to it—varieties of writing that transform and retain, stock up and sift out, accumulate and conquer in particularly meaningful ways. More specifically, I argue that plagiarism prevention and detection in higher education is a conformist project designed to transform—through literal and metaphorical "industrial inversion"—the alterity of plagiarism into one of only a few preferred authorship models. In short, plagiarism services author plagiarism in specific ways and thus author writers and writing in specific ways as well. The extent to which such an enterprise is "capitalist and conquering" is a matter addressed further in chapter 7.

As Andrea Lunsford, Susan Miller, and Martha Woodmansee have pointed out, notions of authorship as a kind of private, solitary, and originary writing activity continue to inform not only legal discourse but scholarly and educational discourse as well. Broadly speaking, in academia we continue to place a premium on "'original' contributions to scholarship" and "'original' student work," enlisting ever more "stringent proscriptions" in the fight against scriptural alterity and other diseases of the page (Lunsford 68). Nowhere are these proscriptions—as well as the kinds of authorial imperatives described above—more readily apparent than in college and university composition courses. As de Certeau points out, "[L]earning to write has been the very definition of entering into a capitalist and conquering society"; indeed, learning to write is its "fundamental initiatory *practice*" (136). The initiatory or "structuring practice" (de Certeau 136) of writing instruction, and more specifically the practices and institutions associated with defining, preventing, and detecting plagiarism, draw their initiatory power from a broad range of literary, legal, ethical, and pedagogical conventions whose cumulative effect is a kind of regulatory climate that continues to affect practice in higher education.

PLAGIARISM AND "SOCIETAL CONTROL"

I take plagiarism as a kind of authoring activity in de Certeau's sense and plagiarism detection as another kind of authoring activity focused on isolating the former for purposes of classification, control, and rule enforcement. Furthermore, in this book I approach plagiarism detection, prevention, policy, and instruction—in short, antiplagiarism remedies—as one of the "real effects" of power as theorized by Michel Foucault (*Power/Knowledge* 97). Arguably, antiplagiarism devices represent one of the prime "effective apparatuses of punishment" (*Power/Knowledge* 97), one of the applied "techniques" or "mechanisms" (*Power/Knowledge* 99) of power aimed specifically at regulating writing activities within and against prevailing notions of legitimate and lawful authorship. However, I am most interested in plagiarism detection and prevention solutions that, as disciplinary mechanisms, also "lend themselves to economic profit" (*Power/Knowledge* 101) by cashing in on prevailing institutional norms. If Foucault is correct in stating that the bourgeoisie "could not care less about delinquents" outside of the "complex of mechanisms" otherwise supporting bourgeois power (*Power/Knowledge* 102), then in my view what becomes increasingly important in studying plagiarism is less the ways in which plagiarists tend to get treated (and treat themselves) as delinquents but rather the particular ways in which a prevailing "complex" of control mechanisms intersects with wider institutional and corporate efforts to garner profit under the aegis of educational rehabilitation.

Antiplagiarism remedies will be treated, therefore, as evidence of much broader economic and commercial practices whose legal and cultural contexts have been introduced above. In particular, I want to make a case for studying plagiarism in light of a larger historical trend toward what James Beninger has called "societal control" (427)—in particular via the several bureaucratic and administrative "information processing" solutions emerging in the nineteenth and twentieth centuries in response to an emerging "crisis in material control" (292). Dissatisfied with what he characterizes as overzealous and misguided efforts to interpret recent history in terms of a technology-driven information revolution, Beninger proposes instead that what we have witnessed in the West over the last two centuries is a much more pervasive "control revolution": a "complex of rapid changes in technological and economic arrangements by which information is collected, stored, processed, and communicated . . ." (427). Beninger maps a series of control crises that throughout the twentieth century have used "increasingly removed" systems of control (292). Citing everything from early railroad switching schedules to later bureaucratic and much later computer-processing measures, Beninger argues that control systems in the age of capital-industrial expansion have themselves spawned their own particular crises requiring second-order control systems (292). In short, as agents of processual control, "information processing and flows need themselves to be controlled" (Beninger 433). Computers and software applications in particular, while often celebrated as harbingers of a new age of information freedom, in fact, according to Beninger, represent simply the latest response to the latest information-management crisis.

Beninger's model, perhaps a bit overzealous itself—particularly in its occasional reduction of political and cultural activity to matters of broad economic urgency—nonetheless provides a useful backdrop against which antiplagiarism services can be viewed. The control revolution was revolutionary, Beninger argues, due to the "development of technologies far beyond the capability of any individual," and this "transcendence" of sophisticated and speedy processing systems suggests a societal commitment to control that trumps whatever innovations a particular technology, or its related commodities, might bring (185). Beninger takes special care to include "massive bureaucracies" among those individual-transcending technologies that came into prominence in the late nineteenth century to control the flow of information. If we take student populations toward the end of the nineteenth century to represent a kind of "flow" requiring bureaucratic control—a point taken up and challenged in the next chapter—then Beninger's model maps well onto educational histories that argue for the emergence of writing programs in the United States as in part a response to a very specific control crisis. Similarly, I would extend Beninger's analysis of control technologies to a very particular technology or mechanism—namely literary and pedagogical *conventions*, such as those pertaining to plagiarism and its detection—that also serve from the nineteenth century onward to regulate information flows in specific ways.

The case for control as an epistemological catchall is tempting for its simplicity but perhaps too broad to have any real bearing on my study of plagiarism detection systems in higher education. Perhaps more useful is Ivan Illich's similarly Marxist, but perhaps more nuanced, distinction between "productive institutions" and "productive systems" in advanced technocratic societies (*Tools* 20). Productive institutions, Illich contends, are one type of societal tool for the production of "tangible commodities" (*Tools* 20). Productive systems, on the other hand, deal in "intangible commodities such as those which produce 'education,' 'health,' 'knowledge,' or 'decisions'" (Illich, *Tools* 20). In very real ways, antiplagiarism "factories," to adapt Illich's example, function as both productive institutions and productive systems insofar as the particular commodities tooled under the rubric of plagiarism detection are both tangible (concrete, saleable) and intangible (abstract, ephemeral). In fact, plagiarism continues to vex in part because the offense appears to be both tangible and intangible. Understood as intellectual property theft, plagiarism looks like an attempt to steal tangible property for personal gain. Understood as ethical violation, plagiarism marks an assault on intangible codes of conduct and therefore can be difficult to spot for purposes of either punishment or rehabilitation.

What particular commodity form plagiarism takes will be addressed in greater detail in later chapters. For now I close this section by suggesting that antiplagiarism solutions are perhaps too easily read as simply the latest mechanism or apparatus of disciplinary power and punishment in higher education. At the very least, where a disciplinary practice is itself an explicit form of punishment or rule enforcement, the status of the practice as a disciplinary mechanism, in Foucault's sense, needs to be calibrated against this deliberate casting of the mechanism as disciplinary fix. Even where plagiarism rules and detection protocols appear to codify a kind of "societal control" over runaway information flows, the question remains as to how and to what end this control works in relation to societal participants—be they students, teachers, administrators, or corporate software companies. Thus, I operate from the premise that indeed antiplagiarism remedies function as one of many mechanisms or "rationally designed devices" (Illich, *Tools* 20) for the regulation of student writing practices. However, my general aim in this book is to question how these particular tools themselves make use of other tools—including a wide range of "artifacts or rules, codes or operators" (Illich, *Tools* 20)—in building and implementing a particular solution to the plagiarism problem. I would argue, in fact, that notions of disciplinary power and punishment sometimes underwrite efforts to sell antiplagiarism devices as a kind of societal healing or, as Illich puts it, "administrative therapy" (*Tools* 46). The status of a service as disciplinary mechanism, in brief, becomes an integral part of its product appeal, much to the delight of its corporate providers.

CONCLUSION: WRITING CONVENTIONS

Plagiarism and antiplagiarism devices build on literary (in particular citation) conventions that have changed very little over the last century or so. Plagiarism as a category is perhaps only meaningful, therefore, when considered against these conventions—or rules, codes, operators—dictating the supposed right and wrong ways to work with texts. In referring to the conventions of literary production, I mean to suggest not only a diverse set of rules, codes, and injunctions designed to regulate the activity, but also the many assumptions and tacit agreements that inform common understandings of writing as either original or something else.

In *Art Worlds*, Howard Becker suggests that the word *convention* can refer to such "sociological ideas" as "norm, rule, shared understanding, custom, or folkway," all of which refer to those "understandings people hold in common and through which they effect cooperative activity" (30). This deliberate broadening of the semantic possibilities of "convention" is useful to my discussion of plagiarism. Antiplagiarism remedies derive their power and sustainability from a well-seasoned amalgam of rules, norms, understandings, customs, and even folkways put to use in particular ways and with the support of historically entrenched structures and institutions. Thus, as Patricia Bizzell has pointed out, drawing on the work of Richard Rorty, conventions are perhaps best understood as "the products of communities, situation-bound but also subject to change" (100). Generally speaking, we agree that a particular normalizing discourse is acceptable because we can agree on its many conventions. Still, particular conventions and discourses begin to change where a given community starts to question the conventional "products" of that discourse. Conventions themselves, therefore, are not inherently rigid, nor even inextricably bound to a set of rules or proscriptions.

Nonetheless, in literary and pedagogical discourse especially, the word *convention* often serves interchangeably with the word *rule*, even though, as Joseph Harris correctly points out, the term "can describe almost anything from a critical habit of mind to a preferred form of citing sources to specific usages and phrasings" (88). As critical habits of mind, the conventions pertaining to authorship and plagiarism prove meaningful even where not explicitly named. Discussing intellectual property law, James Boyle makes the important point that notions of the author as originary creator of content are "coded deep into our speechways and our patterns of thought" (158). This idea of the transformative author is therefore the norm against which assessments of all forms of "information production" tend to be made (Boyle 158). In sum, authoring conventions operate not only through explicit rule sets but also through popular and, in some cases, tacit understandings of modern writing as transformative creation.

Finally, computers and their byproducts suggest a set of conventions potentially different from those normally reserved for print. New media scholars (Manovich, Bolter and Grusin, and Lévy, for example) have theorized the existence of "new media objects" (Manovich, *Language* 36) whose formal properties reflect a departure from traditional authoring conventions and their broader aesthetic regimes. It could be argued, in fact, that the essay or research paper cribbed from digital sources, or even the digitized paper bought, downloaded, and distributed in print form may serve as examples of new media objects—a point taken up in chapter 7. More broadly, computers hooked up to the Internet may in certain ways disrupt our inherited notions of writing as solitary and originary and thus may destabilize the forms and conventions underlying such myths. On the other hand, services such as Glatt and Turnitin may serve to reify traditional authoring conventions, regulating practice that fails to conform to prevailing notions of what writing, for example, can be.

Conventions, in short, only make sense in context—in a given community, at a particular time and place, under certain conditions. Moreover, the learning of conventions (be they rules, habits, or folkways) may not be enough to garner the kind of "insider status" that comes with community membership (Kaufer and Geisler 306). Besides learning conventions, insider status may require adopting a particular set of "tacit beliefs" to assure one's success as a "knowledge-maker" in a given academic community (Kaufer and Geisler 306). In part, I have tried in this chapter to outline the many implicit beliefs that have historically and continue today to inform discussions of authorship, plagiarism, and antiplagiarism remedies. In the next chapter, I endeavor to show that the path traveled by most college and university students learning to write for an academic audience is, in some cases, well worn with age-old beliefs about the role of the author as a "knowledge-maker." Often (but not always) tacitly assumed, these beliefs underwrite notions of authorship, intellectual property, and plagiarism, and so tend to fill in the gaps that often materialize between, for example, a citation convention and a particular habit of mind required of a student writer.

3

Plagiarism in the Early-Twentieth-Century "New University"

PLAGIARISTS HAVE LONG posed a threat to authors. At the same time, plagiarists add value to the very same process they otherwise threaten, insofar as the real or imagined menace justifies ever more stringent prohibitions. Put simply, the modern author would find it difficult to survive without the modern plagiarist as categorical foil. The larger point should be made, then, that plagiarism and original authorship are not "polar opposites" but rather "the obverse and reverse of the same medal" (Lindey 14). Lindey's distinction between "pirate" and "plagiarist" helps clarify this idea that plagiarism and originality—to critics and defenders alike—are two sides of the same literary coin: "[A] pirate makes no attempt to falsify authorship, while the plagiarist compounds the offense by posing as the originator" (3). In other words, the pirate has little to gain in pretending authorship rights to the work pirated; much of the copied material's value, in fact, resides in its assumed authenticity. In posing, however, the plagiarist aspires not only to exploit work already done but also to earn author status for having done original work. Thus, as the obverse of originality, plagiarism also faces in the same direction, in pursuit of the same literary value.

For twentieth-century chroniclers of plagiarism, in fact, the Janus face of originality has figured largely in historical portraits of great authors who, as serious contenders in the realm of literary originality, also bear the mark of genuine plagiarism. For example, Eudora Richardson devotes most of "The Ubiquitous Plagiarist" (1931) to a particularly nuanced form of influence tracking in order to prove the thesis that "plagiarism is in everything that is written" (329). Chaucer and Shakespeare, for instance, drew explicitly (words and phrases, as well as forms and story lines) on the work of earlier artists (Boccaccio and Marlowe, respectively). Thus, the story of plagiarism itself, according to Richardson and others, contains its own origin myth, but one nonetheless anchored in a primary—even primeval—originality. Richardson tells the story this way:

> The first man who told a good yarn to friends gathered at the entrance of his cave undoubtedly discovered later that the product of his brain had been appropriated by one of his listeners and amended without sanction of the author. (Richardson 323)

What separates the "cave" author from the appropriationist listener is, as one might expect, a claim to priority: the "makers of stories . . . can claim greater antiquity for their antecedents" (Richardson 323) and thus forever trump the plagiarist whose product remains inherently secondary and always already overheard.

Plagiarists poised "at the entrance" of authorship, while perhaps privy in their lifetimes to the real or imagined benefits of originality, nonetheless meet less auspicious fates in posterity. As Richardson explains, the "real plagiarist" earns only "oblivion" in the eyes of "future generations" ("Ubiquitous" 330). Conversely, "for authors who have had something to contribute to thought and beauty, whether or not its basis is wholly original, there will be life eternal" (Richardson, "Ubiquitous" 330). A straight reading of Richardson suggests that in the end what separates the real author from the real plagiarist is not just a claim to "greater antiquity" but also, and quite simply, a claim to real authorship in and of itself. A real author (Richardson has in mind such notables as Chaucer, Shakespeare, Milton, Dryden, Coleridge, and Pope) can be something other than "wholly original"—can, in other words, engage in "real" plagiarism—as long as he (the pronoun rarely changes) emerges as a real author. As in other pleas on behalf of influence, Richardson confers the status of "author" in order to rescue the category of original authorship from the taint of plagiarism. Influence tracking, as purification ritual, reveals the omnipresence of plagiarism while simultaneously dismissing its relevance to the long history of "thought and beauty."

Thus, plagiarism and originality may be two sides of the "same medal," but a fine cut down the middle of that medal yields a dualist literary theory committed to the notion that authors have much to contribute and plagiarists do not. Historians of plagiarism—armed with subtle distinctions between copying and borrowing, borrowing and stealing, emulation and reproduction, adoption and adaptation, among others—have gone to great lengths to defend the category of original authorship despite this rather puzzling contradiction. Lindey, another practitioner of influence tracking, posits the following distinction on behalf of literary borrowing: "Copying and borrowing are not synonymous. The one is adoption; the other is adaptation. The copyist hews close to the model; the borrower absorbs, transmutes, reinterprets" (270). Notable here is Lindey's use of categorical markers to stress the idea that plagiarists ("close to the model") engage in outright copying whereas authors (removed from the model) absorb, transmute, and reinterpret whatever gets borrowed. Still, according to Lindey, the term *borrowing* can also imply "concealment of source" (184). Thus, an act of copying, once concealed, in fact suggests an act of borrowing if the author transmutes what has been copied into "something" worthy of an originality claim. In short, literary transmutation redefines an act of copying as an act of borrowing and hence as consistent with original authorship.

Originality can be and often is hewn from something not "wholly original." More emphatically, as side-by-side text comparisons confirm, whole chunks of copied words show up in works otherwise attributed to original authors. In brief, real authors can and do plagiarize. Still, Lindey and Richardson want to maintain that Chaucer and company are real authors despite—and perhaps even because of—the fact that they all stole, copied, and plagiarized. Therefore, they are not "real plagiarists" even though "there is plagiarism in everything that is written." In the end, real authors are real precisely because their continued status as real authors serves an author-centered regime committed to notions of literary originality and, by extension, literary genius. Shakespeare and Pope (and the category of "original author" more broadly) help reify the class that they simultaneously define and occupy.

In listing the excuses most often given by plagiarists and their defenders, Lindey suggests the following: "*Great men are a class apart, with special privileges and immunities*" (238; italics in original). In other words, plagiarism is something of a right to "men" of genius, and genius alone guarantees that right. As an excuse, however, the "privileges and immunities" of greatness do not protect those of lesser, smaller, or weaker grade. Lindey notes the double standard but only in passing: "The plagiarism which, in the case of a genius (especially a dead genius) is hailed as an exercise of royal prerogative, may, in the case of a humble practitioner, be condemned as larceny" (273). In other words, the genius is by default immune to charges of theft and plagiarism, exercising the "royal" right to copy and steal on the way to legitimate borrowing. The "humble practitioner" doing the same thing, conversely, is not immune but damned before the court of imperial privilege. In extreme cases, acts of "larceny" among the humble suggest a deeper and more insidious form of literary kleptomania, and so, as Lindey phrases it, the "psychopathic plagiarist . . . is just as much a medical case as the pathological liar or compulsive arsonist" (254).

Thus, an author-centered system tends to profit, in multiple senses, from a perpetually reified archrivalry between true and healthy authors on the one hand and false and psychopathic plagiarists on the other. Metaphors based in oppositional notions of disease and cure, illness and health, theft and gift, kleptomania and genius, etc. both serve and reproduce that mythical rivalry. In this chapter, I consider how notions of this sort have functioned as dual, and sometimes contradictory, determinants in the fight against plagiarism in higher education. Focusing on early-twentieth-century writing assignments and research conventions, I situate plagiarism and plagiarism detection within a broader set of administrative responses to changing institutional and pedagogical demands at the end of the nineteenth century. In brief, I show that concern about plagiarism in higher education today reflects not only current attitudes about authorship and textual ownership but also a traditional devaluation—even criminalization—of student writing in a system designed to protect real authors. Specifically, where the modern author lends ideological support to intellectual property laws and claims, the modern student writer lends support to an educational system learning to cope with changing student populations within an increasingly turbulent social climate.

Learning to Write in the "New University"

In the United States between 1890 and 1910, student enrollment in institutions of higher learning nearly doubled and, by 1920, had almost doubled again (Brereton 7). Many factors contributed to this turn-of-the-century boom in the college and university market, most notably the progressive push to democratize access to higher education and a commensurate entrenchment of the ideal of meritocracy. Some have traced the enrollment increase to a major economic shift in post–Civil War America: the "new economy" emerging after the war "demanded more college-educated Americans" (Yood 527), particularly those trained in skills relevant to the new service and information processing jobs inherent to the nineteenth-century "Commercial Revolution" described by Beninger. In addition, as Miller suggests, demographic dislocations and relocations after the war "placed American higher education in a new aspect toward its constituencies," particularly in the wake of the 1862 Morrill Act establishing land grant universities in many of the newly reunited states (qtd. in Austin 35). Brereton describes the emergence at this time of a "new university" (6), which came directly out of the progressive "reform impulses" of late-nineteenth- and early-twentieth-century America. The new university offered an alternative to a prewar college system "in danger of becoming irrelevant to a rapidly changing nation" (3). Modifications to postsecondary curriculum reflect this larger reformist agenda. Specifically, the old emphasis on the classics, religion, and ethics gave way, under the new university system, to more professional schooling in increasingly specialized disciplinary genres (Brereton 4).

One major component of the new university education—and one particularly well suited to a burgeoning information economy—was instruction in writing. While the traditional nineteenth-century college required, by and large, a "balanced mix of oral and written work," the new university "valued the written word much more" (Brereton 4). Writing may have been valued more as an academic benchmark in part because an earlier oral emphasis proved difficult to manage in the face of larger student enrollments. Harvard's 1897 "Report of the Committee on Composition and Rhetoric" makes this point explicitly:

> About the year 1870 a change began to make itself felt, first in numbers and then in the methods of the college, which gradually brought about what amounted to a revolution. The classes increased in size nearly fourfold, so as to become wholly unmanageable for oral recitation. . . . (Adams, Godkin, and Nutter 112)

As a management solution, writing thus offered a more efficient instrument for measuring the competencies of a larger—and increasingly diverse—student population. An earlier report (Adams, Godkin, and Quincy) expresses a fear that this "revolution" in higher education in the last quarter of the nineteenth century marks, for Harvard at least, the conversion of what was once a "seminary of higher education" into a "mere academy" where writing instructors are "subjected to the drudgery of teaching the elements" (96). Brereton extrapolates this anxiety to a broader university culture which, in the midst of a "period of ferment" between 1875 and 1925, witnessed the dawn of "mass-production education," particularly in the larger Midwestern, Western, and Southern state universities (15–17).

By the end of the nineteenth century, then, an emphasis on writing led to a disciplinary entrenchment of composition in the form of university writing programs whose general mandate was to educate, or remediate, incoming students in the art of college-level theme or essay writing. Harvard, for example, introduced its English A requirement in 1875 in part to compensate for perceived deficiencies in high school and other preparatory curricula. From the beginning, then, as Brereton and others have argued, the introductory writing course has come saturated with "remedial overtones" inherent to the Harvard model (Brereton 18–19). More to the point, where colleges and universities opted for a first-year writing requirement, the Harvard course set became the industry standard, despite sustained opposition from a few voluble detractors (Brereton 236). In sum, as enrollments nearly quadrupled between 1890 and 1920, introductory writing became a core staple for many incoming college and university students, initiating what Robert Connors called "the almost absolute reign of a freshman composition requirement" in twentieth-century college curricula (13).

Susan Miller has argued that the composition requirement in late-nineteenth-century America functioned as a gatekeeping mechanism as universities—in response to increased social pressure to democratize educational access —opened their doors to more diverse student groups. According to Miller, the course from the beginning targeted those whose gender, class, ethnic, economic, and/or educational backgrounds prefigured their remedial or beginning status in a heavily striated educational hierarchy (73–74). Clearly, educators at this time were wary of changing student demographics, for example as new immigrants entered the state university system in the latter half of the nineteenth century. In 1895, for instance, University of Minnesota instructor George MacLean noted that many of his students were "of foreign birth or ancestry," and while "well prepared in mental development," these students were "ignorant, or at least unskilled, in the use of the English language." MacLean proposed, therefore, that "the fundamental work of the University must be a struggle for correctness" (qtd. in Brereton 186). A Harvard instructor in 1892 complained more explicitly that English instructors had suddenly been saddled with "the burden of the unprepared" (qtd. in Adams, Godkin, and Quincy 75), and three years later University of Michigan's Fred Newton Scott remarked somewhat obliquely that "in the larger universities the day of small and cosey [sic] classes is long past. Now the hungry generations tread us down" (qtd. in Brereton 177).

I offer in passing that while the "struggle for correctness" may have both distressed educators and discriminated unfairly against the "unskilled," Harvard and its imitators met with resistance on the grounds that those populations new to college did not deserve access to skills training in the first place. Lane Cooper's 1913 address to the College Conference on English in the Central Atlantic States, for example, cites "a law of nature" whereby those with "greater capacity" have a "better claim" to English instruction than others. Cooper concludes with a strident plea "for cherishing the more gifted among our students who show promise of becoming influential in maintaining the purity of the English language" (qtd. in Brereton 299). Yale graduate Thomas Raynesford Lounsbury issued a similar complaint in 1911, arguing that the "great American community" has for too long clung to "the faith that anybody and everybody can be taught to use the language with clearness and precision. . . ." This belief in "manufacturing good if not great writers to order," according to Lounsbury, led to the general devaluation of literary training in higher education (qtd. in Brereton 280).

These testimonials suggest that detractors both inside and outside of the new writing programs bemoaned the new "manufacturing" ethos in college and university writing programs. However, for some the best solution to unfriendly or unnatural gatekeeping practices was to close the gate entirely to those of lesser "capacity." While not apologizing for institutional regimes designed at heart to keep the "hungry generations" perpetually hungry, I do nonetheless think a context-sensitive approach is necessary when assessing local responses to the social challenges inherent to the new university. To argue—as MacLean evidently did in 1895—that the University of Minnesota should promote "correctness" in order to train "foreign" students otherwise "unskilled" in English is a far cry from marshalling "a law of nature" to salvage English purity and protect those of assumed greater capacity. Still, I grant the larger point that the new writing emphasis in higher education at the end of the nineteenth century did indeed represent a bureaucratic, managerial solution to a particular crisis in material and social control as the new, larger universities endeavored to stream-line application, instructional, and assessment procedures for a growing and changing student body.

This crisis had grounding in a much broader social and religious unease at the turn of the twentieth century. Radical population changes were just one of the factors lending credence to the popular idea, particularly among American civil religious leaders and social conservatives of the time, that the end of the nineteenth century marked "the end of an era—the Christian era" (Marsden 102). Due in part to the "revolutionary secularization" of education in antebel-lum America, schools and universities became "an important arena for battle" in the general fight against the forces of social and moral decay (Marsden 160). The "spectre" of over-populated cities, widespread poverty, and rampant indus-trialization led many to question an otherwise unshakable faith in American destiny (Marsden 102). Hence, a Victorian-bred leadership witnessing what they saw to be the decline of modern Christian civilization called repeatedly for religious, civil, and educational leaders to "uplift and Christianize," in the words of President McKinley, both the nation's poor and the "heathen" populations abroad (Marsden 21). By the 1920s, many conservative Americans shared the premillenialist notion "that the moral foundations of the nation were rapidly crumbling" and therefore condemned the "vicious habits" of modern society (Marsden 156).

Viewed in this context, the struggle for English correctness that MacLean and others championed at the end of the nineteenth century may have issued from a broader social battle against moral and intellectual disintegration. In gen-eral, then, the introductory writing course from its inception can be viewed as a site of ethical, cultural, and political contestation (Brodkey, Crowley, Miller, Strickland). For some, the contest centered as well (as it does today) on issues of economic exploitation, particularly where the reigning composition requirement required the procurement of a large army of underpaid instructors, graduate stu-dents, and contingent workers. Indeed, Warner Taylor's 1929 nationwide survey of writing programs concluded, in part, that the first-year composition require-ment had prospered for over fifty years in a climate of "cheap labor and mass production" (557). While composition instruction was perhaps undervalued as a labor skill, the practice of writing itself proved valuable within new university and corporate economies. As Donna Strickland has argued, writing in the early twentieth century "functioned in corporations and universities as a prominent tool for the enforcement of discipline in the new phase of capitalist expansion" (461). Thus, within the new university, as Adams et al. wrote in 1897, "facility in written expression" became an essential "implement" or "tool" for negotiating the new curriculum (112). Likewise, a workforce trained in basic composition literacy proved essential to a burgeoning information economy, particularly in the office service sector (Strickland).

Different degrees—even kinds—of composition literacy elicited different values in both university and corporate domains. Strickland points out, for example, that categorical distinctions between technical and mechanical correctness on the one hand and creative or original thinking on the other served not only to fuel ongoing debates over the new university curriculum but also to reify class and gender divisions for purposes of academic ranking and, by extension, professional placement in an expanding service economy. The 1897 "Report of the Committee on Composition and Rhetoric" proves useful in this context. Drawing comparisons between two sets of compositions—one submitted by Harvard undergrads and the other by their Radcliffe counterparts—the authors of the report draw the following conclusions:

> In mechanical execution,—neatness, penmanship, punctuation and orthography,—[the Radcliffe students, all women] show a marked superiority in standard over the papers from the courses of the college proper,—perhaps three (3) only of the whole failing to reach the proper level. In their contents also they reveal unmistakably a greater degree of conscientious, painstaking effort,—the desire to perform faithfully and well the allotted task. On the other hand, in thought and in form, they are less robust and less-self-assertive. A few are sprightly; none of them indicate any especial capacity for observing, or attempt, in pointing out defects and difficulties, anything which might be termed a thoughtful solution of them. (Adams, Godkin, and Nutter 108)

In short, the papers submitted by the Radcliffe women show excellence—indeed, a "marked superiority"—in mechanical and technical skill. However, with regard to "thought" and "form" the female authors show no "capacity for observing" or "thoughtful" problem solving. At turns "sprightly" and "conscientious," the Radcliffe students do reflect "the desire to perform faithfully and well the allotted task," but the report clearly suggests that the more "robust" and "self-assertive" writing will be found in the "college proper." Thus, the new economy certainly favored those students who graduated with good "English" skills. But one might conclude, from this report at least, that where male (Harvard) graduates would be expected to find "thoughtful" solutions to work-related problems, female (Radcliffe) graduates would be asked by and large to perform "faithfully and well" the more mechanical tasks of neatness, penmanship, punctuation, and orthography—in other words, secretarial work and other service-oriented information-processing tasks.

Language learning has thus always been a "crucial locus for power" in higher education (Miller 7). Where students and instructors have come together over the task of composition, course lessons have stressed not only the conventions of good writing and research but also a broader set of disciplinary practices grounded in a late-nineteenth-century need to uphold and propagate bourgeois values and hierarchies. Like Miller, Sharon Crowley takes a Foucauldian approach to analyzing both early and current writing program curricula as a special kind of social engineering intended to appease broader academic and social interests. The purpose of the required course has been, according to Crowley, to make sure that new students learn "the discursive behaviors and traits of character that qualify them to join the community" (8–9). Entering students can expect not only lessons in how to write but also disciplinary instruction in how to "behave, think, . . . and speak as students . . ." (Crowley 9). Thus, for a student in an early-twentieth-century writing course, "mechanical correctness" in the form of correct spelling, punctuation, or word choice might intersect with much broader interpretations of intellectual "cleanliness" (Miller 57) and, as suggested above, gender-specific assessments of professional acumen.

Antiplagiarism remedies function in a way like the universal requirement of introductory writing, representing a specific "ethical technology" (Crowley 217) grounded in both intellectual property law and time-honored literary conventions. Thus, pedagogical interest or investment in any of the several technologies of plagiarism prevention and detection marks a broader political, economic, and cultural commitment to remedial training in a set of socially condoned writing practices.

The "Golden Era" of Plagiarism Litigation

The managerial, mass-production focus of the new university, and the writing program in particular, reflected a deeper cultural and economic turn to larger bureaucratic systems of people and information control. Bill Readings, in his late-twentieth-century indictment of the "posthistorical University," makes a case for how the art of teaching factors into the new "factory" (to recall Illich) of higher education: "Teaching administers students. It accredits students as administrators, and it trains them in the handling of information" (152). While Readings focuses primarily on mid- and late-twentieth-century academia, he posits a broader historical and institutional context within which this kind of administrative accreditation takes place:

> The modern bureaucratic state proposes to reduce the [teacher-student] relation to that of the development and training of technocrats through

> the transmission of education. These attempts can be summarized
> under the rubric of the ideology of autonomy. (154)

Echoing Illich's appraisal of modern education, as well as Beninger's account of
the so-called Control Revolution, Readings laments a long-developing bureaucratization of postsecondary learning. I would argue further, following Readings, that
the "ideology of autonomy" manifests quite explicitly in the rules and injunctions
pertaining to student plagiarism, a point I return to below.

At this stage, however, it would help to review some of the ways in which
the laws of authorship and intellectual property manifested in the new university. Robert Connors has catalogued the many "habits and industries" that grew
up around the introductory composition course at the turn of the twentieth
century (13). Most dramatically, perhaps, the new emphasis on written composition encouraged new markets in educational materials focused specifically on
the teaching and learning of writing. With regard to support materials such as
handbooks, textbooks, and related instruction rubrics and policies, Connors,
Brereton, and others have argued that such artifacts were prevalent in introductory writing courses in part due to the long-standing institutional reliance
on graduate students, part-timers, and young instructors to teach courses rele-
gated, quite literally in some cases, to the basement of higher education.
Taylor's 1929 survey, for example, suggested that more than three-quarters of
writing students nationwide made regular use of handbooks, with the highest
use concentrated in the Western, Midwestern, and Southern states.

Thus, at the turn of the twentieth century, in response to enrollment spikes
in English A and its equivalents, a large textbook industry emerged in effect to
subsidize neophyte instructors unfamiliar with a new standardized curriculum.
Of course, the obverse argument could also be made that large writing programs prospered toward the end of the nineteenth century in part because an
efficient and highly specialized textbook industry laid the foundation for centralized composition instruction. Connors entertains this view in suggesting
that between 1885 and 1910 "what would become Modern composition-
rhetoric was shaped and made smooth by the mechanisms of a modernized,
centralized textbook marketplace" (12). Connors also makes the rather bold
claim that textbooks became at that time "the absolute arbiters of classroom
content and practice" (15). Whether a changed administrative agenda helped
shape the textbook industry or vice-versa (or, more likely, a little of both), the
fact is that new textbook and handbook genres came into prominence in the
early twentieth century in alignment with growing student enrollments and a
widespread commitment to basic writing instruction in higher education.

In almost every case, these early textbooks and handbooks contained rules
and examples pertaining to the proper use and citation of outside sources. University administrations often deployed similar rule sets in fashioning antipla-

giarism statements then distributed to first-year students. The 1913 University of Minnesota "Instructions to Students in Rhetoric 1–2" is a telling example. Provided in pamphlet form to all students enrolled in the course, the "Instructions" warned against the improper "borrowing" of outside materials:

> The themes assigned, unless it is explicitly stated that they are exercises in selection or reorganization, are to be the original work of the student. Whenever he *[sic]* has occasion to use the language of another, even if only a single phrase, he should indicate the fact by quotation marks. The borrowing of ideas from another should be indicated by marginal or footnote references to the original. Failure to observe these rules scrupulously will be regarded as cheating; and the offense will be reported to the Student Council. (qtd. in Brereton 470)

Clearly, the language in this passage reveals a general commitment to the Romantic ideology of creativity. The caveat with regard to "exercises in selection or reorganization" marks a significant distinction between writing as combinatory text assembly (or editing) and writing as creative or "original work." As the instructions imply, acts of literary selection and reorganization, while perhaps superficially relevant to reading, research, and writing assignments, will most likely not be regarded, in and of themselves, as "original" works of composition. This distinction between selection and original work reformulates a very old distinction positioning the work of mere copyists against the original works of true masters.

The instructions further stipulate that "the language" and "ideas" of others should be set off in quotation marks or cited in either "marginal or footnote references to the original." Failure to do so "scrupulously" will constitute a form of cheating, and "the offense will be reported to the Student Council." This language may not surprise educators, or even current or one-time students, who have come across similar pronouncements in writing courses or elsewhere. Brereton attributes the seemingly harsh tone and content of the Minnesota instructions to the prevailing "authoritarian" ethos of the new university in general and the larger state universities in particular. Displaying the "strictness imposed at the time," the rules also seem to suggest that "in composition, students are on trial [and] not really a part of things until they get through their ordeal" (Brereton 19). Strictness was arguably the order of the day at the University of Minnesota, if these instructions are any indication. However, to take a slightly different view, students—at the University of Minnesota and elsewhere—may indeed have been "on trial" in particular ways that had more to do with a wider social anxiety about plagiarism litigation than any unbridled harshness or strictness on the part of institutional administrators.

As noted in chapter 2, the quotation mark—once used to highlight commonly accessible authoritative language—is now used more often to protect words belonging to someone else. Signifying the "reconfiguration of language as property" in the modern age, quotation marks themselves mark an instance where "legal right" intersects and indeed overlaps with "grammatical rule" in that each depends on "the same conferral of ownership over one's words" (de Grazia 290). Clearly "ownership" in this sense denotes an explicit claim to linguistic property made on behalf of its presumed creator. Read one way, the Minnesota instructions bear witness to that kind of ownership in recommending a protectionist stance in relation to "the language of another." The careful distinction between using actual "language," which requires quotation marks, and borrowing "ideas," which requires a marginal or footnote reference, mirrors an intellectual property distinction in effect by 1913 that underwrites copyright claims to the material expression if not the inherent ideas of an authored work. The single phrase, in this sense, can be owned outright as a specific material expression of an idea. On the other hand, ideas, which under basic copyright law cannot be owned as tangible property, can nonetheless—in a scholarly research context—be borrowed from the "original," and this borrowing should be marked with footnotes.

The important point here is that the rules pertaining to the incorporation and citation of textual sources suggest in this specific academic setting a potentially more rigid interpretation of property and ownership than that conveyed by intellectual property law itself. Read literally, the instructions convey the principle that "ideas" too can be protected, and in effect owned, and therefore can be borrowed but only in accordance with a specific set of citation conventions. Citation as honorary acknowledgment of a particular borrowing pays out, as it were, to "the original" if not to the owner or holder of copyright. Meanwhile, explicit use of another's specific linguistic expression requires the use of quotation marks to protect the other's exclusive right to linguistic patterns ("single phrase" or otherwise). Failure to acknowledge ownership of either kind constitutes the "offense" known more generally as plagiarism.

The Minnesota instructions offer, in brief, a preemptive solution to one problem that might arise in student attempts to incorporate sources. The question remains as to why instructions of this sort would be necessary or desired in the first place. One possible answer is that the Copyright Act of 1909—passed just four years prior to the Minnesota instructions—inspired greater administrative oversight of student writing activities in a general effort both to curb potential copyright infringement and to teach the spirit of the new law. As Lindey has shown, the congressional report accompanying the 1909 bill stated that the law was intended "primarily for the benefit of the public," giving "a bonus to authors and inventors, not to favor them but to stimulate writing and invention for the good of 'the great body of people'" (104). Two decades later, however, some would question and challenge—as Lindey does in the early 1950s—the public "benefit" ostensibly awarded by the new bill. One anonymous critic writing for *The Nation* in 1929, for example, suggested that the Copyright Act, while promising on the surface to protect authors, "actually cost the writer" insofar as the law justified greater scrutiny with regard to potential infringement ("Plagiarism Racket"). Thus, one could read the Minnesota instructions not just as an instance of authoritarianism in the new bureaucratic university but also as one local response to a much broader societal interest in issues of authorship, copyright, intellectual property, and, therefore, plagiarism. While appearing stern and authoritarian on the surface, the rules also register, I would argue, a broader institutional anxiety with regard to students who, along with their instructors, were learning to write in what Lindey identified, tellingly, as "the golden era of plagiarism litigation" (134).

Beginning around 1913—notably, the year Minnesota published its pamphlet and, coincidentally, the year playwright Max Marcin was sued for his play *Cheating Cheaters*—this "golden era" of plagiarism litigation picked up speed in the 1920s, slowed down a bit in the 1930s, and then "bowled along merrily in the 40's" (Lindey 134). By 1930, at least, accusations of plagiarism "had assumed the proportions of a racket" (Lindey 267). As more than one critic writing at the time would suggest, this racket could be traced in part to the new Copyright Act, which provoked a new variety of literary "blackmail" initiated by authors and publishers claiming copyright infringement in strict accordance with the new statutes.

I do not mean to argue, as Lindey does, that the 1909 Copyright Act in and of itself inspired greater interest in plagiarism as a literary and/or intellectual property crime. Twenty years prior, critics spared little venom in attacking the "hangers-on of literature" who, "sustained by the malignancy of envy" and a corollary sense of "inferiority," brought charges of plagiarism "simply to gratify feelings of vindictiveness and spite" (Adams 502). Still, Lindey convincingly documents a marked increase in plagiarism (by which he means specifically copyright) litigation in the first few decades of the twentieth century. This increase can be explained in part by stricter copyright laws coupled with the presence in the background of large publishing, motion picture, radio, and later television industries whose goods had become increasingly accessible to an ever-widening consumer market. In brief, anyone successful in proving intellectual property theft in 1890 may have satisfied "feelings of vindictiveness and spite." By 1910, the same plaintiff had a better chance to make a good deal of money as well. I would argue, therefore, that the appearance (or at least entrenchment) of a "brisk, lucrative hold-up game" in the early twentieth century goes far to explain a corollary concern in higher education over issues of copyright protection and plagiarism. The architects of the Minnesota instructions, for example, may not have had the "plagiarism racket" explicitly in mind in authoring their injunctions, but an increasingly intense litigation climate may certainly have galvanized these and other institutional efforts to promote and standardize preemptive antiplagiarism rhetoric.

Plagiarism and the Modern "Research Attitude"

One other remedy introduced during the golden era of plagiarism litigation was the student research paper.[4] In 1941 the *Harbrace College Handbook*, by then in its sixth year of publication, included for the first time a full chapter on this particular assignment model, which soon became a standard feature in handbooks and a regular requirement in composition courses (Connors 96). Earlier rhetoric handbooks, while not addressing research writing explicitly as a discrete assignment rubric, did include rules regarding the proper use and citation of secondary materials, along with related injunctions concerning plagiarism. For example, John S. Hart's 1874 *A Manual of Composition and Rhetoric: A Textbook for Schools and Colleges*, contains a brief section warning against "using the words of other people" without quotation marks: "To use the words of others without acknowledging them to be such, is plagiarism, which is only another name for *stealing*" (54–55). Plagiarism, then, as a notable form of literary theft, was clearly on the minds of rhetoricians long before the Copyright Act of 1909 and even before the heyday of Harvard's English A. However, not until the 1920s would the research paper—an assignment designed explicitly to teach students how to "use the words of others"—emerge as a staple in composition curricula. By then, most handbooks included sections on how to document and cite secondary sources (Simmons 50), and a few years later the use of the research paper in most university writing courses warranted the inclusion of an entire chapter on the assignment in most if not all writing handbooks.

In a twentieth-century new university context, plagiarism detection and prevention can be viewed as part of a much broader educational regime focusing on the management of student research practices and the installation of protective measures designed to ward off potential authoring errors (or copyright transgressions) in the form of "cribbing." The research paper, as suggested above, represents one such measure. However, rather than stopping or mitigating the problem of plagiarism, the research paper assignment may in fact have made the problem worse. As Simmons has argued, student plagiarism became a more serious issue only after drafters of writing curricula began including the research paper assignment (50). One curious property of this assignment model, then, is that it reflects on the one hand a pedagogical solution to an apparent problem of improper student research and, on the other, a regulatory apparatus inherently conducive to the kinds of behaviors it targets for remediation.

Obviously, this argument flirts with a rather dangerous circularity: early writing instructors encouraged bad research habits by assigning papers intended to discourage bad research. More accurately, the research paper assignment emerged in different forms as part of a wider instructional effort to teach students how to navigate libraries and information processing tasks and to avoid pitfalls associated with those tasks. Still, the research writing assignment, especially when viewed in a more contemporary context, continues to betray what appears to be a fundamental contradiction. Alice Trupe argues, for example, that the research paper today often "degenerates" into a "cut-and-paste" exercise demonstrating that "the student has followed certain paths through the club of authorized writers." Trupe further suggests that accusations of plagiarism abound, particularly in the age of the Internet and electronic databases, because "students are far more likely to use electronic texts than print sources for their research, making the cut-and-paste exercise obvious for what it is." In other words, an abundance of electronic texts, coupled with the cut-and-paste functionality of today's word processors, facilitates and may even encourage the use of source materials in ways suggestive of plagiarism.

Whether the cause or the effect (or both) of twentieth-century cribbing habits, the research paper exemplifies a broader point I would like to make in this chapter. In brief, as a pedagogical solution to ostensibly improper student writing, the research paper marked one of several "ethical technologies" associated with the introductory composition requirement. As Connors puts it, anticipating Crowley, the research assignment "proposed to teach more than just a genre; it meant to teach the entire process of 'ethical' research" (321). A growing concern for proper citation—the use of quotation marks, footnotes, and other "minutiae" of scholarly practice—reflected a "growing concern with intellectual property" at the turn of the twentieth century (Connors 321). Thus, the assignment formalized a process of ethical inquiry (acknowledging debt to the original) balanced against a juridical concern for protecting intellectual property (respecting ownership claims) while teaching its manifold laws. In this way, the research paper assignment—and, more broadly, any assignment concerned with using and citing the language or ideas of another—taught a double lesson in both property and propriety. The stakes may continue to be high in student plagiarism cases not only because infractions have traditionally warranted disciplinary responses that often take on the look and feel of copyright litigation but also because failure to reflect the proper "research attitude" (Connors 322) in higher education reflects a failure to abide by deeply embedded moral standards.

Connors's appraisal of the "research attitude," then, is important to note as itself a revisionist account reflective of more current (late-twentieth-century) attitudes regarding the use of library materials and outside sources in general. The research attitude—in short, a respect for copyright and literary decency[5]—

is part and parcel of what Connors cites as the "modern attitude itself" (322). The modern research attitude implies, in brief, an understanding of the student writer as "a medium, not an originator":

> [The student's] task is to explore the library or the words of the world, not timeless wisdom or his own experience. He *[sic]* is to be trained to pick and choose carefully among myriad facts, coming ideally to that selfless position of knowing secondary materials so well that he merges with them. (Connors 322–23)

Anticipating Readings's indictment of the "post-historical" learning experience, Connors defines the modern student researcher as an exploratory automaton. His obvious caricature situates a primary world of "timeless wisdom" and one's "own experience" against a secondary, bibliocentric world of "words" and "materials." In offering this critique, Connors appears to take issue, as other writing scholars will later, with the rote training that a research paper assignment requires, preferring instead perhaps assignments that tap a writer's unique and personal experiences. I focus on this passage, however, not to challenge Connors's preferred aesthetic but rather to underscore the highly charged invocation of an ideal "selfless position" emerging in the aftermath, so to speak, of authorial merging with secondary sources.

Connors's assessment of the "modern attitude" reflects what I see as a long-standing tension between notions of writing as a quasi-religious quest for autonomous creation (original work) and writing as a form of proactive property enclosure requiring strict injunctions against potential threats to ownership. This tension manifests in the tools and apparatuses used traditionally to teach writing. In particular, the research paper assignment—just one example of the mechanisms or administrative therapies designed to teach the "modern attitude"—regulates against illicit and improper cribbing of others' work. At the same time, the assignment, from its inception in the early twentieth century, has invited a particular kind of merging with "secondary sources" through the ostensibly rote work of exploring libraries and "the words of the world." This latter experience of merging suggests an alchemical transmutation (through adaptation, absorption, incorporation) of the language and ideas of other literary materials for purposes of assuring one's position as a "knowing" subject. For better or worse, to write right—or well—in accordance with this research writing formula, is to merge (become one with) while remaining detached from secondary sources.

Thus, the research attitude in early-twentieth-century higher education is "the modern attitude itself" but in a sense perhaps not fully articulated by Connors. Operating at the heart of these early accounts of plagiarism specifically and research writing generally are dual concerns for literary inclusion (merging, incorporation, transformation) and property exclusion (protected rights to ownership, rules against infringement). In other words, as real or imagined piratical thieves, plagiarists transgress textual boundaries and so violate intellectual property laws; as bad alchemists, plagiarists fail to improve upon the language or ideas of another. Plagiarism has thus posed a perennial problem—and market opportunity, as I will argue in chapter 7—precisely because it pits the pursuit of property rights and the regime of property protection squarely against the pursuit of literary transformation and the lure of pedagogical development. Given the epistemological duel at the heart of this dual construction, it makes good sense that institutional mechanisms designed to teach authorial merging would simultaneously punish boundary transgressions, since failures to transform properly translate well, or so the logic goes, into failures to respect property.

CONCLUSION: PLAGIARISM AS ERROR

As a special violation of at least two authoring conventions, plagiarism tends to get marked as an authoring error, as a deviation (as the term suggests) from a code of behavior or from particular values of truth, decency, and accuracy. Plagiarism, in other words, resembles an act of deviant traveling, wandering, or straying outside the proper path or bounds of accepted authorship standards. As Crowley has suggested, the mechanisms and apparatuses that define and describe authoring errors tend to remain static over time, hardened into convention—for example, in the handbooks, policies, and assignments pertaining to writing instruction. Moreover, while the particular errors made by students might change, and even while teachers may modify their "definitions of error" to suit particular contexts, still the "institutional paraphernalia that name those errors" do not change (Crowley 232).

In fact, one argument I make in this book is that the "institutional paraphernalia" at the heart of antiplagiarism remedies both change and stay the same as error-checking mechanisms in higher education. Insofar as plagiarism detection solutions stress the dual values of scriptural inclusion and property exclusion, they reify intellectual property and authoring conventions already well established by the time of the first official writing programs. However, as guidelines or techniques for defining and identifying—and perhaps even correcting—student authoring errors, antiplagiarism solutions have changed significantly in recent years, particularly as the same tool used ostensibly for errant "cut-and-paste" exercises has proved useful itself in the fight against illicit or immoral acts of cutting and pasting.

I should acknowledge, of course, that to name (identify, label, define) and to remediate (correct, right) errant activities are often separate processes and not necessarily coextensive in either a learning or a legal context. A handbook, plagiarism policy, or research assignment, for example, might name the error of improper use or citation, but the extent to which such an error will be processed (punished, ignored, or even encouraged) depends on several factors, including among other things the presence or absence of academic honor codes, prevailing relationships between teachers and students, course topics, assignment parameters, class size, administrative oversight or lack thereof, etcetera. Crowley's point is nonetheless worth heeding, particularly when looking at a particular apparatus for naming authoring errors (such as computer-based detection software) that by definition operates in tandem with, or even in lieu of, related apparatuses for error processing.

Early writing programs offered an ideal market for error-defining paraphernalia, including the rule sets or instructions, handbooks, textbooks, and assignment models designed exclusively for introductory writing courses. Plagiarism detection services available at the end of the twentieth century resemble these earlier paraphernalia insofar as the detection process suggests yet another instance of institutionalized error naming. Turnitin.com, for example, borrows the handbook rule set as part of its pedagogical, therapeutic program. It teaches the promise (as well as the duty, responsibility, dream) of a particular kind of literary transmutation, consistent with earlier writing models and in keeping with the twentieth-century "research attitude" described by Connors. At the same time, it provides evidence useful for identifying, and perhaps punishing, those writers who, like the "cribbers" before them, engage in activities that violate intellectual property and copyright law.

The question remains as to how the products of Web-based plagiarism detection—such as Turnitin's "Originality Report"—get used (i.e., read, interpreted, applied) by teachers, students, administrators, and other agents in specific educational settings. As with handbooks, there is no necessary correlation between evidence offered as an indication of error and an error in fact marked, corrected, punished, or perhaps ignored. Still, as an "ethical technology" introduced, in particular ways, into the overall writing process—as a service that quite literally marks or even corrects the potential errors of text appropriation—Turnitin and its competitors promise to change the rules of plagiarism detection by revising the relevant terms, formal properties, and practical conditions of that process. Just how the site of plagiarism detection—and more generally, writing itself—operates in our own "era of plagiarism litigation" will be discussed in greater detail in chapter 7.

4

Plagiarism and the Alchemical Tradition

THOMAS MALLON, IN his 1989 book *Stolen Words: Forays Into the Origins and Ravages of Plagiarism*, offered the following advice to the writer concerned about plagiarism:

> [T]he writer need not blush about stealing if he makes what he makes completely his, if he alchemizes it into something that is, finally, thoroughly new. (25)

Nearly a century earlier, in 1892, W. H. D. Adams made a related claim in *The Gentleman's Magazine* on behalf of the "great writer" who, in borrowing someone else's literary material, "passes the rough ore through his own mint, stamps the gold with his own die, and turns out the new piece as his own coin" (502). In the same article, Adams objects to what he sees as undue criticism leveled against writers of genius who profit by using other people's "ore." Indeed, he wonders why it must "always be made a reproach against genius that it has changed copper into gold" (Adams 507–508).

In keeping with this alchemical metaphor, plagiarism has often been defined as either the failure to transmute borrowed copper into gold or, perhaps worse, the deliberate attempt to pass off the base metal as its precious counterpart. In E. F. Benson's 1899 "Plagiarism," we find this definition writ large, albeit in the industrial language of material use and potential:

> Unintelligent theft is theft which does not see and show in the material stolen a higher possibility for its use than that in which it was previously employed. To fail in this is to be convicted of plagiarism. (977)

Half a century later, Alexander Lindey adapts the alchemical metaphor in arguing that writers can "lift material" so long as they "improve it" (238). Indeed, "inspiration" is most evident where a writer's "ideas, impressions, intuitions, memories, fancies and emotions . . . fuse into a coherent and meaningful whole, ready to be expressed" (Lindey 248).

The metaphorical association of alchemical transmutation with literary transformation, or more generally with writing as a process of textual refinement or perfection, has been a staple theme in the West for centuries. Moreover, where "rogues and charlatans" have bedeviled the long history of alchemy, spoiling with their "trickery" the reputations of those engaged in more "honest attempts at transmutation" (Holmyard 93), plagiarists have likewise earned "rogue" status at various historical moments with their own brand of fraudulent or false alchemy. The trope of alchemical transmutation became a common theme for rhetorical, poetical, and religious writings as early as the seventh century AD, emerging as a powerful symbol suggesting, among other things, "regeneration and transformation to a nobler and more spiritual state" (Holmyard 29). In this chapter, I trace the symbolic trajectory of alchemical transmutation in literary and educational theory, beginning with a brief sketch of alchemical themes through the end of the seventeenth century. I will argue, in short, that the contemporary equation of plagiarism with false or failed textual transformation revises a medieval alchemical tradition in the service of modern, humanist notions of spiritual improvement and mental or cognitive development.

ALCHEMY, DIVINITY, AND CHRISTIAN REMEDY

The practice of exoteric alchemy—or the attempt to transmute base metals (lead, tin, copper, iron, and mercury) into precious metals (silver and gold)—derived from the artisanal craft and technical traditions of Alexandrian Egypt (Holmyard; Hopkins; Long). Hopkins traces the alchemical pursuit of material perfection to Aristotle's theories of universal matter. Early European alchemists, as self-proclaimed inheritors of Aristotelian philosophy (hence the pursuit of a "philosopher's stone" endowed with the power of transmutation), hoped to demonstrate, through alchemy, "the triumph of perfection" over "primitive evil" (Hopkins 37). For practicing alchemists in the Christian West, alchemy developed into a "devotional system" where the substantial transmutation of base metals stood in symbolically for the "transformation of sinful man into a perfect being . . ." (Holmyard 15). Since its formal introduction in the Latin West in the twelfth century (Long 144), alchemy has been a site of both operational and doctrinal investigation, with alchemical work focused on both material and spiritual perfection (Long 145). Moreover, the alchemical pursuit of the philosopher's stone, also known as the Elixir or Tincture, marked a corollary pursuit of not only the power of transmutation but also the power to prolong life into eternity (Holmyard 15). For alchemists of medieval Europe, then, the philosopher's stone was symbolically equated with the figure of Christ (Holmyard 160).

As mentioned above, the terms of exoteric alchemy have often been used as agents of theological, philosophical, and mystical inquiry (Holmyard 15). The pursuit of the philosopher's stone has also communicated the related search for a particularly potent remedy for human evil and imperfection. Thus, as esoteric spiritual remedy, alchemy involved the pursuit of a "universal medicine" grounded in the belief that the process of perfecting base metals might lead the way to physical healing in the human body (Long 144–45). Indeed, Paracelsus would later chide his alchemist contemporaries for missing the point of chemical research, the object of which was not so much to make gold but to prepare medicines for human use (Hopkins 216). Still, for alchemists practicing well into the sixteenth century, the quest for the philosopher's stone was nothing less than the search for spiritual perfection and purification through the divine transmutation of the soul.

Petrus Bonus's early-fourteenth-century defense of alchemy, *Pretiosa Margarita Novella* ("The New Pearl of Great Price"), provides a good example of the language in which this quest was written. For example, Bonus describes the "ferment" of alchemical transmutation as either "the Stone itself" or "that which perfects and completes the Stone" (qtd. in Holmyard 143). To accomplish alchemical transmutation, the alchemist must attend not only to this dual nature of the Elixir but also to the ways in which alchemical ferment behaves both like and unlike other more familiar agents of physical transformation. Bonus takes as his governing model the leavening properties of bread dough, suggesting that "our Stone is the leaven of all other metals, and changes them into its own nature" (qtd. in Holmyard 143). In other words, as dough will rise with the introduction of leaven, so surrounding metals will rise to a higher state (silver, then gold) in reaction to the leavening properties of the stone. However, as Bonus points out, leaven, while of the "same nature" as dough, cannot raise the dough until "it has received a new quality which it did not possess before" (qtd. in Holmyard 143). The philosopher's stone works in a similar fashion: "our Stone cannot change metals until it is changed itself, and has added to it a certain virtue which it did not possess before" (qtd. in Holmyard 143).

Bonus's account makes clear that change in a medieval alchemical context involves not only the transformation of a base substance but also the changing nature of the stone itself. With a "certain virtue" added to it, the philosopher's stone becomes both alchemically transmuted metal and (simultaneously) endowed with the power to transmute other metals. Bonus adds that ordinary leaven "receives its fermenting power through the digestive virtue of gentle and hidden heat." Our stone, as well, is rendered capable of fermenting, converting, and altering metals by means of a certain digestive heat, which brings out its potential and latent properties, seeing that without heat neither digestion nor operation is possible. (qtd. in Holmyard 143)

The similarity stops there, however, for the difference between ordinary leaven and the alchemical "ferment" is that "common leaven loses nothing of its substance" whereas alchemical digestion "removes from our ferment all that is superfluous, impure, and corruptive, as is done by Nature in the preparation of gold." In brief, alchemy finds its apotheosis in the purification of the philosopher's stone through the "digestive" removal of all that is unnecessary, tainted, and potentially destructive (Holmyard 143).

Following a devotional system concerned with divine transformation and soul purification, esoteric alchemists by the middle of the fourteenth century worked to distinguish their brand of alchemy from the strictly exoteric variety. Even the secular Latin Geber (or pseudo-Geber, thought to be the fourteenth-century Franciscan Paul of Taranto) admonished the adept to "trust in God" and avoid the "falsehood" associated with the pursuit of mere material transformation:

Our Art is reserved in the Divine Will of God, and is given to, or withheld from, whom he will; who is glorious sublime, and full of all Justice and Goodness. And perhaps, for the punishment of your sophistical work [work directed solely to material transformation], he denies you the Art, and lamentably thrusts you into the by-path of error, and from your error into perpetual infelicity and misery.... (qtd. in Holmyard 154; gloss in original).

Two points are worth noting here. First, pseudo-Geber warns the skilled alchemist against placing too great an emphasis on the mere transmutation of base metals. Second, he foregrounds the art of alchemy as an exclusively esoteric—or hermeneutic—tradition "reserved in the Divine" and "given" and "withheld" in accordance with God's will. Thus, for those aspiring to the "glorious sublime," alchemy reveals its secrets through the glory of God's "Justice and Goodness." Conversely, for those laboring under the influence of "sophistical work"—or work rooted in the artisanal operations of material transmutation—the rewards are none and the punishments severe. In short, the exoteric alchemist lands "lamentably" in the "by-path of error" and slips thereafter into perpetual wretchedness.

Without adhering too religiously to this chapter's founding metaphor, I would argue in passing that Lindey's remark, discussed earlier, regarding textual copying as distinct from material absorption bears some likeness to this fourteenth-century alchemical doctrine. "The copyist," Lindey claims, "hews close to the model; the borrower absorbs, transmutes, reinterprets" (270). Genius, in other words, operates at a particular remove from borrowed (transmuted) materials, and this remove in the context of pseudo-Geber's advice to the adept amounts to a sublime transfer of creative reserve to the "Will of God" or "divine grace." The copyist, on the other hand, in the context of mid-twentieth-century textual practices, falls into the "by-path of error" (or plagiarism, perhaps) by working too close to the literal model, to the material itself, rather than aspiring to the virtuous process of divine transmutation. Thus, borrowing from a chemical (if not outright alchemical) tradition, Lindey arrives at the following aesthetic judgment:

> We can duplicate in a test tube all the chemical ingredients that are found in living organisms, and yet fail to bring the combination to life. So, too, we can isolate and analyze the elements that enter into the making of a work of art, and still not discover the precise nature of the process by which those elements are synthesized into an animate whole. (246)

The "precise nature" of this process, I would argue, is alchemical, but in the esoteric sense discussed above. To make a work of art is to alchemize "chemical ingredients" in such a way that the whole of it comes to life, animated before God and human witnesses. To do otherwise—to rest content, perhaps, with the combination itself or with combinatory exercises in and of themselves—is to reside on the near side of synthesis, close to the model, where the mere appearance of a whole nonetheless reveals its failure to self-animate. The "divine grace" of alchemical transmutation, in brief, bears some likeness to Lindey's "process" of aesthetic synthesis and inspired animation. The "Divine Will of God" finds its postindustrial corollary in the "critical moment" of inspiration, and those engaged in the uninspired work of mere copying (as base alchemy) descend to the by-path of error and become, in a word, plagiarists.

Shelving this provisional analogy for now, I would like to focus briefly on the ways in which the themes of medieval alchemy share common ground with ancient, Renaissance, and later modern textual and pedagogical traditions. As Long has pointed out, alchemy made its way into the twelfth-century Latin West by way of "the translation of Arabic alchemical texts, which themselves derived in part from the late antique textual traditions" (144). Medieval alchemists, appropriating many of the themes and practices of Arabic and antique textual traditions, borrowed many of their conventions as well, engaging for example in "deliberate attribution of alchemical texts to authoritative past authors . . ." (Long 145). This tradition of pseudo-authorship was adopted by alchemical authors for a number of reasons, including the desire to ward off "criticism and persecution" for their texts (Long 145). Also, alchemists saw themselves "participating in an ancient tradition of sacred wisdom," and so, rather than pursue novel contributions to this ancient tradition, they "sought to discover an already established body of ancient wisdom," relying on authorial attribution both to substantiate their work and to subvert their roles as primary authors (Long 145).

One alchemical treatise of lasting significance through the end of the seventeenth century was the pseudepigraphical *Summa perfectionis*, written presumably by the fourteenth-century Franciscan, Paul of Taranto (Long 146). Paul's defense of alchemical tradition would remain an important fixture in Western thought and would contribute to the development of alchemy as a "significant and influential discipline" in the two centuries following its publication (Long 147). Paul concludes his treatise with three key notions, which, for our purposes, would later prove to be important touchstones for emerging humanist theories of education. Paul maintains, first, that alchemical secrets are held and shared in accordance with the "Divine Will of God." Secondly, anticipating later Renaissance rejections of "bookish" scholarship, Paul proposes that alchemy is not to be learned "by reading books" but rather must be sought in "one's own nature" and in "God" (Long 147). Finally, in a move that arguably complicates the alchemical convention of pseudo-authorship discussed above, Paul contends that not ancient authors but "his own experience" grounds the tenets proposed in his treatise (Long 147). Paul's emphasis on "experience" suggests a later Renaissance rhetorical stress on the priority of experiential knowledge in education, as evidenced, for example, in the late-sixteenth-century pedagogical essays of Michel de Montaigne.

As I will demonstrate below, these three tenets—in brief, that esoteric (alchemical) knowledge is divinely inspired, grounded in experiential knowledge, and "withheld" from the unworthy—inform later aesthetic, philosophical, and more importantly educational traditions, among them a Renaissance poetics of literary emulation and more recent nineteenth- and twentieth-century theories of writing and research. In attempting this admittedly broad transhistorical leap from fourteenth-century alchemy to postindustrial pedagogy, I do not mean to suggest a strict practical lineage (the use of esoteric alchemical doctrine to teach writing, for example) but rather a thematic concordance over time that bears out in special ways in contemporary approaches to plagiarism as failed or false authorship. Granted, to historicize plagiarism as a modern or postmodern form of failed/false alchemy is perhaps to add little to its history, especially if the tropic allusions cited in the opening of this chapter are taken seriously as indices of professional, academic understandings of plagiarism as a kind of productive error or scriptural misadventure. However, my focus throughout this and other chapters is on plagiarism as a salient signifying form in the history of modern communication generally and education specifically.

To historicize plagiarism, therefore, in relation to an alchemical "devotional system" is to question the ways in which theories of learning and knowledge acquisition—and by extension remedies targeting what are often characterized as learning errors—continue to signify in ways reflective of earlier systems. Thus, the alchemical metaphor with which I began this chapter is here used as a signifying gateway into related communicative practices dealing explicitly with student plagiarism and its prevention and detection.

In pursuing this link between alchemical and educational traditions, I take my lead from Ivan Illich's claim in *Tools for Conviviality* that the modern effort to put all people through "successive stages of enlightenment" is "rooted deeply in alchemy . . ." (18). Illich traces this alchemical legacy back to John Amos Comenius, a seventeenth-century Moravian bishop who used the language of alchemy "to describe the art of rearing children" (*Tools* 18). It is useful to note that in crafting his pedagogical method, Comenius, like Paul of Taranto three centuries before him, rejected bookish reading in favor of the experiential pursuit of knowledge. For Comenius, the student becomes wise by studying "the heavens" and "the earth" and "not by studying books . . ." (qtd. in Mulhern 365). As discussed further in the next chapter, a modern emphasis on experiential learning (to complement if not replace book learning) will continue to inform pedagogical theory well into the twentieth and twenty-first centuries. For now, though, I focus on Illich's subsequent claim that industrial production was first "fully rationalized" in the realm of education (*Tools* 19). Pedagogy's "new chapter" nonetheless borrowed, Illich suggests, from antiquated notions of alchemical transmutation. Indeed, industrial-age education standardized "the search for an alchemical process" that would spawn a "new type" of human being better suited to modern, industrial life (*Tools* 19).

Illich's somewhat broad account of modern industrial education can be traced to the work of John Dewey, who, in his 1900 *The School and Society*, for example, states his belief in "the mind as a growing affair, and hence as essentially changing . . ." (102). Dewey's organic account of mental growth and change amounts to a psychological inflection of the successive alchemical "stages" described by Illich. Indeed, Dewey's progressive pedagogy placed a high premium on "educational transformation" (*School* 104), and in his 1902 *The Child and the Curriculum*, he deploys the transmutation metaphor with some surprising results. Arguing against the popular German model of education through interest (Mulhern 468), Dewey contends that the best way for a student to learn and grow in relation to a given topic is not to find interest in the material but rather "to transform the material; to psychologize it . . ." (30). Eventually Dewey states his psychological agenda outright: "Mental assimilation is a matter of consciousness; and if the attention has not been playing upon the actual material, that has not been apprehended, nor worked into faculty" (30).

It would be ludicrous to reduce Dewey's robust and complex pedagogical theories to these few select passages. I aim simply to highlight thematic connections between psychological notions of mental "attention," "apprehension," and "faculty" and alchemical notions of exo-and esoteric transmutation. To "psychologize" material is, crudely put, to transmute base metals into gold or, more accurately, to perform an esoteric operation rendering the individual better through successful transmutation of received content. More specifically, "assimilation," as the "matter of consciousness," is also an apprehension, a cognitive bringing-forth of attention through the child's taking into faculty the material relevant to his or her life. Through attention—or rather, the attention "playing upon the actual material"—material assimilation (or growth, transformation) becomes possible. Attention in this context provides the ferment, the Elixir by which to affect assimilation and conversion. In short, if Illich is right, then Comenius's seventeenth-century adaptation of alchemical technique to the "art" of raising children continues in this early-twentieth-century adaptation of behavioral psychology to the science of developing young minds. In the guise of developmental pedagogy, the alchemical myth of transmutation finds purchase in the promise of material "worked into" faculty.

Dewey's approach to material assimilation is obviously part of a much broader postindustrial educational philosophy based, as Illich argues, in an understanding of education as a site of human progress and improvement. Worth mentioning here, then, is the late-nineteenth-century emphasis on education as a key battleground for the fight against religious and moral decay and the defense of civilized progress. For turn-of-the century liberal theologians—whose influence at the time reached broadly into secular society—"the progress of the Kingdom of God" was often linked to "the progress of civilization . . ." (Marsden 24). Assuring civil-divine progress required appropriate methods for protecting and transforming minds and souls otherwise seduced by modern temptations if not given over already to the questionable habits of modern life. Joseph Angus, in his 1873 "Duty of the Church in Relation to Mission," outlines a methodology for human progress reminiscent of doctrinal alchemy and the search for divine transmutation: "The divine method of human improvement begins in human hearts through evangelical truth, and it spreads from within outwardly till all is renewed" (qtd. in Marsden 12). Like the philosopher's stone, capable of "altering" surrounding metals "by means of a certain digestive heat," the human heart, steeped in "evangelical truth," enlarges and emerges outwardly to renew a world threatened with decay and ultimate annihilation.

Generally speaking, a nineteenth-century secular defense of civilized society—and with it a progressive emphasis on developmental learning and "educational transformation"—went hand in hand with a broadly religious commitment to the pursuit of spiritual and moral perfection. Early in the century, for example, John Wesley (founder of Wesleyan Methodism) noted that Scripture "commanded one to 'be perfect'" and held, therefore, that "this state must therefore be obtainable" (Marsden 73). In contrast to an earlier Puritan emphasis on a perpetually sinful life filled with struggle, Wesley proposed on behalf of an emerging American revivalism that "sin" was by and large a "voluntary act of will" (Marsden 73). Believers could therefore seek liberation from both "sinful acts" and, perhaps more important, from "the disease of sinful motives and the 'power' of sin'" (Marsden 73). Adopting Wesley's concept of spiritual "sanctification," Yale theologian Nathaniel Taylor argued that "nothing is either sinful or righteous unless it be a free act of will," and therefore humans are capable of choosing "the good" whenever confronted with a moral choice (Marsden 74). In choosing to do good, one can thereby choose to "be perfect," casting off sinful acts and finding a remedy, "by God's grace," for the disease of sinful motives.

In sum, where nineteenth-century theologians debated the voluntary or willful nature of sin, conservative humanists, in many cases adopting the language of evangelical (and later fundamentalist) Christianity, bemoaned the "vicious habits" of a turn-of-the-century citizenry showing signs of strangeness in a changing world. In both cases, the quest for spiritual, intellectual, and cultural improvement catalyzed hope for a twentieth-century America liberated from sinful acts (decadent immorality) and regressive modernism (urban poverty, industrialization). Education, in this context, functioned widely as a key site of spiritual, intellectual, and cultural reform, and learning to write implied not only a commitment to mastering English and the varied skills of information processing, but also a related commitment to societal progress through the cultivation of strong mental "faculty" and perfect "human hearts." Thus, central to Dewey's and other modernist accounts of learning through "material" assimilation are related notions of literacy as a kind of platform (or luminous "page") essential to that assimilation.

REMEDIUM AND THE BIRTH OF SCHOLASTIC READING

In his introduction to *In the Vineyard of the Text*, Ivan Illich describes his work as a commemoration of the birth of scholastic reading in early-thirteenth-century universities. The first half of the book, however, is devoted to a close study of twelfth-century monastic reading habits. The primary focus of Illich's study is Hugh of Saint Victor, the French monk whose *Didascalicon*, written sometime around 1130, was one of the first books written "on the art of reading" (5).[6] Hugh's treatise on reading begins with a mandate reminiscent of doctrinal alchemy and the search for Christ in the form of an Elixir or philosopher's stone. Hugh writes: *Omnium expetendorum prima est sapientia* ("Of all things to be sought, the first is wisdom"). The wisdom an aspiring monk seeks, according to Illich, is "Christ himself" or, for those learning to read in accordance with Hugh's curriculum, "Christ as Remedy," "Example," and "Form" (10). The monastic reader in search of wisdom (as Christ, as Remedy) is one willing to go into a kind of readerly "exile" wherein all "attention and desire" is focused on the pursuit of divine wisdom (Illich 17). Reading the illuminated page is thus "remedy" because it restores light to a world lost in the darkness of original sin (Illich 20).

In Hugh's world of reading, the light of the page as divine form or exemplum heals the reader with the medicine of Christ as Remedy. This twelfth-century concept of *remedium* (remedy, medicine) thus intersects with contemporary alchemical interest in divine healing through transmutation and later, for Paracelsus, the production of medicines through chemistry. Illich clarifies the importance of *remedium* to an early-twelfth-century reader: "God became man to remedy the disorder . . . in which humanity, through Adam's sin, has been steeped" (10–11). The highest remedy is thus "God as wisdom," and for Illich the arts and sciences both "share in being remedies for the same purpose" (11). For monastic readers, the chief medium of study (*studium legendi*) is of course the book, which allows the reader to find again the light lost to original sin (21).

One prerequisite for monastic *remedium* was training in the art of memory storage and recall. Hugh, for example, encouraged his students "to expand and refine their memory skills through the construction of an interior treasure chest" (Illich 35). As an instructor in the art of reading, Hugh thus revised for a twelfth-century reading curriculum the "antique art of the rhetor," teaching memory work as a companion skill to "monastic mumblers" uttering the words before them (Illich 42). Later scholastic memory strategies, drawing on the ancient Greek notion of "memory palaces," would also emphasize this idea of memory storage. However, for these later scholastic readers the book itself connoted "the treasury, the mine, the storage room" in which memory could be not only stored but accessed (Illich 95).

On the eve of scholasticism, in fact, the monk of Hugh's *Didascalicon* gives way to a new kind of reader whose approach to book reading and memory work would be vastly different than that encouraged by Hugh. By the early thirteenth century, the word *study* would no longer refer to a meditative quest by the light of the page for Christ the Remedy, but rather to the storing and sorting of knowledge via an assiduous search—or research—through the indexical landscape of the new page layout (Illich 65). Moreover, for thirteenth-century scholars the new methods of knowledge acquisition, and scholastic reading in particular, were reserved for "people who do something special" within the bounds of an increasingly exclusionary university structure (Illich 81). In 1310, nearly two centuries after the publication of Hugh's treatise, Paul of Taranto would conclude his *Summa Perfectionis* with a similar injunction (discussed above) against sharing alchemical secrets with the "undeserving." However, where Paul conceded the right of revelation to the "Divine Will of God," for thirteenth-century scholars a new regime of clerical professionalism warranted a new variety of secular secrecy. By default, scholastic reading—and knowledge acquisition in general—became the province of those working within the walls of the new scholastic university, with lay readers systematically excluded.

The new scholastic reader, as described in broad strokes by Illich, enters a life of individualized knowledge acquisition that differs radically from the life of exile reserved for the monk dedicated to the lifelong pursuit of wisdom. Moreover, for this new reader, a new set of reference tools would facilitate the search for and acquisition of knowledge within the bounds of scholastic inquiry. Scholastic readers, as writers or perhaps copyists, also used their books in a new way—"no longer as fodder for their own meditative rumination, but as building materials that could be used in the construction of new mental edifices" (Illich 105). The page, in short, became a "bookish text" that, by analogy, "shaped the scholastic mind" in accordance with a "scribal revolution" that would help set the stage for the well-chronicled print revolution of the fifteenth century (Illich 116).[7]

As argued in the next section, early modern writers such as Michel de Montaigne would launch a rhetorical attack precisely on the regime of bookish, pedantic scholasticism described broadly here. Against what he perceived to be bad habits of bookish reading and scholarly foraging, Montaigne would propose a new pedagogy of skeptical inquiry grounded in reading and writing techniques that, while derivative of classical rhetorical models, also prefigured later modernist approaches to textual assimilation, authorship, and plagiarism.

READING MONTAIGNE READING

Often identified as an early modern progenitor of later modern and even postmodern theories of authorship, Montaigne can also be read, like his contemporaries, as a late Renaissance adherent to classical rhetorical models, such as those commonly attributed to Cicero, Quintilian, and Seneca. In this section, I read Montaigne in light of the above discussion of alchemy and, specifically, plagiarism as a kind of fraudulent or failed transmutation of textual material.

To begin, I should note that alchemy found little support in the new scholastic university of the early Renaissance but nonetheless grew into an important shadow discipline in the fourteenth and fifteenth centuries. Indeed, in its complex coordination of philosophical and theological doctrine and operational practices, alchemy continued to intersect with humanist scholarly activity well into the sixteenth century and beyond (Long). While he was certainly no alchemist, Montaigne's rejection of "pedagogical scholasticism" made him "a nemesis to the neoclassical hegemony in France, and later in England" (Marchi 119). Thus, his theories on authorship suggest a useful, if complex, counterfoil to prevailing notions of scholastic study as characterized by Illich. My aim in this section will be to measure Montaigne's antique textual inheritance against corollary alchemical and scholastic traditions at play in the late sixteenth century when Montaigne penned (and later re-penned) his *Essais*. In particular, Montaigne's emphasis on textual transmutation in the pursuit of wisdom and the perfection of the soul will guide my analysis. In the next chapter, I will trace Montaigne's legacy to contemporary composition theory and, more specifically, current efforts to revitalize research writing practices using a neo-Montaignian model.

In his two essays on learning—"On Schoolmasters' Learning" ("Schoolmaster") and "On the Education of Children" ("Education")—Montaigne addresses the question of classical imitation as both a pedagogical and an authorial concern. Montaigne's statements on literary incorporation and transmutation, in particular, intersect with broader questions about learning and educational technique. Before addressing these two essays, I will cite the much-quoted preface to the *Essais* in order to frame Montaigne's project in self-portraiture and authorship more broadly. Echoing Erasmus, Montaigne begins by assuring the reader that he wishes to be recognized in his "simple, everyday fashion, without striving or artifice" ("To the Reader").[8] In painting his own literary portrait, Montaigne strives to convey his "own self" and promises, in the effort, to reveal everything: "Here, drawn from life, you will read of my defects and my native form. . . ." Montaigne's rhetorical emphasis on native form complements an inherent relationship between his "own self" and the many authors he has encountered during a lifetime of reading. In both "Schoolmaster" and "Education," Montaigne writes the rhetorical "self" by writing through his scholarly inheritance, formalizing the process in ways both reflective and disruptive of prevailing scholastic techniques.

Montaigne distinguishes his literary practice from the rote imitation of his scholastic contemporaries. Like birds in search of grain, writes Montaigne in "Schoolmaster," "our schoolmasters go foraging for learning in their books and merely lodge it on the tip of their lips, only to spew it out and scatter it on the wind" (154). He goes on to confess that this "foolishness" applies to his own situation as well:

> Am I not for the most part doing the same when assembling my material? Off I go, rummaging about in books for sayings which please me—not so as to store them up (for I have no storehouses), but so as to carry them back to this book, where they are no more mine that they were in their original place. (154)

Montaigne places himself in the ranks of those foolish foragers "rummaging about" in scholarly texts. This admission could be explained as an example, among several in the *Essais*, of the "modesty topos" common to Renaissance rhetoric (Brush 3). However, as Marchi has argued, the passage also reflects a "perpetual tension" in the *Essais* between Montaigne's own words and "previously written texts" (113). This tension has proved puzzling to generations of critics who want to maintain that Montaigne, on the one hand, claims "independence from classical models" and, on the other, relies on classical models both directly and indirectly throughout the *Essais* (Ancekewicz 134). Irving Babbitt's 1908 testimony is perhaps indicative of modern responses to this tension. According to Babbitt, Montaigne wrote an "original book" that nonetheless "often impresses the reader as a mere cento of quotations" (230).[9]

In his own defense, Montaigne marshals a grounding skepticism to justify his patchwork technique: "We only know, I believe, what we know now: 'knowing' no more consists in what we once knew than in what we shall know in the future" (154). In other words, to know is to assay knowledge, and to do so now, in the essay. Thus, received knowledge ("what we once knew") gives way to experiential knowledge ("what we know now") in the service of self-revelation. Writing as rummaging codifies this exercise in skeptical inquiry. Montaigne echoes this point in "Education": "My aim is to reveal my own self, which may well be different tomorrow if I am initiated into some new business which changes me" (167). Initiation and change, therefore, distinguish the skeptical project of the essayist from the mere foraging of scholastic readers. Moreover, faced with a literary-pedantic tradition that stresses the "opinions and learning of others," Montaigne urges that "we ought to make them our own" (155). The path to one's "own" requires a methodical reading of literary material ingested, digested, and thus assimilated into the soul of the knower. Montaigne puts it this way in "Schoolmaster": "What use is it to us to have a belly full of meat if we do not digest it, if we do not transmute it into ourselves, if it does not make us grow in size and strength?" (155). In "Education," Montaigne answers his own question: "[T]he stomach has not done its job if, during concoction, it fails to change the substance and the form of what is given" (169).

Montaigne's version of digestion and concoction is itself a product of his own consumption of Quintilian and (or via) Erasmus. In particular, Quintilian's notion of "innutrition" informed Erasmus's sense of "inward digestion" (Randall 38). As Randall points out, tropes of digestion functioned in neoclassical rhetoric to warn against the dangers of copying (32). In "prescribing modes of proper imitation," Renaissance rhetoric prioritized "the work of *transformation* required to shift the imitation from servility to inspiration . . ." (Randall 32). This transformation work—reminiscent of the rigors of esoteric alchemy—required intensive practice and technical mastery leading, in the end, to literary perfection:

The means to this end were, first, the assiduous study of the rules of
composition by means of the reading and interpretation of the words
of the masters, and then their paraphrase and, eventually, translation.
In all instances, transformation, applied to the form of the work, was
an essential step, for it is in this phase that the genius of the author,
prohibited from inventing subjects, was exercised. (Randall 37)

Montaigne, himself a product of intense "assiduous study," argues for a similar
pedagogical regimen throughout his essays.

Montaigne closes "Schoolmaster" by making a case for the importance of
literary transmutation in educating the young. He proceeds by drawing an important distinction: "Learned we may be with another man's learning: we can
only be wise with wisdom of our own" (155). Learning is thus the product of
reading and the conveyance of knowledge from "books" to "memory" (154). As
Elizabeth Eisenstein has pointed out, the "denunciation of book learning"—or
bookish scholasticism more broadly—had become so common by the end of
the sixteenth century that the denunciation "became itself a bookish cliché"
(151). More to the point, Montaigne's emphasis on "wisdom" echoes Hugh's
"*sapienta*" and the twelfth-century monastic emphasis on reading as therapeutic "reunion with wisdom." For Montaigne, to read and digest classical knowledge is to heal the "imperfect" soul through the inculcation of wisdom:

[W]e are not merely to stick knowledge on to the soul: we must incorporate it into her; the soul should not be sprinkled with knowledge
but steeped in it. And if knowledge does not change her and make her
imperfect state better then it is preferable just to leave it alone. (158)

Where an esoteric alchemical tradition emphasized divine transmutation
through the allegorical transformation of base metals and the removal of taint,
Montaigne proposed an "educational practice" grounded in the transubstantiation
of knowledge and the refinement of soul. In the latter case, a soul made better
through assiduous study, knowledge incorporation, and reunion with wisdom is
also a reading pupil fashioned and formed into a well-nourished scholar. Adapting
Illich's reading of Hugh's *Didascalicon*, I would argue that a monastic quest
through reading for Christ as Remedy reappears under the rubric of Renaissance
pedagogy as a spiritual search for wisdom and perfection offered in contrast to the
scholastic heaping of knowledge. In the end, what the schoolmaster lacks, according to Montaigne, is the proper orientation with regard to knowledge and knowledge use. Nonetheless, for both Montaigne and the rummaging schoolmaster, the
quest for wisdom begins in the assiduous study of received knowledge ("the opinions and learning of others"). Thus, in the search for wisdom as a "natural property" (161), Montaigne must nonetheless stay close to material "sayings."

The search for wisdom described at the end of "Schoolmaster" continues in "Education." Montaigne begins by defining his own writing process: "I undertake to write without preconceptions on any subject which comes to mind, employing nothing but my own natural resources" (164). Montaigne's strategy to avoid the appearance of "striving or artifice" requires, once again, a rhetorical bypass around the problem of received knowledge: in using "natural resources," the self appears in "native form." Addressing the problem of imitation, however, Montaigne employs the modesty topos in full force:

> [I]f (as happens often) I chance to come across in excellent authors the very same topics I have undertaken to treat . . . then I acknowledge myself to be so weak, so paltry, so lumbering and so dull compared with such men, that I feel scorn and pity for myself. . . . What I myself have thought up and produced is poor feeble stuff, but I let it go on, without plastering over the cracks or stitching up the rents which have been revealed by such comparisons. (164)

Ancekewicz argues convincingly that these and similar "fictions" in the *Essais* are part and parcel of a broader Renaissance concern for "the truth of falsehood . . . underlying language, self and history" (62). In short, the modesty claim, along with companion claims to material transmutation, functioned for Renaissance authors to ward off accusations of arrogance and false pretense. An author admittedly "so weak, so paltry, so lumbering and so dull" compared with the "men" of antiquity he so ardently ravaged could not be accused of mere copying when the "fiction" of authorship itself remained so close to the surface. The "je" of the essays must therefore engage in continuous "self-criticism and deprecation" in order to "retain the status of origin" (Ancekewicz 143). Simply put, self-lacerating acknowledgments of one's derivative status secured the Renaissance author's claim to originality and, for Montaigne in particular, the rhetorical construction of self in "native form."

Still, Montaigne insists on distinguishing between the thoughts of others ("excellent authors") and his own ("What I myself have thought up"). "Our souls," he admits, are "shackled and constrained to what is desired by someone else's ideas; they are captives, enslaved to the authority of what they have been taught" (170). The captive soul must therefore seek liberation from antique authority by means similar to those reviewed above. Montaigne appends his earlier discussion, however, by introducing a new term in the language of textual transmutation—namely, *reason* and the reasoning power of the learning pupil. For Montaigne, reasoning transmutes someone else's opinions into the selfsame opinions in different form, as one's "own." A philosopher's stone of a decidedly different order, reasoning coaxes the transmutation and assimilation of received knowledge. It is "by his own reasoning," Montaigne writes, "that [the pupil] adopts the opinions of Xenophon and Plato, they are no longer theirs: they are his . . ." (170). In keeping with the trope of digestion, the pupil emancipates self from the authority of other writers not by "learning their precepts" but by "drinking in their humours" (170).

Here Montaigne introduces a reading technique poised somewhere between Hugh's quest for mystical reunion and the scholastic search for mental building blocks in the works of antiquity. Significantly, to incorporate and transmute the precepts of others is also to forget or hide the original source. "If he wants to, let [the pupil] not be afraid to forget where he got them from, but let him be sure that he knows how to appropriate them" (170). In short, the "boy" learning, on the one hand enslaved by ancient knowledge, is on the other encouraged to use his own resources by forgetting the knowledge gained from reading others. As Randall argues, forgetting in this context suggests a "transition in Renaissance aesthetics from a poetics of memory and memorization, to one of forgetting . . ." (41). This recourse to a poetics of forgetting, once again, helps stabilize the fiction of original authorship. In brief, a claim of "cryptomnesia" among Renaissance authors served well to foil accusations of wanton borrowing and imitation (Randall 42).

To forget what one has absorbed is to incorporate knowledge such that it nourishes and enriches one's faculties of good judgment.[10] Montaigne writes:

> Bees ransack flowers here and flowers there: but then they make their own honey, which is entirely theirs and no longer thyme or marjoram. Similarly the boy will transform his borrowings; he will confound their forms so that the end-product is entirely his: namely his judgement, the forming of which is the only aim of his toil, his study and his education. (171)

Fittingly enough, Montaigne ransacks Seneca almost verbatim in this passage, confirming Donaldson's point that Renaissance accounts of "the hazards and proprieties of literary imitation tend to be largely recycled from influential classical authors" (119). Moreover, the "doctrine of aesthetic dissimulation, of hiding away" (Donaldson 122) reproduces a classical emphasis on concealment in the guise of a Renaissance insistence on "re-creation" or "reinvention" (Ancekewicz 37) through literary emulation. As Seneca wrote, "[O]ur mind . . . should hide away all the materials by which it has been aided, and bring to light only what it has made of them" (qtd. in Richardson, "Plagiarism" 109). For Montaigne, as well, the path to good judgment requires some careful concealment: the pupil should "hide the help he received and put only his achievements on display" (171). To display one's achievement—defined here, in sum, as the incorporation (forgetting, hiding) of received knowledge through the transmutation of borrowings—is to meet the rewards of assiduous study: "The profit we possess after study is to have become better and wiser" (171). Thus, the educated child—like the alchemical adept—arrives at the apex of wisdom found in the pursuit of spiritual transformation.

My reading of Montaigne thus far has been for the most part a rereading, and one which by and large reflects what Ancekewicz characterizes as a move in Montaigne criticism since the 1970s toward a treatment of the *Essais* as a rhetorical experiment in self-reflexivity (16n). Other readers have taken a more literal view of the text as "expressive of the views and thoughts of the writer or author . . ." (Ancekewicz 21). Without addressing the finer details of these two approaches, I would like nonetheless to consider representative examples of each in order to introduce a broader discussion of reading, writing, and textual transmutation in a late-twentieth-century communication context. In the next chapter, I consider the ways in which recent composition theorists have read (adopted and adapted) Montaigne in the interest of pedagogical reform.

In *From the Perspective of the Self: Montaigne's Self-Portrait* (1994), Craig Brush develops a rhetorical reading of Montaigne but to a radically "expressivist" end, bringing the self Montaigne alive in accordance with the project of self-portraiture outlined in the *Essais'* opening address. Adopting Wayne Booth's argument regarding the fictional "coherence" of the *Essais*, Brush proceeds to build a series of "plausible scenes" in which the fictional Montaigne can be imagined composing his essays (35). Responding in particular to the well-documented fact that Montaigne annotated his 1580 copy of *Essais* for reprinting in 1588, Brush wonders how the author might have gone about the work of marginal notation:

> [T]he most plausible scene would feature Montaigne reading a favorite author alone in his tower library, being struck by a particular passage, and reaching for his copy of the *Essays* to find the proper place to incorporate its content in his own work. (49)

Granting on the one hand the inherent derivations of Montaigne's writing, Brush seeks to bypass the editorial stratification of the *Essais*[11] in favor of a preemptive originary moment. "There will be times when it is important to catch Montaigne in his original words, rather than their later amended form . . ." (52). Worth noting here is Brush's confidence that an original Montaigne exists in the first place, despite the author's acknowledged practice of incorporating his "favorite" authors throughout all drafts of the essays. For Brush, Montaigne's readerly (perhaps fictional) pursuit of native form should reveal an original form underneath, perhaps beyond, the "later amended form" surviving in modern editions (in all editions, in fact, after 1580). In any event, it is important, according to Brush, "to catch Montaigne" in that original form.

Brush admits, however, that it would be wrong "to overlook the role of reading in Montaigne's search for himself and for human nature" (181). Herbert Lüthy, in his 1962 "Montaigne, or the Art of Being Truthful," makes a related point with regard to reading and appropriation:

> The best introduction to [the *Essais*] might be simply: Take it and read! or better still: read it and take!—for everyone is free to take what suits him *[sic]*, as Montaigne himself took whatever suited him, in order to make it his own. . . . (12)

Deploying the Renaissance trope of cannibalistic innutrition, Lüthy echoes Montaigne's argument regarding literary transmutation and the construction of self through the assiduous study of ancient wisdom. Likewise, he anticipates Marchi's point that modern thinkers would later find in Montaigne's writings the implied appeal "that readers continue his writing . . ." (13).

Terence Cave's 1982 "Problems of Reading in the *Essais*" focuses on the "practice of reading" (79) in Montaigne. Citing the presence in the *Essais* of well over a thousand direct quotations (in addition to even more paraphrased or translated passages), Cave suggests that direct quotations

> are the most self-evidently foreign bodies in Montaigne's text, the least digested elements of his discourse. They thus provide a test case for the way in which his readings are integrated into a new context. (93)

Reading as writing is understood here as a process of integrating—or incorporating—received materials into a "new context." The new context, in this case, is the domestic domain of Montaigne's "original, authentic intention." Responding to Montaigne's practice of unattributed quotation, Cave questions the sixteenth-century writer's motivation:

> Montaigne's quotations have "weight," it would seem, because they come from the most famous authors (or authorities). But the device of presenting them anonymously would seem rather to strip them of their credentials and thus deprive them of their function as a citation of authority. One could go further and say that they are released from their allegiance to another text, and thus free to become incorporated into Montaigne's. (98)

As noted above, Montaigne sought to liberate a soul "enslaved" to authority. In Cave's analysis, "quotations," not souls, are held in "allegiance" to other texts, then freed through anonymity and the loss of "credentials" to "become incorporated" in a new literary context. The main question for Cave, then, is one of readerly approach, that is, how best to read Montaigne in a modern context when the author seems to be deceiving the reader with anonymous quotations: "The tricking of the reader is a symptom of the persistent desire to eliminate the difference between foreign materials and the text of the *Essais*" (98). Cave's reading suggests that Montaigne, striving throughout the essays to present himself in "native form," uses anonymous quotation to eradicate difference between himself and quoted authorities.

By and large, Cave's analysis exemplifies what Marchi more recently characterized as the "appeal" of Montaigne to nineteenth- and twentieth-century modernists who have found in Montaigne's "free use of tradition" a difficult analytical problem (119). In fact, if Marchi is right in arguing that Montaigne's essays invite—perhaps even demand—that future readers continue the writing begun in the sixteenth century, then Cave's problem-solving efforts may suggest that the best way to write Montaigne is to figure out how best to read him. Cave's reading of Montaigne's "trick," for example, may speak more to the critic's objective to eliminate difference than to a desire in fact traceable to the text of the *Essais*. In any event, Cave must entertain the somewhat startling conclusion that the essays are perhaps "'simply' the orchestration of a vast reading experience" (101).

That the *Essais* may be the outcome of Montaigne's reading (and foraging) practices, however, complicates their inherited status as a collection of writings. To resolve this "paradoxical dynamism" (Marchi 7) in the work of Montaigne, Cave posits that the multivocal character of Montaigne's essays suggests "a dialogue of many voices, past and present; or of a series of windows opened on the not quite forgotten pages of Montaigne's library" (102). In the space of the garret, in other words, the author (as cryptomnesic alchemist) purges himself of the taint of authoritative influence and emerges in the pseudo-unified semblance of a modern writer. Or as Cave puts it, Montaigne's *Essais*, as historical artifact, provide "a history or story which confers some degree of unity on an otherwise fragmented self" (108). The book, then—or, to adapt Illich, the "bookish text"—registers in its historical unity the evidence of textual transmutation and, as a consequence, the clear mark of a unified authorial subject.

I propose by way of conclusion that the issue at stake when considering plagiarism as failed or false creation is not so much writing per se but rather reading and the textual, if not strictly alchemical, transmutation of received knowledge for reuse in a writing context. Marilyn Randall points out that Montaigne wrote at a pivotal time in the history of arts and letters and does, in fact, embody a set of conflicting rhetorical strategies that turn on issues of authorship and originality in writing. During the late medieval and early Renaissance periods, even as scribes embraced more modern notions of authorship, "they continued to invest authority in the *auctoritas* of the ancients" (Randall 35–36). However, while *auctoritates*, or "statements of truth," were handled as "common property" among medieval authors, Renaissance authors engaged in a "continual battle to accede to authority on the part of human authors . . . a struggle sufficiently exemplified by Montaigne . . ." (Randall 36). In short, living writers "were becoming more like *auctores*" (36), and Randall situates Montaigne as "one of the most modern" of them all and, more tellingly, as "a potential model 'plagiarist'" (36).

Montaigne's writing process is perhaps best understood, therefore, not as a monodirectional, influential regime of textual absorption (as Cave, for example, might have put it), but rather as a bidirectional or mutually transformative process whereby bodies incorporated via transformational reading activities include not only texts but the ones who read them. Thus, a postmodern rereading of Montaigne provides at least one avenue for a revised approach to plagiarism and antiplagiarism remedies. As I discuss more fully in chapter 6, such rereadings are instrumental to late-twentieth-century revisionist writing pedagogies—particularly where Montaigne reappears as both model plagiarist and model author in broader efforts to revamp student research writing.

CONCLUSION:
TRANSMUTATION IN THE NEW UNIVERSITY

As stated in the last chapter, the new university of postindustrial America had its beginnings in the small, provincial colleges of the eighteenth and nineteenth centuries. Thus, Irving Babbitt's defense of reading and "humane" learning, published in his 1908 *Literature and the American College*, could be interpreted as a nostalgic plea on behalf of a waning college system overshadowed by the new, larger university. Babbitt's target, however, is specifically literary, and I close this chapter by way of his discussion of the "decline of humanism" in twentieth-century higher education. The decline, according to Babbitt, operates in tandem with the rise of "Rousseauism" and a corollary "decay in the higher uses of memory" (244). To make his case for rescuing humanism from the ravages of a nineteenth-century "race of eccentric individualists," Babbitt draws an explicit comparison between the individualist par excellance, Rousseau, and his sixteenth-century forebear, Michel de Montaigne.

Babbitt's critique of Rousseau targets the latter's unmitigated rhetorical self-reflexivity. Like Montaigne, Rousseau endorsed a humane pedagogical formula centering on the fortification of young minds in defense of a priori nature. Rousseau opposed the traditional view "that human nature is evil and must be changed or disciplined" and recommended instead that education strengthen an essentially "good" soul against the distorting forces of society (Mulhern 449). In making similar claims about scholarly training for the young, both the eighteen-century Rousseau and the sixteenth-century Montaigne wrote unabashedly of their own lives and experiences. However, according to Babbitt, each author approached his respective project in self-portraiture differently: "[I]n the final analysis Montaigne is interested in Montaigne because he is a human being"; Rousseau wrote about Rousseau, on the other hand, "because he is Jean-Jacques" (228). For Babbitt, whose early-twentieth-century humanism resurrects a late-Renaissance respect for *auctoritas* and classical wisdom, Rousseau's superficial obsession with the self-Rousseau pales in comparison to Montaigne's profound excavationist project in the realm of human nature. Montaigne, then, is the better model of the "humane man" who, with a memory "richly stored," also possesses "the sound sense perfectly expressed that is found only in the masters" (244).

In his defense of humanist learning, Babbitt touches on a few key themes also addressed in this chapter. For example, his emphasis on learning as a kind of memory storage recalls both Hugh's twelfth-century tutorial on the "treasure chest" and Montaigne's later invocation of the memory "storehouse." As discussed above, Hugh's mnemonic device reproduced the earlier Greek art of constructing "memory palaces" to aid the rhetor's recall of memorized details. Hugh's memory pedagogy gave way in the latter half of the twelfth century to a scholastic emphasis on the book as itself a storage vessel. To read, in the scholastic sense, was to engage in a kind of bookish rummaging later denounced by Montaigne. Babbitt's early-twentieth-century call for a resurgent humanism through "the revival of the almost lost art of reading" (244) is therefore reminiscent not only of Montaigne's dismissal of scholastic "foraging" but also of Hugh's monastic emphasis on reading as a form of inspired memory work. For Babbitt and perhaps his humanist contemporaries, a memory "richly stored" conveys the "sound sense" of wisdom pursued or, to adapt Montaigne, the soul "steeped" in knowledge incorporated.

Moreover, Babbitt's quest for the lost arts of reading revives under the banner of humanism an alchemical interest in the search for perfection through material transmutation. The "humane man," richly stored with the "best in literature," also finds recourse to the "sound sense perfectly expressed . . . in the masters" (244). As discussed above, the alchemical search for the philosopher's stone meant for Paul of Taranto and his adepts the divine search for wisdom through experimentation and self-purification. For Babbitt, however, the "sound sense" of humanism finds its perfect expression in the masters whose aesthetic sensibilities bring, through modern reading and memory work, the light of wisdom. Babbitt's "revival," in other words, is nothing less than a redressed resurrection of the quest for inspired Remedy. Still, in contrast to the doctrinal alchemy of Paul and his adepts, Babbitt's fundamental healing experiment—reading—has already located its philosopher's stone in the "perfectly expressed" wisdom of the masters. A search for perfection, in short, is realized in the perfectly expressed words of dead geniuses.

In short, Babbitt wants more students to read more masters, to drink in their "humours," to incorporate, transmute, and make them their own. To make reading work for the reading and writing student in the twentieth-century college requires an arguably nonindividualist emphasis on inherited wisdom, classical knowledge, the opinions of others, and the interjection of the "pupil" into the treasury or mine of modern information storehouses. The twentieth-century experiment in research paper writing can be read, therefore, as a new-university solution to Babbitt's problem of a decadent humanism and the need for more artful reading. Babbitt would likely have rejected this conclusion, but the assignment arguably combined a humanist interest in reading as a means to "sound sense" and masterful wisdom with a postindustrial emphasis on writing as a functionalist exercise in material search and acquisition. Thus, I would argue that critical assessments of the research paper assignment as a perennially troubling and troublesome task, to students and teachers alike (see Zemliansky and Austin on this point), may miss the point that the assignment has always spelled trouble for a reason. Namely, as an exercise in adjudicating memory richly stored in either the student's own storehouse or the university's expanding library (or both), the research paper also required a healthy respect for intellectual property law and the protected tenets of original authorship.

Note that Babbitt's main gripe with Rousseau was that his goal in the end was "to be the extraordinary man, or original genius" (228). A significant distinction informs this claim: Rousseau the individualist endeavored to "be" extraordinary and original, and thus, according to Babbitt, generations of Rousseauists committed to teaching students to be extraordinary individuals derailed the scholarly effort to teach "sound sense" through an assiduous study of the masters. A "humane man" such as Montaigne, on the other hand, aspired not to be an extraordinary or original genius but rather to know or assay the genius in "human being." Babbitt's individualists, in short, want their students to be extraordinary individuals. His humanists, on the other hand, want their students to know what it means to be extraordinary. The practice of research paper writing—poised, I would argue, somewhere between an individualist striving after originality and a humanist search for the original—bedeviled students and teachers alike in demanding both at the same time. Plagiarism thus presented a serious problem for a twentieth-century educational system struggling on the one hand to nourish and grow students into healthy originals and, on the other, to teach a healthy respect for the laws of origin.

Finally, plagiarism must be understood not only as an act of errant or fraudulent writing but also as an "act of reading" (Kewes 6) that ends in the ostensibly wrongful or inadequate appropriation of materials read. As others have suggested (see Kewes, Randall, and Howard, for example), to approach plagiarism as an act of reading is to pay stricter attention to what Kewes calls the "material form" of that which is plagiarized. For example, reading and copying from a bookish text may result in a different kind of plagiarism than cutting and pasting text from an Internet Web site, a point I return to in chapter 7. Kewes also suggests that "the development of information technologies and the surge of desktop publishing could be said to have produced a new breed of appropriator . . ." (8). I would argue more generally that new institutional and practical approaches to information processing have spawned several new breeds of readers and writers, appropriators and plagiarists, mediators and originators (not to mention humanists and individualists), who have all nonetheless inherited an author-centered intellectual property regime that both wins and loses in this new age of widespread scriptural breeding. The art or sin of plagiarism, therefore, must be handled—therapeutically or judiciously or both—within the bounds of this new information environment.

5

How to Avoid Plagiarism

READING FOR RESEARCH purposes in most writing classrooms requires close attention to diverse sources of information and the eventual use or incorporation of those sources into writing subsequently submitted for evaluation. While research methods, assignment models, and evaluation procedures may vary, the process of incorporation often turns on related acts of textual assimilation (appropriation, integration) manifesting in deliberate attempts on the writer's part to summarize, paraphrase, or directly quote language encountered in primary and secondary source documents. Such acts of text incorporation, often dismissed as rudimentary, are in fact quite complicated, and failure to follow the rules judiciously can lead to accusations of misappropriation, or even plagiarism or copyright infringement.

In seeking out guidelines for how best to negotiate the conventions of text incorporation, students, educators, and scholars alike may turn to research writing handbooks. The research handbook, as one of the potential "tools" or "technologies" (Gee 20) available for navigating research conventions, provides an example of disciplinary "genre knowledge" (Berkenkotter and Huckin ix) distilled and promulgated for wide use in printed or digital form. Research handbooks thus embody the more conventional strategies for managing research writing conventions. With this general understanding of the research handbook in mind, I endeavor in this chapter to analyze text incorporation conventions as constructed in research handbook discourse. For this exercise, I focus in particular on the incorporation conventions modeled in the Houghton Mifflin (2002) *Handbook for College Research*.

I should note first that handbooks, like textbooks in general, record and fix the dominant tradition of right practice within a given communicative network. As Kurt Spellmeyer puts it, "[T]extbooks are pedestrian materials, . . . removing knowledge from the precarious worlds out of which it has emerged . . . and transporting it, now dead and sealed in wax, to a very different kind of place" ("Great Way" 45). The handbook in particular, defined in Webster's Ninth as a concise reference book covering a particular subject, not only "seals" genre knowledge but offers it in a concise form designed to be carried, literally, by hand as a ready reference. Michael Kleine, citing the inherent arbitrariness of written rhetorics, goes farther in describing them as "a kind of transcendent discourse" garnering and propagating "foundational truth" (137). It remains to be seen, however, whether writing handbooks are invariably as closed and detached as characterized here. One aim of this chapter is to investigate how the handbook may in fact work—and get used—as a viable set of guidelines for right practice in writing. As a concise reference, the typical handbook may prove to be the most "ready" means available for negotiating success as a student writer.

My primary example, the Houghton Mifflin (2002) *Handbook for College Research* (hereafter referred to as the *Handbook*), is here understood as a written text available for use in a communicative system in which students and teachers, as disciplinary actors, participate. Furthermore, the *Handbook* reflects just one material artifact of a particular discursive genre—in this case academic student research writing. As Bekenkotter and Huckin point out, beginning college and university students are asked to learn the rules and conventions that other members of that community might use toward the mastery of genre knowledge (118). Genre knowledge is required, in other words, to access what Gee calls the "'Big D' Discourses" of communicative networks (17). To be part of a discourse community, according to Gee, is to be "recognizable" as someone able to put together the "language, action, interaction, values, beliefs, symbols, objects, tools and places" relevant to the community and its disciplinary knowledge (18). This kind of recognition work, of course, works both ways: given correct behavior, others "*recognize* you" as a legitimate actor in a given setting (Gee 17–20). In short, to be recognized as an effective writer, students must learn to recognize good writing and its associated rules of correctness. As I will show in this chapter, these rules are partially encoded in the text appropriation conventions commonly found in research writing handbooks.

Some may object that an analysis of this sort is not relevant to today's writing, reading, and research pedagogies. As Gale and Gale have noted, textbooks (and by extension, handbooks) are notoriously out of touch with current practice, failing to represent "the rapidly changing and richly diverse" discipline of writing (4). So, one might ask, why bother with handbook rule sets in the first place? A related objection might be that even where handbooks are instrumental to writing instruction, they are at best minor components of a much more complex and richly nuanced learning experience. Both of these objections may underestimate, however, the relevance and authority of handbook conventions to beginning student writers, even where the handbook itself remains peripheral to classroom activities. Kleine makes the important point that first-year college students, confused about the rules of conduct for academic writing, may seek out "textbook rhetoric" as a reliable "authoritative text" (137). Moreover, first-time teachers—

adjuncts, graduate students, and other instruments of academia's growing contingent workforce—may look to the handbook as both a convenient guide and a definitive "source of truth" in academic research writing (Kleine 138).

Some may question, as well, my exclusive focus in this chapter on the Houghton Mifflin *Handbook*. Admittedly, the value of this analysis lies almost entirely in the extent to which this particular handbook reflects what is common (perhaps endemic) in other handbooks and other standardized rule sets more generally. To make my case for studying the Houghton Mifflin *Handbook* as a valid sample, I quote at length from section 63 (on compilation) of Charles Baldwin's 1902 *A College Manual of Rhetoric*:

> First, cite always; quote rarely; use phrase without quotation never. This last counsel ought to be superfluous; but from a confusion of too copious notes even educated people will make half-conscious borrowings; and until this habit is broken nothing can be learned. . . . Facts are not copyrighted; but unless a writer is accepted as himself an authority, he is expected to tell where he found them. Form, that is order, grouping, is private property, copyrighted, not to be reproduced without paying royalty, not worth reproducing anyway, since the whole point of writing at all is thereby lost. Phrase is as strictly private as its maker's purse. It may, of course, be quoted, with citation as of fact; but frequent quotation is tiresome and unprofitable. Use without quotation is theft.

In this passage, Baldwin addresses—in condensed formal language—the related conventions of citation, quotation, use of factual evidence, and literary "theft," four concerns also discussed in the Houghton Mifflin *Handbook*. Furthermore, as noted below, Baldwin's advice to honor the "form" of quoted material (its "order, grouping") as "private property," reflects similar advice in the *Handbook* to honor the "sentence structure" of an "original" as belonging to or owned by its author. Thus, I would argue that the *Handbook* is not only a representative sample of today's research writing handbooks but also remains true to the spirit, and at times the letter, of this 1902 text. Indeed, that the basic rules, etiquette, aesthetic, and injunctions associated with using and quoting secondary sources have changed very little over the last hundred years is one of the central concerns of this chapter.

My chapter title—"How to Avoid Plagiarism"—suggests another concern. In almost any writing handbook, the rules for correct quotation, paraphrase, and summary are invariably described as either remedies for excessive copying or preemptive strategies for how to incorporate authoritative language—in the multiple senses addressed in chapter 4—in a manner befitting academic discourse. This dual agenda of academic researching writing—avoiding plagiarism while finding one's voice as an academic writer—is captured nicely in Joseph Harris's (1997) *A Teaching Subject*. Harris proposes that one way to access "the voice or stance" of a student writer is to examine how he or she engages in appropriation activities or, to use Harris's language, how the student "quotes and uses the words of others" (46). Harris identifies the "problem of quotation" as one of

> trying to keep an upper hand over the languages and materials you're working with, of trying *not* to slip into a form of ventriloquism in which you can no longer tell the words of others—readers, writers, teachers, editors, authorities—from your own. (46)

My general aim in this chapter is to consider the "problem" of textual appropriation very much as Harris has described it here. What are the rules, that is, of "trying to keep an upper hand" in writing and how are these rules constructed (defined, explained, exemplified) in the research writing handbook? Also, what conventions come into play in helping students avoid "ventriloquism" in citing the words of others? Finally, how do the rules for avoiding plagiarism intersect with the themes, concerns, and traditions discussed throughout this book?

How to Read Writing Handbooks

The handbook has been around—in name at least—for a long time, but toward the end of the nineteenth century the writing handbook per se emerged as a "popular genre" providing "a brief compendium of rules and precepts" for the beginning student writer (Brereton 315). As a numbered set of "prescriptive rules" (Connors 88), the writing handbook grew in some cases out of preexisting college and university rule sets. For example, University of Oregon dean Leulla Carson adapted her own set of rules for the 1907 *Handbook of English Composition: A Compilation of Standard Rules and Usage*. Woolley's *Handbook of Composition* (discussed further below) appeared that same year and would later influence the 1935 *Harbrace College Handbook*, which has served since its publication as a model for almost all handbooks appearing thereafter (Connors 94–96).

As Hawhee argues, writing handbooks serve two "institutional purposes": first, they determine "important subject matter" in a given discipline; and, second, they "discipline the writer" toward a particular subject position within the institution (504). If handbooks socialize students in this manner, via the prevailing rules and precepts of college composition, then it remains to be seen just what those rules and precepts are and how they have changed over time. To begin answering those questions, I focus now on Woolley's 1907 *Handbook* as an early example of a genre whose rhetoric, while "conservative and reductive" according to Connors (94), nonetheless set the tone for a developing and arguably influential genre in the field of writing instruction. Plagiarism policies and rule sets, wherever they might appear, almost invariably duplicate handbook conventions either explicitly—by echoing or directly quoting (in fact, plagiarizing) handbook rules—or implicitly by framing discussions of plagiarism in the kind of reductive rhetoric Connors attributes to handbooks in general.

Introducing his handbook, Edwin Woolley states up front that the rules contained therein "may perhaps be charged with being dogmatic. They *are* dogmatic—purposefully so" (qtd. in Brereton 359). To demonstrate why this kind of purposive dogmatism is necessary, Woolley narrates a parable about "a youth, astray and confused in a maze of city streets," who needs directions in order to find his way within this potentially confusing urban environment (qtd. in Brereton 359). Here and elsewhere in the long but repetitive story of writing handbooks, analogies such as this, positing rule following as a kind of map reading or geographic navigation, are common. Indeed, handbook authors for at least a century have promoted their books as "guides" to beginning writers, and hence a certain "stringency of some of the rules" should perhaps be expected. In keeping with this theme, Woolley's *Handbook* also compares a novice writer to a beginning piano student "held rigidly, during the early period of his study, to certain rules of finger movement . . ." (qtd. in Brereton 359). Like the piano student, the writing student would do well to observe "rigidly and invariably" the rules pertaining to correct composition (qtd. in Brereton 359). As these narratives suggest, the youth "astray" in the maze of writing conventions is also, by definition, the one who deviates from rigid and invariable observance of the rules. Particular instances of deviation (or deviance) can prove to be either accidental (getting lost) or intentional (choosing the wrong path), a distinction of enormous importance with regard to plagiarism detection.

Handbook discourse of this sort will likely surprise no one. In fact, while the tropes and parables may change, the basic story with its calculated foreboding stays much the same over time, confirming Connors's point that writing handbooks from the start operated within a tradition of conservative and reductive rhetoric "which still continues to this day, with [only] a few notable exceptions" (94). In short, as either teaching supplement, informative framework, or reliable standby, writing handbooks have historically echoed a broader master rhetoric intent on describing and managing issues of right and wrong with regard to student authoring activities. At the point of basic literacy "skill," this rhetoric writes student bodies into a master narrative designed to help "confused" writers stay on the path to authorial conformity.

My aim in this chapter is to test these broader claims—about handbooks and composition instruction in general—against a specific set of research writing conventions. To do so, I draw on Halliday's claim that linguistic structures—phrases, clauses, and sentences—"function 'ideationally' in representing reality" (qtd. in Fairclough and Wodak 275) and that language therefore "works ideologically"

(Fairclough and Wodak 262). In analyzing the rules for correct quotation, paraphrase, and summary, I attempt to explain what the rules are, how they are used, and how other readers might come to understand or misunderstand their application in practice. While I endorse a particular reading of the *Handbook* guidelines under review, I grant that this explanation does not preclude either particular understandings of the text (in a writing classroom, for example) or other critical explanations. It is my hope that in offering one explanation of these guidelines, I will leave room for just such alternative understandings and explanations with regard to these or similar rule sets. I agree with Chouliaraki and Fairclough that there is a "limit to what a text can mean" (67), but I do not claim to have reached that limit in my own analysis.

I should note, finally, that where I discuss linguistic patterns and grammatical turns within the text, I am more concerned with underlying structures and less with the author's—Robert Perrin's—particular authoring choices at any given moment. It is not my intention to belittle Dr. Perrin's investment in and dedication to the work of assembling the *Handbook*. I believe, however, that it is crucial for the sake of this analysis to emphasize the multivalent and distributed nature of the textual creation under review, especially since handbooks by definition serve to encapsulate existing conventions and rules of practice within a discipline. In that spirit, wherever agency proves an issue, I will refer to and cite the author of the handbook as strictly the *Handbook* so as to underscore the complex disciplinary, corporate, and communal forces that lie behind a text of this type.

Discipline and Credit

Whether intentional or not, acts of textual misappropriation (plagiarism) in the academic world are often met with severe penalties of the sort otherwise reserved for copyright violations (Woodmansee and Jaszi 9). For this reason, I focus on those pages in the *Handbook* that deal directly with issues of source incorporation—via summary, paraphrase, and quotation—and, more specifically, the strategies for avoiding plagiarism. I consider these pages relevant to the broader discussion in this book because, in describing and modeling strategies for avoiding plagiarism, the *Handbook* must, in condensed form, account for those underlying principles of textual transformation often glossed in more general discussions of the topic.

In section 10c of the *Handbook* (110–12), the text deals ostensibly with note-taking strategies. Here we encounter definitions that will prove useful to the ensuing analysis. The *Handbook* advises the student researcher to "take notes flexibly" and then reviews the "[f]our common kinds of notes" typically used to assimilate different kinds of information: factual notes, summary, paraphrase, and quotation. The last three—summary, paraphrase, and quotation—are most important to this study, but I will address all four briefly.

Factual notes, according to the *Handbook*, "record technical information . . . to be incorporated in your own sentences." Summaries, however, do not record factual particulars but rather restate "the substance of a passage in condensed form." At the same time, summaries must be original in the sense that they "must be written entirely in your own words," or more precisely, "in your own words, phrases, or short sentences." A paraphrase is a particular kind of summary in that it too restates the "substance" of a passage in modified form. Unlike summaries, however, paraphrases typically "contain approximately the same amount of detail and the same number of words as the original." Quotations, finally, are verbatim reproductions wherein textual material is reproduced "word for word," including spelling and punctuation.

The *Handbook* provides the following guidelines for determining when it is appropriate to quote a source directly:

- *Style*. Is the author's language so distinctive that you cannot say the same thing as well or as clearly in your own words?
- *Vocabulary*. Is the vocabulary technical and therefore difficult to translate into your own words?
- *Reputation*. Is the author so well known or so important that the quotation will lend authority to your paper?
- *Points of contention*. Does the author's material raise doubts or questions or make points with which you disagree?

As reflected here and in the previous paragraph, the literary techniques of summary, paraphrase, and quotation require that the writer make a series of determinations with regard to (1) his or her own text and (2) the text to be used as a possible source. In particular, the researcher is asked to draw distinctions between (1) a statement and a restatement; (2) a statement and its inherent substance; (3) an original statement and one translated into one's own words; and (4) an abbreviated, condensed restatement and one that approximates the "detail" and "words" of the original. To take notes from other sources, in brief, is to perform a complex set of operations requiring careful attention to minute linguistic differences between "my own" and an "author's" textual property.

Similar distinctions inform the *Handbook's* discussion of plagiarism: "To avoid plagiarizing, learn to recognize distinctive content and expression in source materials and make a habit of taking accurate, carefully punctuated and documented notes" (115). Here, the *Handbook* describes plagiarism as a behavior whose avoidance requires a learned ability to "recognize" distinctive form and content in source documents read for purposes of research. In doing this recognition work, one should also "make a habit" of keeping organized and accurate notes that effectively separate one's own content and expression from that determined to belong to others. This dual practice of recognition work and habit formation is hardly menial or incidental. As both Ambrose and Goodwin learned so well (see chapter 1), errors in adjudicating these subtle differences can lead to serious consequences. And to be clear, I am not suggesting that the advice quoted above does any disservice to the beginning student writer. On the contrary, as Susan Miller has wisely suggested, students might "properly wish to master" these rules—and via the kind of concise (if arguably draconian) language offered here—in order to better understand what passes as legitimate textual practice in today's academic settings (112). My aim, then, is not to debunk the conventions—in this or any handbook—and certainly not to argue that recognition work and habit formation are inappropriate to postsecondary education. Rather, my purpose is to identify and understand precisely what it is that we are asking students to recognize when we introduce techniques and conventions of this order.

To return to my example, the *Handbook* proceeds to explain that "avoiding plagiarism" requires close attention to a rather nuanced set of text-based "qualities." These qualities can be summarized as follows: what makes a particular source distinctive is, in the order given, a distinctive "writing style," a "distinctly" original or "individual" research (i.e., material that is "easily distinguishable" from other attributed material), and/or a "personal" or "unique perspective" on the subject as well as a "unique order (sequence) or arrangement" of "ideas or concepts" (115). In sum, what makes an author or a source distinctive and unique is the uniqueness and distinctiveness of the source or author. Moreover, an author's uniqueness and distinctiveness, as reflected in the *Handbook*, can be recognized in the use and/or repetition of particular "patterns" of phrasing, wording, organization, or ideas. Recognition work for the imagined reader, then, resolves to a complex kind of pattern recognition in learning how to identify the unique content and expression of distinctive authors.

The *Handbook* also advises the student writer not to "appropriate" the ideas and expressions of others "without giving them proper credit." As discussed in earlier chapters, credit given in the form of citations satisfies the lease laws of academic discourse insofar as ideas or expressions borrowed are returned, nominally, to the source and author. This give-and-take relationship serves yet another purpose. As most dictionary definitions suggest, the verb *appropriate* can mean not only to take or annex but also to distinguish—or set apart—something or someone for a particular purpose or use. (This is the sense in which federal appropriations committees appropriate funds for particular uses.) The *Handbook* seems to convey this second sense of appropriate as well. When one appropriates source material for research purposes, one takes or sets apart not just (or not exclusively) the original ideas of the originating author but also the distinctive prose patterns of the original. What one borrows, in either case, is the uniqueness and/or originality of the author.

To learn how to do this, of course, is to learn how to recognize those distinctive qualities that make an author worth quoting. In short, to make determinations of this order, one must learn to distinguish distinctiveness. The *Handbook* makes this point explicitly: "To avoid plagiarizing, learn to recognize distinctive content and expression in source materials . . ." (115). To be sure, there is nothing particularly startling or unique about this logic. The 2003 *MLA Handbook for Writers of Research Papers* states that the "essential intellectual tasks of a research project" require that student writers "rigorously distinguish between what they borrow and what they create" (69). To borrow and to create, in this context, are decidedly different activities, and knowing the difference can help one avoid the "pity and scorn" often associated with acts of plagiarism (Gibaldi 66). Likewise, one's ability to distinguish the several qualities inherent to authoritative discourse can help one avoid the error of misappropriating and failing to credit what otherwise merits a mark of distinction.

Research writing in general, as the MLA handbook makes clear, requires that students arbitrate these small and large matters of borrowing and credit, citation and creation, at every turn in the writing process. The goal of this activity is to "synthesize previous research and scholarship with your ideas" on a particular subject (Gibaldi 69). The MLA handbook also assures the student writer that he or she should "feel free" to borrow and use the ideas and expressions of others—and clearly the work of synthesis that lies at the heart of research writing requires this kind of freedom, this range of movement. However, MLA (Gibaldi) is quick to point out that material borrowed "must not be presented as if it were your own creation" (69). Herein lies an important distinction echoed in the pages of the Houghton Mifflin *Handbook*. The work of literary creation, simply put, must be kept distinct from the work of literary borrowing. Nonetheless, the labors unique to each come together, merge, interact in the "synthesis" known as research paper writing. In the next section, I consider the rules attached to this latter process of research synthesis.

QUOTE, PARAPHRASE, AND SUMMARY

In the "Plagiarism" section of the Houghton Mifflin *Handbook*, we find "examples of plagiarized and acceptable summaries and paraphrases" (116). These examples serve as models for how to achieve literary synthesis and to avoid the trap of plagiarism. Drawing on my brief discussion of summary, paraphrase, and quotation above, I will look only at the language the *Handbook* uses to characterize differences between acceptable and unacceptable borrowing practices. For the sake of expediency, I will bypass the examples themselves and concentrate on the explanatory language that follows each.

For clarity's sake, however, I offer this synopsis of the concluding portion of section 10d, "Taking Notes from Sources" (113–17): The *Handbook* advises the imagined reader to consider two paragraphs excerpted from Appleby, Hunt, and Jacob's book *Telling the Truth about History* (Norton, 1994). The reader is then encouraged to review model summaries and paraphrases, half of which are "acceptable" and half of which are "plagiarized." Key words and phrases italicized in both sets of examples serve to highlight moments of faulty appropriation.

After citing three discrete examples of ostensibly "plagiarized" text, the *Handbook* provides the following explanation:

> The italicized phrases are clearly Appleby, Hunt, and Jacob's, even though the verb tenses are changed. To avoid plagiarism, place key words, phrases, or passages in quotation marks or rewrite them entirely in your own words and form of expression. (116)

The practice under review here is summary, and as discussed above summaries do not record particulars but rather "present the substance of a passage in condensed form." Summary, in brief, presents a translation or transubstantiation of textual content, in this case the distinctive content and expression of Appleby, Hunt, and Jacob. Appropriated words and phrases, even where "verb tenses are changed," belong to the authors and therefore must be given "proper credit."

The *Handbook* goes on to suggest two possible revisions: (1) place "key words, phrases, or passages in quotation marks" or (2) "rewrite" these words, phrases, or passages "entirely in your own words and form of expression." Correct summary, in brief, requires either (1) acknowledging distinctiveness with the use of quotation marks (i.e., marking ownership with punctuation credit) or (2) transforming "someone else's" words into "your own." In the latter case, a summary, as the presentation of someone else's substance, can also be, in theory at least, a perfectly distinct presentation of "your own" form. However, making changes of this sort to a text—i.e., transforming it from someone else's into my own—does not necessarily eliminate the risk of plagiarism. Change, we might say, is foolproof only where it is wholly transformational. Or as Stearns puts it, borrowing is only "legitimate" when it "proceeds to transform the original material by means of the borrower's creative process" (6–7). I have made this point earlier, but it is worthy repeating in this context: only complete transformation turns borrowing into creation.

Paraphrase, like summary, restates a passage in one's "own words." But the paraphrase restates differently in that it contains "approximately the same amount of detail and the same number of words as the original." A paraphrase, then, is both the same as and different from the original statement from which it derives: the same in that it matches detail and word count; different in that it only approximates the original statement, and this because it restates the statement in different words. My question at this point is: In restating a statement that approximates the detail and words, or even the idea, of the original, may I thereby claim the restatement as my own—as a creation, in other words, as opposed to mere copying or borrowing? I turn back to the *Handbook* for an answer:

> Changing selected words, while retaining the basic phrasing and sentence structure of the original, is not acceptable paraphrasing. Appleby, Hunt, and Jacob's thought pattern and prose style are still evident in the passage. (117)

Above, with regard to summary, the *Handbook* cautiously suggests that change of a particular kind (writing an abbreviated version of a passage "in your own words") will amount to the kind of formal adjustment necessary to avoid plagiarism. Here, with regard to paraphrase, we learn that transforming "selected words" is not enough if the paraphrased passage still conveys the "phrasing and sentence structure of the original." The explanation offered in the *Handbook* is clearly reminiscent of an earlier discussion about "qualities worth noting" when appropriating material from authorial sources. To avoid plagiarism, one must take note of the author's distinctive style and unique syntactic arrangements. Here the *Handbook* explains in similar fashion that the example is plagiarized precisely because the "prose style" belongs to Appleby, Hunt, and Jacob. More specifically, the passage, while similar enough to reflect the original idea, is nonetheless too similar to the authors' distinctive pattern to qualify as "your own." Taking the *Handbook* as our guide, we can conclude that an author's "thought pattern," as well as his or her "prose style," must be recognized as such in order for the researcher to avoid plagiarism.

I take at face value this notion that "ideas or concepts" can be distinctive to an author and also retained, through subtle transformations of content, in words then claimed as my own. I grant that such transformations are not only possible but, perhaps, demonstrated readily throughout this book. I submit, however, that the primary purpose of paraphrase and summary (and quotation by extension) is not to honor distinctive authoring traces, but rather to convince the reader that my own trace is itself worthy of distinction. The prize—the gold, if you will—at the end of this exercise in ideational transmutation is to stake a claim to uniqueness and distinction whose justification lies less in the word-thought patterns themselves than in the extent to which those patterns are recognized as unique and distinctive.

As discussed in chapter 3, to "own" language—particularly the ideas and expressions inherent to a piece of writing—is likened to owning a tract of land or any piece of material property. But the attribution "your own" stands in for something quite different: namely, that special kind of recognition work required to draw those sorts of distinctions that writers must make in order to avoid plagiarism and achieve a particular status—in the case of the *Handbook*, the status of "author." Put simply, to find my own voice as a writer is to own up to genre knowledge. This rule (tactic, technique) of "your own" is ideological insofar as it marks one of the categories within which people—writing students in particular—"figure out" the rules of a given community.

CONCLUSION:
SYNTHESIS AND ALCHEMICAL TRANSMUTATION

As suggested throughout this analysis, the rules pertaining to quoting, paraphrasing, and summarizing source materials are rules that writing students are not taught so much as expected to pick up—perhaps via changes in "habit" such as those recommended by the *Handbook*. As Nick Carbone has pointed out, however, writing teachers may assume too eagerly that students know "all that we do" and that the conventions we might typically rehearse in class are "self-evident and readily learned by those who are good students . . ." (236). No doubt, the rules of text appropriation might be "readily learned" in the manner in which much else is learned: via rote imitation, study, experimentation, and time spent working on particular tasks, such as those essential tasks common to most research writing assignments. Carbone's point is well taken, though, that the conventions, while eventually learned in most cases, are not necessarily "self-evident," even to the best of our "good students."

In fact, I have endeavored in this chapter to demonstrate that the rules governing text appropriation activities, even as rendered in the concise reference book explored above, tend to mystify rather than clarify the process of textual synthesis at the heart of research writing practices. Obviously, research writing manuals, such as the MLA handbook and the Houghton Mifflin *Handbook for College Research*, can be helpful insofar as they call attention to textual synthesis as fundamental to academic research writing. Still, while it remains true that "writers draw on, respond to, and rework both their own previous writings and those of others" (Harris 68), the rules yield little on how that work of "rework" requires, before all else, a working understanding of prevailing copyright, property, and authorship conventions. In teaching students how conventions work, in other words, we fail to show them how they "work ideologically."

My argument, then, is that research writing guidelines, such as those found in the *Handbook*, endeavor to objectify and standardize what remains, in the end, a local rite of socioliterary passage into a specialized community of practice. Rather than disguise this rite in the camouflage of clear and distinct distinctions, we should first name it boldly and even strive to qualify its relevance to rhetorical practice at large. In fact, rhetoricians are clear on the point that *Imitatio* (modeling, imitation) requires more than just mere copying. Texts transcribed from one context must be, in turn, transmuted and recontextualized—in a word, alchemized—in order to present something new, something decidedly *my own*.

That move from transcription to transformation is also a maneuvering. For students writing research papers, in particular, every act of legitimate transformation, if recognized, may serve to authorize access to, and positioning within, a desired knowledge community. Likewise, when writers try to distinguish between quotation and summary, summary and paraphrase, paraphrase and plagiarism, and so on, they are not learning rules so much as learning how to recognize the rules at work, in their own and others' writing. This particular kind of recognition work is key to understanding how to avoid plagiarism.

6

Plagiarism, Research Writing,
and the Spirit of Inquiry

IN THIS CHAPTER I apply some of the previous chapters' conclusions to late-twentieth-century writing practices. In particular I look at writing approaches that have centered specifically on the *Essais* of Michel de Montaigne as a model for modern—and perhaps postmodern—reading and essay writing. My aim is to show how Montaigne's rhetorical pursuit of the "spirit of inquiry," as well as Hugh's search for Remedy through reading, inform late-twentieth-century secular approaches to research writing as an applied search for knowledge, wisdom, and redemption.

ASSAYING MONTAIGNE IN THE MODERN ESSAY

The academic essay has long been a staple assessment tool in higher education. Viewed by some as a focused exercise in skeptical inquiry, and by others as the paragon of self-expression in writing, the modern essay is typically traced to the *Essais* of Michel de Montaigne (Owens 85). Elizabeth Eisenstein proposes a similar genealogy in describing the essay as a clever solution to a particular public relations problem unique to post-Gutenberg Europe. In the sixteenth century, according to Eisenstein,

> no precedent existed for addressing a large crowd of people who were not gathered together in one place but were scattered in separate dwellings and who, as solitary individuals with divergent interests, were more receptive to intimate interchanges than to broad-gauged rhetorical effects. Perhaps the most ingenious solution devised to meet the new situation was the informal essay which was first successfully used by Montaigne. (230)

Of interest here is Eisenstein's claim that Montaigne's essay form offered an effective apparatus for contending with the problem of individualized reading. In a post-Gutenberg world, there was as yet no "precedent" for addressing the interests of "solitary individuals" operating in isolation from the broader public. Thus, the essay form "devised" by Montaigne provided a convenient answer. Eisenstein also seems to suggest that Renaissance readers' openness to "intimate interchanges" in effect paved the way for Montaigne's informal technique of assaying. Whether historically accurate or not, this concept of the personal, intimate, expressive essay as a viable writing solution to the problems of modern reading has been instrumental to composition theory through the end of the twentieth century.

A telling example is found in Palumbo's 1978 "Montaigne in the Composition Class." Claiming that the personal essay enacts "a kind of thinking and writing" that is "free" from the "established" formats of expository writing, Palumbo traces this free-form character of the essay back to Montaigne, who in composing his essays "lets his mind range over vast areas of thought and experience and reading" (383). Palumbo contends, furthermore, that Montaigne performed this mental exercise in a concerted attempt "to find congruence and continuity in this patchwork" (383). Michael Hall's more recent "Montaigne's Uses of Classical Learning" successfully bridges the concerns of composition with a broader concern for successful reading and cultural assimilation. Montaigne, Hall argues, teaches us how "to digest the wisdom of the ancients and make it our own. What better preparation could we offer today's teachers and students?" (74).

Spellmeyer's 1989 "A Common Ground: The Essay in the Academy" takes a broader approach to essay writing as an exercise in self-portraiture. Essays, for Spellmeyer, place a particular emphasis on "the actual situation" and "the personal nature" of the writer (264). Spellmeyer traces the situatedness of modern essay writing to Montaigne: "From its inception with Montaigne," he writes, "the essay purports to disclose the reflections of an actual person in response to actual events . . ." (264)—a claim that in itself echoes Montaigne's statement about "native form" in the preface to his *Essais*. Also worth nothing is Spellmeyer's faith in the dialogic character of essay writing; the movement from "disjunction to dialogue," he contends, is perhaps best realized in the "transgressive from" of the Montaignian essay (Spellmeyer, "Common" 271). Such descriptions of the personal essay as a more progressive "way of thinking dialogically" (Spellmeyer) or as a kind of unfettered "thinking and writing" (Palumbo) are reminiscent in general of Montaigne's commitment to "knowing" as a form of "knowing now" in the act of assaying. Moreover, Spellmeyer and others adopt Montaigne's rejection of scholastic foraging in order to build their own cases against more staid (established, constrained) modes of scholarly prose. Bruce Ballenger takes this approach in his 1999 *Beyond Note Cards*, a primer on research writing which I will consider extensively here as an example of the Montaignian legacy in contemporary composition theory.

Rejecting the traditional research paper as inherently constrictive, Ballenger recommends an alternative in the guise of the "researched essay."[12] Adapting John Dewey's inquiry-based emphasis in *Democracy and Education*, Ballenger frames the research writing assignment as an important site for helping students develop "a more democratic relationship" with what Bakhtin called "authoritative discourse" (14). In dialogic relationship with secondary sources, according to Ballenger, students come to understand and perhaps enact democratic participation through the act of research writing. However, this relationship with authoritative discourse works best if student researchers "develop a faith in their own agency" and "a sense of ownership over their own words" (14). Zemliansky has characterized Ballenger's democratizing project—and "social-constructivist" theories of composing more broadly—as a means to promote "interaction between the writer and sources" in a way that is customarily missing from the traditional research paper (213). In particular, the kind of compositional exercise endorsed by Ballenger "may help remedy" what many see as a broader student (and often teacher) aversion to research writing (Zemliansky 213).

For Ballenger, the research essay remedies insofar as it gives students broader access to "the genuine spirit of inquiry" (16). The expression comes from Montaigne in "On Educating Children":

> Put into [the pupil's] mind a decent, careful spirit of inquiry about everything: he *[sic]* will go and see anything nearby which is of singular quality: a building, a fountain, a man, the site of an old battle. . . . In this commerce with men I mean him to include—and that principally— those who live only in the memory of books. By means of history he will frequent those great souls of former years. (175).

For Montaigne, the "spirit of inquiry" prompts an experiential tour through the monuments of one's time and the well-peopled landscape of history. The pupil's "commerce" with the living finds its complement in a conversation with the "great souls" of the past who live now in books—but books understood in the scholastic sense of treasury, mine, or storage room, as discussed in chapter 4. Ballenger's sense of "inquiry" is similar, but for the modern student researcher the unleashing of the "spirit" of inquiry is tantamount to "[f]reeing the research paper from its tightly tethered attachment to the nineteenth-century research ideal" (58). Tracing traditional research instruction to "Enlightenment notions of truth, knowledge, and perception" (57), Ballenger goes on to suggest that "these notions are largely discredited by contemporary scholarship" and yet still persist in conventional college research writing curricula (57).

In setting the stage for Montaigne, Ballenger defines the writing self "as an active agent, dialogically involved in listening and responding . . . and in the process transforming and being transformed" (73). This transformative, dialogical process, reminiscent of classical literary and alchemical ideals of transmutation, stands in stark contrast to the older "habits of mind" that gave rise to the traditional research paper. Ballenger's discomfort with this traditional model of research writing compels him to imagine Montaigne in a similar bind:

> I like to imagine that Michel de Montaigne, who first coined the word *essai* to describe his experiments in self-reflective writing, was among the first writers to bristle like our students at the fifteenth century version of the traditional research paper. (76)

"In short," Ballenger continues:

> Montaigne was educated to write the conventional Renaissance research paper—formal in language and structure, well planned, and composed with ancient sources whose authority was well established and whose words reflected accepted truths. (77)

Ballenger's target at this point is not so much the "epistemological assumptions" of Enlightenment or nineteenth-century thought but rather the rote, patterned, foraging practices of sixteenth-century schoolmasters. In other words, Montaigne's "playful irreverence" for received models reflects his discontent "with the truth of received knowledge" (77). In brief, "Montaigne got tired of writing research reports and wanted to write research essays" (77). Here, Ballenger constructs a fictional Montaigne engaged in a calculated turning away from "received knowledge" in favor of the more immediate, skeptical form of knowing available through essay writing.

Moreover, Ballenger's Montaigne uses his lived experience as a "valuable *source* of knowledge" (78). A student writer's lived experience, as well, provides a valuable source accessible as a kind of empirical content. As a legitimate source, personal experience can, in effect, be cited. Or put another way, experience substitutes as a form of authority equivalent to secondary authoritative discourse. The underlying goal of the research essay, in sum, is a focused experience in identity formation via expressive engagement with internal and external sources. Ballenger puts it this way: in trying out the research essay writing experience, students "must try on a new identity as knowers, as writers in charge of sorting through and making sense of other people's knowledge as they try to make it their own" (87–88). Thus, the assignment promises to bring forth an epistemologically sound and democratic identity in unfettered "commerce" with authoritative sources.

I quote Ballenger's argument at such length not to undermine its purported objective (assignment reform) but rather to highlight the broader theoretical issues behind his wish to free research writing from a troubled past. The project is commendable for its overall emphasis on new, more democratic learning activities. However, in rejecting the past, Ballenger must also draw on the past to substantiate his argument for change in research pedagogy. Thus, his invocation of Montaigne's essayist project does more than foreground a new or revised assignment model; it also substantiates a larger effort to "create a new epistemology in his readers" (Zemlianksy 172) grounded nonetheless in neoclassical, or at least neo-Montaignian, rhetorical strategies. This new epistemological framework for source-based writing reproduces an established theoretical emphasis on reading (or research) as a spiritual quest for divine remedy, good judgment, or, in Ballenger's case, good "habits" of material appropriation (9). Research, in Ballenger and elsewhere, is understood generally as "a creative, knowledge-seeking act" (Zemliansky 152), and Ballenger's revisionist project in particular "treats research writing as a process of seeking . . ." (Zemliansky 178). My aim, then, is not to denounce the general equation of source-based writing with the "spirit of inquiry" but rather to historicize these and other educational projects in the context of a broader history of human searching.

In fact, the debate at the heart of *Beyond Note Cards* is not just between Montaigne and his scholastic contemporaries, nor between traditional and transgressive research writing strategies, but rather between competing "habits of mind":

> There is [in research] this wondering and remembering—questioning and reflecting—a looking outward and inward that is exactly what we are trying to teach when we teach the research essay. It is now habit with me. But how do we teach it to our students, most of whom don't share the habit? (Ballenger 98)

Articulated in this passage is a performative aspect of research writing that one masters via practice, keen vision, and, perhaps, assiduous study. While the performance has become "habit" for Ballenger, the challenge remains to teach this habit to students who have not yet mastered the ability to wonder and remember, question and reflect. The research essay—as an exercise in learning good habits of perception—positions teachers as the guardians of that perception and students as growing minds (in Dewey's sense) and identities in need of deepening and development. Ballenger's assignment rubric may certainly free students from the constraints of traditional research paper writing, but they are nonetheless tethered to the work required to both recognize a preferred "genre" and be recognized as able-bodied performers of preferred habits of mind. In sum, the research essay, while perhaps different in form, proves to be not much different in function than the traditional research paper, even in this new, more democratic guise.

In defining his assignment, Ballenger provides an account of the "note tak-ing stage" of student research writing, and his account has significant bearing on my ensuing discussion of plagiarism. In taking notes, students "struggle to take possession of other people's words" (Ballenger 109). This effort to gain "posses-sion" of source material begins in an act of reading. Note taking, via any of a se-ries of methods that Ballenger generously models, moves students "back and forth between what they're reading and what they think about what they're read-ing" (109). This process—a reading/thinking process of textual assimilation— "helps many students see their encounters with sources as occasions for *conversations*, not monologue" (109). Ballenger concludes, therefore, that rather than "'taking' notes," students "can 'essay' them" (112). In other words, as a pre-liminary stage of research writing, students can take notes in a focused attempt to dramatize "conversations" with sources. Or simply, students can self-navigate an experience of literary transmutation by essaying notes before drafting an essay.

The return at the end of *Beyond Note Cards* to the topic of essay writing per se makes sense in this context. For Ballenger, the act of writing an essay, like skating backward on ice, evokes "a fascination with the self in motion" (113). The "self" at the center of this new epistemological formation bears some like-ness to the unified reading self that Terence Cave posits as a tactical response to the rhetorical fragmentation in the *Essais* (see chapter 4). It also resembles, if more obliquely, the monastic self approaching wisdom through "studious striv-ing" (Illich 17). By Illich's reckoning, Hugh's proposed reading technique, like Ballenger's suggested process for research essay writing, "is a commitment to engage in an activity by which the reader's own 'self' will be kindled and brought to sparkle" (Illich 17). Hugh's monks were also engaged in a kind of di-vine recognition work: "In the light of wisdom that brings the page to glow, the self of the reader will catch fire, and in its light the reader will recognize him-self" (21). What Ballenger's reader-qua-writer recognizes, however, is not so much the "sparkle" of newly kindled wisdom but rather the scintillating aspect of a self "in motion" through the progressive stages of knowledge incorporation. Pages read (and written) may not glow in the sense imagined by Illich on be-half of monastic readers, but Ballenger's "fascination" arguably adds a certain luster to the work of assaying the research essay.

GOOD WRITING HABITS AND THE
EXPERIENCE OF INSPIRED SERMONIZING

Ballenger's research writing model depends quite explicitly on the earnest devel-opment of good habits of mind relevant (and perhaps limited) to that particular model. The broader equation of education with the eradication of bad habits and the reinforcement of good ones can be traced to Aristotelian philosophy and, more recently, nineteenth- and early-twentieth-century educational psychology, religious fundamentalism, and the general precepts of social Darwinism. Cremin traces the origin of development theories in education to the "psychonomic law" of Granville Hall, who in turn draws on Spencer's science of evolutionary change and progress (101). Hall's thesis posits individual development as progressing "through a series of stages" that coincide generally with human racial development "from presavagery to civilization" (Cremin 101). To progress or develop normally—as an individual or a "race" of human beings—requires "living through each of the stages" in anticipation of the next (Cremin 102). Hall's psychonomic law, hypothesizing a formal link between individual and racial development, inspired radical changes in "American pedagogical opinion" at the end of the nineteenth century (Cremin 103).

This widespread shift of attention to the nature, needs, and development of the individual student can also be traced to William James's progressivist emphasis on the "powers of conduct" and habit formation (Cremin 107–108). Exercising such powers of conduct, and developing appropriate behavioral habits, students prepare themselves for success in the outside world. Or as James writes: "Habit is thus the enormous fly-wheel of society. . . . It alone is what keeps us all within the bounds of ordinance . . ." (16). This broader connection—between habit formation and the development of good ethical conduct—can be traced further to Hegel's theory of education:

> Education [Pädagogik] is the art of making human beings ethical: it considers them as natural beings and shows them how they can be re-born, and how their original nature can be transformed into a second, spiritual nature so that this spirituality becomes *habitual* to them. In habit, the opposition between the natural and the subjective will disappears, and the resistance of the subject is broken; to this extent, habit is part of ethics. . . .(195)

The "end-product" of education, to recall Montaigne, is the development of what Hegel here defines as "a second, spiritual nature" made habitual through education. For Locke, as well, education served to instill good "Habits" while controlling less reasonable "Desires" and "Inclinations." Ballenger's research essay assignment can thus be read as a technical process designed to elicit an ethical transformation whereby the "opposition" between the natural and the subjective "disappears." Secondary "spirituality" is marked in this case by the learned habit of negotiating secondary sources, or authoritative discourse, located in "outside texts." The art of successful textual transmutation is thus bound to the "art of making human beings ethical."

Plagiarism in this context represents a bad habit, an ethical violation—in short, a failure to transform or, perhaps worse, a fraudulent or abandoned search, through writing, for good habits of ethical inquiry. Likewise, plagiarism scandalizes the pedagogical pursuit of the "spirit" of inquiry realized in the quest for commerce and conversation with authoritative sources. To fail or fake the spirit of good commerce is, simply put, to perpetuate a decidedly uninspired writing. Moreover, to revisit my argument in chapter 4, there is in plagiarism and other breaches of good writerly conduct a particular "strangeness" that underscores, where it manifests, the moral decay of a society threatened by "vicious habits." Learning good writing and research habits will thus uplift those "human hearts" who, through either wrong choice or corrupt faculty, might otherwise succumb to the temptations of sinful appropriation.

Anticipating this line of argument, Harold Love has pointed out that the secular debate over plagiarism in the modern West continues a long-standing religious debate concerning authorial originality and claims to divine inspiration (164). For seventeenth-century Puritan sermonizers, the "centrality of inspiration" encouraged originality in the form of the inspired, improvisational sermon (Love 160). Puritan originality did not issue from the author but rather was "the product of the experience in which the human author took part" (Love 162). The inspired impromptu utterance of the Puritan sermonizer authored the word of God, and the verbal or written sermon was thus regarded as "an inferior substitute" (Love 158). Moreover, to the Puritan minister, "the borrowed or plagiarized sermon was doubly abhorrent" (Love 158).

The transition to "secular notions of originality" in the West begins, according to Love, in an Anglican revision of this Puritan claim to divine inspiration (163). The Anglican sermon, while imminently reusable as a printed text, lacked the improvisational zeal of the Puritan equivalent (Love 163). Orthodox Anglicans, who feared surrendering this "notion of inspiration" entirely, thus redrafted the inspired text as something not external to the mind (as their Puritan rivals would have it) but rather as something "mysteriously generated from the mind's own resources" (Love 164). Later drafters of the Copyright Act of 1710 would rule in favor of this general model of authorship, a legislative choice that later opened the way for a secular understanding of writing as a "literary" creation "inhering in a particular, unrepeatable experience" (164).

Thus, the inspired, knowledge-seeking activity of research writing described in Ballenger and elsewhere—or more broadly a postmodern resurrection of neoclassical ideals of text incorporation—can also be traced to an Anglican emphasis on the pursuit of inimitable experience nonetheless grounded in a kind of textual merging or communal commerce with authoritative sources. In this context, Lindey's description of (prototypically male) originality in his 1952 *Plagiarism and Originality* helps summarize a major point of this chapter:

> Originality is individuality. It is the artist's gift of viewing life through the prism of his sensibility, his own way of reacting to experience, his

own way of expressing his reactions. It is the vital force which inheres in his personality and constitutes his uniqueness. It is, so to speak, his thumbprint, his aesthetic signature, so distinctive as to be instantly recognized. (20)

PLAGIARISM AND THE PATCHWRITING FERMENT

The idea that student plagiarism may figure at times as a kind of misunderstood sharing of textual resources has inspired some composition theorists to recommend more generous and forgiving approaches to student writing behaviors often characterized (and punished) as uninspired stealing. Rebecca Moore Howard, in particular, has championed what she calls "patchwriting" as an intermediary step in processes of literary transmutation ("Plagiarisms" 796). The term *patchwriting* itself recalls Montaigne, who identified "patchwork" as a weaker form of rhetorical invention made better by recourse to a poetics of literary transmutation. Defined by Howard as a "subset of the category of plagiarism" ("New Abolitionism" 89), patchwriting is "copying from a source text and then deleting some words, altering grammatical structures, or plugging in one synonym for another" (qtd. in Price 103). As Price argues, quoting Howard, a student's intentional or unintentional attempts at patchwriting should be regarded not as "intentional cheating" but rather as "'a move toward membership in a discourse community'" (103).

Price's review of Howard's patchwriting process will be taken up in greater detail below. For now, I focus on Howard's own discussion of patchwriting as a writing activity common to today's scholarship ("Abolitionism" 90). As Lunsford clarifies in introducing Howard's work, this process of copying, deleting, and altering source text is "what advanced scholars in the field think of as good scholarly practice of weaving sources together" ("Forward" xii). Scholarly patchwriting, in other words, bears some likeness to scholastic foraging, if perhaps with a greater emphasis on the transmutational value of textual interweaving. Howard's patchwriting motif—as a late-twentieth-century revision of the sixteenth-century ideal of literary incorporation—in some ways resembles the note-taking stage of research addressed toward the end of Ballenger's *Beyond Note Cards*. As Howard puts it in a rather effective revision of Montaigne, Bakhtin, and arguably the seventeenth-century Anglicans:

There is no "my" "own" language; there is only the shared language, in its shared combinations and possibilities. When I believe I am not patchwriting, I am simply doing it so expertly that the seams are no longer visible—or I am doing it so unwittingly that I cannot cite my sources. ("Abolitionism" 91)

The experience of patchwriting is reminiscent of the habit of mind developed through assiduous practice in the art of textual weaving. Likewise, patchwriting can at times figure in the unwitting (or cryptomnesic) "hiding" of borrowed sources.

Furthermore, Howard endorses patchwriting as a means for students to enter a "new discourse community" ("Ethics" 85). Her main complaint, however, is that patchwriting, while evidently commonplace among scholars and other community experts, is often wrongfully confused with the morally "bad" or "transgressive" practices of student plagiarism ("Abolitionism" 91). Thus, in telling students that patchwriting (as a subset of plagiarism) is bad, teachers and policy makers in effect tell them "that learning is bad—which amounts to our telling them that they must always remain on the bottom of the textual hierarchy" ("Abolitionism" 91). In other words, patchwriting functions within an economy of textual ranking: "Learning, we tell them, will move them up the textual ladder. Yet by outlawing the learning that is patchwriting, we are obstructing rather than facilitating that movement" ("Abolitionism" 91). Howard then calls on educators to envision a writing program that treats the patchwriter "not as an ethical transgressor nor even as a bumbler, but as a student laudably striving to learn" ("Abolitionism" 94). In sum, patchwriting, as an honest attempt at textual transmutation, should not be punished but rather encouraged, like Hugh's monastic reading, as a studious striving after wisdom and self-improvement.

Answering Howard's call, Price has made the case for revised institutional policies and standards that reflect what she calls "context-sensitive understandings of plagiarism" (88). Acknowledging many of the troubling aspects of plagiarism treated in this book, Price recommends that institutions and writing departments depend less on standardized plagiarism policies and more on "context-sensitive" rubrics open to modification over time. Price points out that Howard's own plagiarism policy "explains patchwriting as an *interim* step on the way to learning to paraphrase and summarize well and stresses that it 'is never acceptable for final-draft academic writing'" (103). In other words, patchwriting is part of a learning process—akin to Ballenger's note-taking stage—that also includes the more formal procedures of paraphrase and summary accepted in formal academic ("final-draft") products. As Howard puts it, patchwriting "may not be a desirable final stage for one's academic writing, but it is a valuable and hence laudatory transitional stage" ("Ethics" 87). Patchwriting, as a community membership activity whose outcome is scholarly expertise in more formal academic customs, is also tantamount to learning how to avoid plagiarism. Therefore, policy statements, according to Price, can do better to explain plagiarism as a learning activity as opposed to an error or crime (104). Given a clearer set of policies, students and teachers can then be held "responsible for their part in learning these conventions" (104).

Price advances the laudable claim that statements of convention and custom, with regard to plagiarism, can be modified to better suit the particular contexts in which plagiarism is or can be an issue. Nonetheless, both Price and Howard argue that students and teachers should become familiar with a particular custom—patchwriting, in this case—as an "*interim* step" on the way to learning another set of customs, namely how "to paraphrase and summarize well" (Price 103). The final emphasis on the need to learn "well," in brief, bypasses the larger question of how this "learning" works in the first place. Therefore, the proposal does not resolve the problem of faulty or fraudulent text incorporation, since students (and teachers) are still held "responsible" for learning to summarize and paraphrase "well" in final-draft writing. In the end, Price's well-intentioned call for revised standards and policy appears to issue from an overriding acceptance of what Lunsford has termed "the silent supports of traditional authority" ("Refiguring" 76) as well as a tacit approval of a given set of conventions and customs as unimpeachable mainstays of institutional experience.

Price also calls for greater student involvement in institutional policy decisions with regard to plagiarism. Student participation in revising and interpreting policy statements, she argues, would highlight their positions as "individuals not just subject to obeying rules but also responsible for interpreting, upholding, and, perhaps, even helping develop them" (107). In encouraging this kind of student participation, however, Price appears to be trading in one form of obedience for another. In her effort to make students responsible for understanding, maintaining, and "helping develop" plagiarism policy, the local (even context-sensitive) regime of power nonetheless holds sway over all acts of even responsible adjudication. To be a member of an academic community, in Price's account, is to participate—by invitation—in the "ritual recoding," in Foucault's terms, of plagiarism policy (*Discipline* 111). To be clear, I am not arguing in principle against involving students, or teachers for that matter, in administrative decision-making processes. Still, I question the underlying rationale for endorsing this kind of "administrative function" (Readings 152) on behalf of teachers and students. To involve students in the rituals of recoding plagiarism does nothing to change prevailing relationships, unless the goal of this exercise is to institutionalize ever more efficient forms of administrative discipline in the guise of democratic participation.

Price returns to Howard to close out her argument. Echoing her earlier statement that Howard's patchwriting leads the way to scholarly summary and paraphrase, Price states further that patchwriting "emphasizes the process by which information that one reads becomes assimilated into one's knowledge base and way of thinking" (108–109). Here, Price posits knowledge incorporation as the *sine qua non* of patchwriting. Nonetheless, as mentioned above, patchwriting is not necessarily a fully transmuted result, but rather an interim step in a process (like the "note-taking stage" as understood by Ballenger) on the way to textual assimilation. To be fair, understanding exactly *when*, not to mention *how*, knowledge becomes fully "assimilated into one's knowledge base" remains the most difficult challenge facing a pragmatic approach to plagiarism and research writing more broadly. In pursuit of a better understanding, I focus on the steps of textual incorporation as modeled below.

The "next step beyond patchwriting," according to Howard, is "effective summary," which Howard models by way of the following exercise:

> Read the source quickly to get its general ideas, perhaps reading only the first sentence of each paragraph. Then reread, more slowly. Go through it a third time and take notes. Then let some time elapse—a half hour should be enough—and *with the book closed, write your own summary of it* . . . . Once you have drafted your summary, go back to the book and check to see if any of your phrasing resembles that of the source; if so, quote it exactly. Provide page citations for both your paraphrases and for quotations. Also check your version to see what you forgot: what you forgot is usually what you didn't understand. (qtd. in Price 108–109)

In citing this somewhat daring formula for textual transmutation, I note first of all that knowledge assimilation, which Price aligns with patchwriting, is here positioned as relevant to a later moment of "effective summary." It is unclear if these temporal markers (and the general logic of "steps") are to be read literally, but in the interest of better understanding the writing process under review, I read them literally and imagine that a student who has once assimilated information during patchwriting then goes into (or back into) the source in order to write an effective summary. The hypothetical reader-writer then performs a set of iterative reading and note-taking activities, after which the book is closed and "time" (maybe thirty minutes) passes. Turning away from the book, the student then writes a summary, and after writing it, goes "back to the book" to check for resemblances between the summary and the information source read before.

On the surface, Howard's instructions appear to contradict the claim, advanced by Kaplan and others, that critical reading activities, unlike writing activities, "leave no visible trace behind them" (215). Indeed, as a literal (written) embodiment of a student's close reading activity, the summary as described here functions as just that "trace," although it remains unclear how that trace (as writing, as text) might help us gauge or measure the particular "events" or "episodes" of reading in and of themselves (Kaplan 215). This distinction, however—that reading leaves no trace while writing does—assumes that reading and writing are always distinct activities and analyzable or measurable as such. Howard's summary writing exercise implicitly challenges that assumption and suggests the corollary hypothesis that reading and writing events can happen contemporaneously—can in fact be the same event—particularly where the time of reading and rereading a source overlaps with the time of noting ideas and writing them down. Arguably, then, reading and rereading a source text can in fact leave a highly visible trace, and that trace, in this case, is the written summary.

My two questions at this point therefore target this implied move in Howard's formula from, so to speak, invisible reading to visible writing. First, what relationship exists (if any) between knowledge assimilated during an act of patchwriting and a later restatement in the form of a summary? Second, after time has elapsed between and after readings and note-taking episodes, how might one distinguish between assimilated material and source material still tied to its origin? In other words, in checking to see if any "phrasing resembles that of the source," is the writer to assume that resemblances spotted during this check belong, ipso facto, to the source, or can the writer otherwise assume that resemblances are, in fact, traces of assimilated information now stored in "one's knowledge base" in the aftermath of reading?

In posing these questions, I do not mean to make light of Howard's very practical exercise. My goal rather is to highlight, within this model process, the potential contradictions that emerge when trying to map—in the language of modern pedagogical method—the activity of text incorporation. In Howard and Price as in Ballenger, the push for a particular read-write procedure (patchwriting, summary, or note taking) as the preferred means to a particular end (successful literary transmutation) relies finally on the formation of preferred habits of mind to function as both the tools of successful transmutation and the index of that success. That Howard's patchwriting or summary procedures might work for a particular writer is not the point. The question remains as to how, when, and where the work comes to pass, so to speak, as a recognizable, and thus recognized, good habit of mind. In other words, at what point—and via what process—does a "summary" become an "effective summary"?

As I see it, Howard's effort to describe a process for writing effective summary conceals the time of writing summary (incorporating knowledge) in the movement toward writing effectively. Once again, the signs of effectiveness, as in Ballenger, reside not in the process described but rather in the outcomes of effective writing—in this case exact quotes, page citations, and correctly identified paraphrases. Thus, the time of reading toward a writing outcome is subsumed in the space of a written summary, in the product of a successfully navigated process. It remains to be seen whether or not the time of literary transmutation as described here can in fact be measured or gauged as a prescribed—and delineable—subroutine in the teaching and learning of writing. I suspect that time is better spent attending to the kinds of recognition work that prevail in writing activities, particularly where students and teachers convene over writing and reading habits often glossed in the search for more effective processes. In this case, to make the time of assimilation glow and sparkle (to adapt Illich) is to assume that summary already exists (your own, to be precise) and that you recognize your summary, and thus yourself, in the pursuit of effective writing. In short, the summary writing process—a process of textual transmutation—assumes a given, and preexisting, outcome otherwise hidden in the final display of mastery.

What intrigues me, finally, in Howard's summary-writing description is not so much the elaboration of checks and resemblances, but rather the heuristic value of time, which in this case bears a noticeable likeness to the yeast-like "ferment" of Petrus Bonus's alchemical formulations (see chapter 4). In the "some time" elapsing between "read" and "summary," the source has mysteriously transmuted into "your own summary of it." The passage of time implicitly guarantees that a source read by a student eventually prevails in the form of "your own." Indeed, there abides in this articulation of how to write "effective summary" the assumption that a pure summary emerges—*ad interim*—in the wake of time elapsed. A second look at the instructions confirms that understanding: there is "your summary," first drafted after a few passes through the text, and then there is "effective summary" which comes to pass after checking phrasing, quoting accurately, and providing citations. There are no pointers offered, however, for how to navigate that time of transmutation, how to read and move and think in space for a half hour, more or less, before closing the book and sitting down to draft your own summary. Instructions lapse with regard to the time variable, I would imagine, because there really is no knowing what happens on the way from reading to writing—except perhaps to say that summary is either the Stone itself, or that which perfects and completes the Stone.

CONCLUSION: PRELIMINARY RECOMMENDATIONS FOR RESEARCH WRITING INSTRUCTION

The reproach against student plagiarism as failed or fraudulent transmutation goes hand in hand with an approach to academic writing as rightful transformation of text and self toward membership status in an academic writing community. This approach—where it manifests, for example, in the teaching of academic research writing—does not always speak directly to the social consequences of membership and exclusion as they intersect with more practical concerns, such as how to transmute authoritative discourse, how to avoid plagiarism, and how to navigate a written summary, effective or otherwise. Nonetheless, where research writing is taught, opportunities exist to recast learning relationships as "sites of *obligation*, as loci of *ethical practices*" (Readings

154), whose outcomes are not better "training" but, perhaps, a better under-standing of the ethical, political, and cultural issues surrounding the reading and taking of source materials and the practical outcomes of doing so.

In particular, to treat plagiarism as a social "act of reading" is to pay closer attention to the several pragmatic scenes of research writing. By teaching and defending note taking and assaying, patchwriting, methodical incorporation (as summary), and other context-specific solutions to the problem of plagiarism, compositionists go far to demystify plagiarism and to open up research writing to a set of inventive reading processes. However, as I will argue further in my concluding chapter, a revised pedagogy for research writing would benefit from a broader poetics of reading framed by revisionist accounts of *remedial* reading practices, many of which find purchase in today's composition techniques, such as the digital *remediation* of textual content in the pursuit of effective writing.

7

Internet Plagiarism
and Plagiarism Detection

IN THIS CHAPTER I focus on one recent development in the history of plagiarism, namely, the purported increase in academic plagiarism at the end of the twentieth century and the recent deployment of plagiarism detection software as one solution to the problem. I should note initially that Internet plagiarism, as a culturally significant category as well as a juridical and pedagogical concern for today's colleges and universities, does not always resemble its pre-Internet, or print age, equivalent. Thus, I begin by dismissing the assumption that plagiarism online reproduces in digital form its offline, paper-based, cousin. At the same time, I choose not to assume unconditionally—as many in higher education do—that an increase in plagiarism at the turn of the twenty-first century is due in large measure to the widespread use of the Internet and computers as digital editing machines.

For now, I adopt Kewes's claim that a thorough understanding of plagiarism requires some exploration of the physical media through which plagiarized content tends to flow (4). The physical medium known as the networked personal computer—arguably the most important communication innovation of the late twentieth century—inspires a new set of questions with regard to plagiarism, its reception, and its real and imagined remedies. In this chapter, therefore, I look at the computer and the Internet as two recent innovations which, viewed separately and together, complicate the plagiarism problem in particular ways for twenty-first-century educators.

As Ivan Illich argued in 1993, the radically new tools of scholastic reading introduced in the late thirteenth century would remain "fundamentally unchanged" until the appearance of the "text composer program of the 1980s" (*Vineyard* 96). In the eighties, according to Illich, a new set of tools and conventions inherent to the digital writing machine would once again alter the modes and modalities of literary production. Indeed, Seymour Papert, writing

121

in 1980, had already begun to anticipate new methods for teaching literacy grounded in "the use of a computer as a writing instrument" (419). Six years earlier, in 1974, hypertext guru Ted Nelson heralded the dawn of a new communication age in which "computer technology" would facilitate "the revision and improvement—the transformation—of all our [preexisting] media" (318). Taking his lead from Nelson,[13] Lev Manovich has argued more recently for a "new" or "post-media" orientation with regard to today's computer technologies ("New Media" 23). For Manovich, the late-twentieth-century text composer or writing instrument envisioned by Illich and Papert respectively has evolved into a more robust postmillennial "media processor" (*Language* 25) capable of "accessing and using in new ways previously accumulated media" ("New Media" 23). The new digital composing machine introduces a form of "post" or "meta" mediation precisely because "it uses old media as its primary material" ("New Media" 23). Years of analog production, Manovich insists, have yielded a "huge media archive" whose contents now serve as the "raw data" for post-media communication practices ("New Media" 22).

If one accepts the spirited pronouncements of Illich, Nelson, Manovich, and others, then indeed the end of the twentieth century marked a watershed moment in the history of literary, and more broadly artistic, production. For Manovich, this moment was tantamount to a revolutionary avant-garde betrayal of old media forms and practices in favor of "new media" objects produced at the intersection of human labor and computer processing (*Language* 36). As Manovich puts it, today's experimental artists, abandoning a modernist preoccupation with innovation and originality, are "no longer concerned with seeing or representing the world in new ways" ("New Media" 22). Rather, today's post-media artists engage in the rearticulation and repackaging of "raw" media content garnered from a rich stockpile of already packaged television, film, audio, and text objects. Below I will consider this argument further in relation to Web-based plagiarism detection software, which, while hardly representative of the kind of artistic production Manovich has in mind, nonetheless suggests what I see as a curiously similar variety of "raw data" processing and content rearticulation, albeit in the guise of plagiarism surveillance if not literary experimentation.

For now, I focus more specifically on the following questions, all of which will guide my discussion in these last two chapters: First, what does plagiarism look like in the age of computers and the Internet, and how does Internet plagiarism compare to its pre-Internet versions, as described partially in the preceding chapters? Furthermore, in what ways have current debates over plagiarism and antiplagiarism solutions changed (or not) in the wake of recent innovations in text composing technologies? In a similar vein, what is the overall mood in higher education with regard to plagiarism and academic dishonesty more broadly, and how have institutions endeavored to deal with the problem of plagiarism, particularly as it migrates to online and other computer-based environments? Finally, how do today's plagiarism detection services work, where did they come from, and, as particular solutions (among others) to the ongoing plagiarism problem, how do they reflect the many legal, pedagogical, and aesthetic concerns addressed so far? I begin by considering Internet plagiarism as a recent development in the story of plagiarism in higher education.

COMPUTERS, THE INTERNET, AND THE PLAGIARISM "EPIDEMIC"

If recent trends are any indication, then the fundamental transformation in media practice theorized by Illich, Nelson, and Manovich has some grounding in fact. As Hawisher et al. report, personal computer use in the last decades of the twentieth century (from 1978 to 2003) rose sharply in the United States as computers entered the home and the classroom and, perhaps more important, as post-media writing machines were adopted by many students "as the composing tool of choice" (645). Currently, the school, the workplace, local communities, and homes serve as "the major gateways through which people in the United States have gained access to computer technology over the last twenty-five years" (Hawisher et al. 670). Access to PCs has led as well to a recent surge in personal Internet use in the United States and abroad. According to Hawisher et al., by 2003 well over six hundred million people worldwide had regular access to the Internet and had "moved their communication activities online . . ." (659).

The recent spike in computer and Internet use has led some to theorize the emergence of a "new breed of appropriator" who surfs the Internet in search of "stretches of text" to download and incorporate into documents otherwise resident on the appropriator's own computer (Kewes 8). Opinions are mixed with regard to how well, and how extensively, this "new breed" has infiltrated the halls of higher education. Some lament the "disturbing and fast-growing problem" of Internet plagiarism—and cheating more broadly—among today's student populations (Desruisseaux). For Harold Noah and Max Eckstein,[14] cheating, plagiarism, and other varieties of student "misrepresentation" have reached "epidemic proportions" in the age of the Internet, leading Noah to claim that cheating "is now ubiquitous in the United States and overseas" (Desruisseaux). Such views are consistent with earlier historical eras in which the introduction of a new text-production tool has produced a certain "resistance" or even "hostility" in all sectors of society (Kaplan 211). When the ballpoint pen and the typewriter first came into use, for example, some educators feared that each, in its own way, "would undermine the quality of students' writing or might promote plagiarism" (Kaplan 211).

My own research[15] suggests that some students do plagiarize (and cheat more generally) as they always have but also that student, teacher, and administrator perceptions regarding student cheating activities vary widely. In particular, a 1997 *Psychological Record* study found that 36 percent of undergraduates surveyed had plagiarized at one point or another in their college careers. In addition, a study compiled in the late nineties at the Rochester Institute of Technology (R.I.T.) reported that 25 percent of undergraduates surveyed admitted to cutting-and-pasting from the Internet without using proper citation. However, in the same study a much heftier 75 percent claimed that their peers plagiarized regularly. Similarly, a 2002 R.I.T. study concluded that "students think much more plagiarizing is taking place than they actually report doing" (Kellogg). While only 8 percent reported having "often" or "very frequently" cut and pasted text into a paper without citation, more than one-half reported that their peers had done so "often" or "very frequently" (Kellogg). In addition, a whopping 90 percent reported that their peers "often" or "very frequently" copy text without citation from "conventional sources" as well (Kellogg).

Such findings may reflect what researchers call the "third-person effect," or the tendency for people "to overestimate when asked about others' undesirable behavior" (Lamb). However, while it may be tempting to hypothesize that students plagiarize significantly less than they think they do, Scanlon cautions that the "accumulated data is possibly fallible because students, despite anonymity, are often reluctant to admit that they have plagiarized" (Lamb). These and other caveats notwithstanding, it is reasonable to conclude, based on the majority of these studies, that some students plagiarize from time to time, and some probably do it "often" and perhaps "frequently." More important, students by and large seem to believe that regular plagiarism among their peers is a significant issue in today's institutions of higher learning.

Regardless of the real or imagined frequency of plagiarism, the question remains as to why students who do plagiarize do it in the first place. Research suggests that students plagiarize for several reasons, including desperation before looming deadlines, anxiety about meeting professor demands, pressing family expectations, and intense competition among peers hoping to gain advantage in a professional world where college degrees hold an ever shrinking cachet. Furthermore, some students are more willing to assume the risks associated with plagiarism, believing generally that the deed will likely go unnoticed on today's larger, more anonymous, college and university campuses. Many teachers believe that students plagiarize because they are ignorant of, or confused about, the rules and conventions of source incorporation and academic conduct more broadly. Moreover, as one might expect, those bemoaning the new plagiarism epidemic in higher education often target the Internet as the most salient, if not the sole, cause of student misconduct. For example, Julia Miller, chair in 1998 of Binghamton University's Academic Honesty Committee, attributed "much of the increase in plagiarism to the newest information resource available to students: the Internet" (Catts). Similarly, in 2002, University of Iowa associate provost for undergraduate education, Lola Lopes, reported that "observations among professors suggest that the availability and popularity of the Internet has *[sic]* made plagiarism easier and more prevalent" (Mueller).

Some cite the recent proliferation of Internet paper mills as the chief cause for today's scourge of student plagiarism. Before proceeding I should acknowledge, as Orgel does, that "long before the Internet there were outfits supplying papers on demand and students buying them" (57). In fact, for many years at Harvard the *Encyclopedia Britannica*'s research service "was an egregious supplier" (Orgell 57), and subsequent paper mills would simply duplicate and refine in-house services of this kind. Buerger, as well, describes the long history of "commercial traffic in academic assignments," arguing in fact that today's educators face the same issues that an earlier pre-Internet generation faced in contending with mail-order term paper services (253). According to Buerger, term paper mills "were a national phenomenon" by the 1960s (268), and today's traffickers have simply moved their wares online "in response to a potentially unlimited market and a climate of fundamentally unfettered trade" (312). Buerger goes on to describe the "changing battlefield" in higher education, where institutions threatened by this new Internet-based "commercial trade" in papers have no choice but to adopt "new weapons" appropriate to a new threat (312). Buerger is clear on this point:

> [Internet paper mills] remain the most obnoxious to educators. This is in part because of the blatant disregard, which borders on contempt, that these sites show for established academic mores, and partly because of the distaste that educators feel for businesses which appeal to students' base instincts or prey on the desperate. (322)

Some educators choose not to blame online paper mills, or the Internet more broadly, for the perceived lapse in student morality at the turn of the twenty-first century. For example, Sally Cole, executive director in 1998 of the Duke-based Center for Academic Integrity, claimed that "the level of plagiarism has not increased dramatically with the availability of information on the Internet" (Eschbacher). More recently, the 2002 R.I.T. study cited above reported that the Internet has not had a noticeable effect on plagiarism activities. In fact, the researchers went so far as to suggest that the purported increase in plagiarism in recent years is more likely due to a changed academic climate in which professors are typically more inclined to report it. It could be argued, as well, that today's professors may exaggerate claims due to an already entrenched assumption that students plagiarize "often" and perhaps "frequently," particularly in the age of "vast" information access. Kacie Wallace, associate dean of students for judicial affairs at Duke University (home of the Center of Academic Integrity), puts it this way:

> It's very hard to say that more students are cheating. . . . There's a greater awareness among students and faculty, and obviously more cases are being referred. [The increase] could be a factor of people knowing where to refer it, [plagiarism] happening more often, [or that] more people are aware. . . . (qtd. in Hauptman)

Wallace concludes that it may be unwise to attribute the perceived increase to an actual boost in plagiarism activities, since other factors—including "greater awareness"—may contribute to that perception (Hauptman). Cornell student Matt Lowenstein (class of 2006) punctuates the point nicely: "I don't think professors and administrators would make a big deal [of plagiarism] if it wasn't a problem" (qtd. in Williamson).

Whether the cause of Matt Lowenstein's "big deal" is the Internet itself, overzealous plagiary-hunters, or one of the many other causes addressed above (or a combination of all), the common perception is that a digital "battle" is indeed underway in which savvy undergraduates, pitting themselves against increasingly savvy professors and administrators, try to strike with plagiarized material before defensively weak opponents can know, so to speak, what hit them. As Buerger suggests, many on the receiving end of this attack have taken up the cause of eradicating the scourge outright. Buerger argues in favor of establishing an academic culture "in which ethical behaviour is the norm" and in which students are kept "out of ethical harm's way" (115). Today's schools, colleges, and universities, he insists, should find ways to "shelter students from the temptation to be unethical" (115–16). McCabe and Drinan have taken a similar tack in response to the "seemingly relentless increase in the level of cheating among college students." Citing the prevalence of "serious academic dishonesty on written assignments" in the mid-nineties, McCabe and Drinan also point out that "students now define plagiarism much more leniently than students did 30 years ago," a phenomenon perhaps "masking" an increase not otherwise reflected in the data. Thus, faced with an increasingly dishonest academic "climate" in higher education, McCabe and Drinan, through Duke's Center for Academic Integrity,[16] have endeavored to help institutions develop effective "strategies" for dealing with plagiarism and other ostensibly dishonest student activities.

Both with and without help from the center, a number of institutions have adopted a range of strategies to deal with the problem of student cheating. With regard to plagiarism in particular, some have turned to assignment reform[17] as a first step in stemming the tide of student misconduct, tailoring assignments "to eliminate possibilities of students passing copied work off as their own" (Giovannetti). Other strategies include: (1) tougher rule enforcement and the introduction or entrenchment of institutional honor codes; (2) "awareness" campaigns on campus and through university forums; (3) better promotion of academic honesty among the student body; and (4) a general commitment to educating students and faculty on issues related to intellectual property and plagiarism. In addition, some schools have resorted to logistical solutions, such as saving student papers over the years in order to compare submitted assignments against a cumulative archive.

Moreover, many in higher education have sought Internet-based solutions to the problem of Internet plagiarism. Thus, a "new breed of appropriator" spawned in the age of networked computers has met its proverbial match in a new clan of "twenty-first century plagiary-hunters" who, as Kewes points out, are often "instructors wishing to check the self-sufficiency of their students' essays" (8). Academic plagiary-hunters search the Internet—using currently popular search engines such as Google—for potential similarities between submitted papers and other documents stored on the Web. Indeed, some have cited Google as the "best and most comprehensive Internet tool available to professors in battling plagiarism" (Nowakowski). Adapting this Internet search procedure to entrepreneurial ends, antiplagiarism solutions such as EVE(2) and Turnitin.com promise, in effect, to streamline and expand the plagiary-hunter's online search for plagiarized content. In the next section, I consider these and other plagiarism detection solutions which, at the turn of the twenty-first century, offer a particular kind of "shelter" from the temptation of Internet plagiarism.

PLAGIARISM DETECTION SOFTWARE

The first few decades of the twentieth century saw a marked increase in copyright litigation due in part to stricter copyright laws and wider public access to print, radio, film, and, later, television content (see chapter 3). Alexander Lindey defined the then-popular recourse to copyright litigation as a "brisk, lucrative hold-up game" favoring enthusiastic plagiary-hunters hoping to earn large settlements from growing media companies. In the last decade of the twentieth century, as I hope to demonstrate below, an equally "lucrative" plagiarism game materialized in the form of plagiarism detection software. While not strictly aligned with copyright litigation (in general, the services check for copied passages if not copyright violations per se), turn-of-the-century post-media detection services nonetheless promised to help treat or remedy the perceived "epidemic" of student plagiarism. Fueled by what some have called a new "gotcha" ethos among today's educators, a new industry has emerged in the always volatile world of plagiarism detection (Howard, "Forget About Policing"). This development has inspired Howard to remark that today's colleges and universities are currently in a "state of siege," using technology to defend academia against the "attack" brought on by a moral climate "in precipitous decline" ("Forget About Policing").

The new software-based plagiary-hunters make use, albeit on a much larger scale, of the very same technologies and techniques used by plagiarizers to appropriate online material. This phenomenon led Biz Bledsoe, writing for the *Arizona Daily Wildcat* in late 2002, to remark that the "most ironic, or for plagiarists, horrifying, aspect of the new technology is that the Internet owns both sides of the plagiarism market." Indeed, evidence suggests that ambitious term paper dealers and reactionary plagiarism detectors have taken up different "sides" in the plagiarism battle. In an effort to better understand this new lucrative market in plagiary-hunting, and in order to address the several questions raised at the beginning of this chapter, I will analyze four plagiarism detection services currently on the market: Glatt Plagiarism Services, EVE2 (Essay Verification Engine, version two), Plagiarism-Finder, and Turnitin.com.[18]

Glatt

Glatt Plagiarism Services, the oldest of the four services considered here, offers three software solutions "to help deter and detect plagiarism": Plagiarism Teaching Program (GPTeach); Plagiarism Screening Program (GPSP); and Plagiarism Self-Detection Program (GPSD). The screening program, provided for use "in academic institutions or . . . for cases of copyright infringement," is intended to help educators amass "substantial evidence" to support plagiarism charges. Claiming to be the "first comprehensive computer software program specifically designed for detecting plagiarism," the Glatt service deploys a version of the "cloze" reading procedure pioneered by journalist Wilson Taylor in 1953.[19] In brief, the cloze method, designed to determine language redundancy in written texts, eliminates the nth word (for Glatt, the fifth word) in a given passage and replaces every deleted word with a blank space. To check for plagiarism, the teacher gives the student a cloze-modified version of the submitted paper and then asks the student to "supply the missing words." Where a student fails to remember a certain number of missing words, the case can be made that he or she has not authored the text (or portions thereof). To help with this determination, the Glatt software tabulates a "Plagiarism Probability Score" using "a proprietary database, statistical variables, and probability theory." Equipped with the score, the wary teacher can, based on these and other factors ("number of correct responses," "amount of time intervening"), establish with an ostensibly high degree of accuracy whether or not the student plagiarized.

Glatt claims near-perfect results for its service. According to the Web site, the tests have proven "very accurate; NO STUDENT HAS BEEN FALSELY

ACCUSED" (caps in original). Moreover, the service promises "a valid and sensitive measure for successfully discriminating plagiarists from non-plagiarists." Glatt makes the claim, as well, that the evidence provided is "objective" with regard to "plagiarism guilt or innocence." Thus, as a scientifically and mathematically sensitive detection solution—i.e., with objective verification grounded in statistics and probability theory—the Glatt Screening Program proves "especially useful in situations where the original source material cannot be located." In other words, unlike other software-based search programs (discussed below), Glatt does not comb the Internet and term paper databases for evidence substantiating charges of plagiarism. Instead, the service "afford[s] teachers that kind of [valid, objective] evidence by exploiting the uniqueness of each individual's linguistic patterns."

The alleged "uniqueness" of an individual's writing, reminiscent of Romantic theories of authorship, underwrites the statistical accuracy (perhaps infallibility) of the Glatt Plagiarism Probability Score. A student writer who successfully fills in the gaps, from memory, in his or her own writing thereby verifies the uniqueness or authenticity of the submitted document. Thus, Glatt test results prove "very accurate" in establishing not only authorial origin but also "non-plagiarist" status for any who successfully remember what they have written. Indeed, Glatt is quite clear about the kind of memory and identity work a student must do in order to deflect charges of plagiarism. Echoing Lindey's claim that an author's "originality" is like a "thumbprint," Glatt claims that the "procedure assumes that each person has an individual style of writing, i.e., writing styles are as unique as fingerprints." In a rather startling inversion of Montaigne's defense of cryptomnesia or rhetorical forgetting (see chapter 4), Glatt assures the prospective buyer that "we know and can remember our own writing style far more accurately than anyone else." In other words, by remembering or recognizing one's own "fingerprints," a student can effectively bypass charges of plagiarism.

The art of forgetting helped protect the Renaissance author from charges of reckless borrowing. Under the rubric of Glatt's cloze procedure, the student is "asked" to remember what he or she has written in order to avoid a similar charge. This memory test is a kind of drug test reproducing classical memory training but in the service of determining student status as either plagiarist or nonplagiarist. Barbara Glatt, president of Glatt Plagiarism Services Inc., offers the following assessment: "Ultimately, what I'm doing is determining originality of authorship. . . . It's sort of like random drug testing." Thus, Buerger's call for new forms of "shelter" to protect students from the temptation of plagiarism is here answered in Barbara Glatt's pledge to help teachers find out whether or not a student has, in fact, given in to that temptation.

The Glatt service, as a turn-of-the-century solution to the problem of linguistic misuse (of words if not drugs), seeks a remedy for plagiarism in the student's search through his or her own memory for the *n*th missing word. This word, when found, will help complete the formula for stylistic uniqueness that the software otherwise hopes to exploit. This practice in remedial-mnemonic uniqueness testing, the architects of Glatt promise, will "help deter" and "decrease" plagiarism on college campuses. This promise of "decrease," I would argue, harkens back to an early alchemical, and later humanist, interest in the removal of taint, or bad habits, in the search for God or the well-educated child respectively. In brief, the stated goal of "decrease" adds an element of progressive optimism to an activity otherwise trading on the unfortunate (and regressive) "epidemic" of student plagiarism. To remedy the plagiarism problem is to heal an educational system made sick by illegitimate textual practices. Educational and social progress thus requires an activist approach to the eradication of plagiarism; to participate in that action is to serve the broader social pursuit of pedagogical (and moral) perfection.

Moreover, the opportunity to "deter" and "decrease" plagiarism reminds the prospective plagiary-hunter that the goal of plagiarism detection is ultimately not criminalization but the elevation of student writers to a higher level of stylistic originality. With Glatt, for example, an epistemological commitment to "uniqueness" underlies the screening process, and the hunt for plagiarism focuses a much broader attempt to defend preferred authoring conventions against those who, intentionally or not, act in defiance of those conventions. Therefore, academic institutions will most likely continue to benefit from plagiarism detection remedies, even if Glatt and other services eventually have the desired effect of decreasing or eliminating plagiarism outright. Even in that unlikely event, the borders of authorship will still need protection from the perennial threat of "precipitous" moral decline. Detection, in other words, is also a form of inoculation.

EVE

As noted, Glatt offers a screening apparatus designed to assist teachers in those situations where "original source material" cannot be used for comparison. Conversely, EVE (Essay Verification Engine) checks student documents against available sources for purposes of identifying overly similar (plagiarized) textual patterns. Whereas Glatt empties the *n*th word in linguistic strings in order to check for stylistic "fingerprints," EVE measures linguistic patterns contained in whole submitted papers against others found on the Internet. In this case, not student recognition work but pattern recognition software—coupled with the vast memory storage capabilities of today's networked computers—helps the teacher accumulate the evidence required to advance a plagiarism charge.

As stated on the EVE2 Web site, this "powerful tool" can be used "at all levels of the education system to determine if students have plagiarized material from the World Wide Web." Performing "a large number of complex searches," EVE, like Glatt, finds "evidence of plagiarism" but does so by performing a "direct comparison" of a submitted essay to text found on any number of "suspect" sites. Available for download, EVE2 runs as a stand-alone application on the user's desktop. After installation, collected files (student papers, ideally in "plain text" format) can be checked using the "EVE2 Wizard," a setup screen that initiates the search process by offering the user a choice between "quick," "medium," and "extra strength" searches. As the help screen notes, an "extra strength search will take quite a bit longer than a quick search"; however, selecting this option will yield "a better chance of detecting plagiarism." Time saving appears to be a crucial element in the EVE2 sales pitch. Plagiary-hunters for whom time is a "critical factor" can use the "medium" or "quick" option to speed up the search, foregoing a more thorough search in favor of ending the hunt more quickly.

Step two in the EVE detection process requires that the user set search intensity by stipulating a maximum percent value for suspected plagiarism. As clarified on the help screen, the user at this stage can instruct the program to "[c]all the hounds off when xx% has been determined to be plagiarized." In other words, this feature allows the user to halt the detection process (call off the dogs) if, after a certain number of searches, the program determines that "xx%" or more of a given paper already shows signs of plagiarism:

> For example, lets [sic] say EVE has a paper, and is planning to do 1000 searches. You've set the call off the hounds value at 80%. On search 360, EVE2 finds an almost exact copy of the paper, and determines it has matched 88% of the student's paper to this site. EVE2 would then stop searching, thereby saving the time it would take to perform the remaining 640 searches.

After performing the desired search operation, the program provides a "full report on each paper that contained plagiarism, including the percent of the essay plagiarized, and [for plain text files only] an annotated copy of the paper showing all plagiarism highlighted in red." Thus, whether or not the "hounds" are called off early, the hunt for plagiarism comes to an end in the form of a plagiarism "report" akin to that provided by Glatt. In this case, however, the report annotates a "copy" of the paper with the sanguine (perhaps sanguinary) marks of plagiarism detected.

The EVE system inverts, in both practical and symbolic ways, the cloze system used by Glatt. On the one hand, EVE hunts for pattern matches through "direct comparison" with many other documents found on the Internet. Glatt, on the other hand, invites pensive, mnemonic reflection on one single document for purposes of establishing stylistic uniqueness. Nonetheless, while different in this regard, both programs check for plagiarism by attempting to verify both uniqueness and similarity. In the Glatt context, similarity operates as a form of proof that the text is not plagiarized, insofar as words filled in by the self-recognizing writer prove to be the same as, or similar to, those deleted from every *n*th position. With EVE, however, similarity between or across documents may serve to establish a suspicious link between a purportedly original work and its actual origin in the text patterns resident on a "suspect site." Deploying text recognition "hounds" let loose on the Internet's vast storehouses, EVE highlights suspicious text strings "in red." Conversely, Glatt "asks" the potential plagiarist to mark his or her own suspicious strings by failing to provide words ostensibly drawn from his or her own storehouse.

Plagiarism-Finder

Like EVE, Plagiarism-Finder offers a downloadable solution to the plagiarism problem. As one of the newer additions to the plagiarism market at the time of this writing, Plagiarism-Finder announces on its homepage that the "Internet makes it easier than ever to plagiarize papers," thus affirming the popular wisdom regarding plagiarism and its prevalence in the post-media world. Plagiarism-Finder offers a service that, similar to EVE, finds plagiarism by seeking out and marking egregious similarity between documents. The service describes itself as a "Windows application" appropriate for any PC "with Internet access." A simple "mouse click" initiates the "check up" or the "examination." Also like EVE, Plagiarism-Finder claims a particular speed advantage over its competitors. EVE makes this claim directly via a *Rolling Stone* testimonial posted on its homepage: "EVE is faster, testing four papers in fifteen minutes, a fraction of the four hours it took Plagiarism.org [parent site of Turnitin.com] to respond." Plagiarism-Finder promises more generally that "[a]fter minutes you receive the results" of your query. A more telling description appears elsewhere on the site: To check a "term paper with 35 pages" takes, using a "broadband DSL" connection, approximately two minutes "with random sampling examination." Moreover, depending on the speed of the user's Internet connection and the choice of "adjusted accuracy" settings, as many as "20 pages" could be checked in just one minute.

For educators accustomed to manual plagiarism detection—or those reluctant to check suspicious papers themselves using Google or another detection tool—both EVE and Plagiarism-Finder offer an enormous time and labor-saving advantage. As noted above, the promise of time saved informs many if not all of the promotional narratives posted on behalf of the respective products. Behind this claim to ease and speed of use is a long history of plagiarism investigation emphasizing the laborious search for similarities between and among ostensibly unique text documents. As discussed in greater detail below, traditional "side-by-side" comparisons (of the sort streamlined by the EVE and Plagiarism-Finder programs) at one time required a small army of plagiary-hunters whose sole occupation was to chase down—in some cases for days at a time—suspiciously similar text patterns. For some, this time and labor, to greater or lesser extent (depending, for example, on one's preferred "accuracy" settings), has been transferred to the technical apparatus known currently as plagiarism detection software.

I should point out, however, that detection services of the sort reviewed so far do not eliminate outright the labor of plagiarism detection. First of all, educators who use computer-based services must still measure the "evidence" provided against any other circumstantial evidence available. Adjudication procedures of this kind take time, as they always have. Secondly, users hoping to maximize detection proficiency must, in some cases, spend time mastering the rules and techniques of textual conversion (or transformation) to compensate for software limitations. EVE, for example, devotes a significant portion of its "help" document to explaining how a potential user might go about "converting" Word and Word Perfect files to "plain text" format. Such a conversion is required, at least with the current version of EVE, if the user wants to get "full reporting" on a submitted document. For any files not converted, EVE will still "locate plagiarism" and "give the teacher a report consisting of the sites where from which plagiarism occured [sic]." However, for Word and WordPerfect files, "the teacher won't be given an annotated copy of the essay." To get that copy—and thus to receive the benefits of full reporting—the teacher must take the time to convert (and perhaps learn how to convert) one set of word-processing file formats into another. With the version of EVE under consideration here, this task of conversion marks one of the lingering labors of plagiarism detection in the age of computers and the Internet.

To summarize, the three plagiarism detection packages reviewed so far offer a number of features that I will identify as follows: (1) choice or *variety* (Glatt's three different "Programs," EVE's and Plagiarism-Finder's multiple "accuracy" settings); (2) suitable *evidence*, proof, or verification of plagiarism or plagiarism-free writing (by testing for similarity and/or uniqueness); (3) a detailed *report* (or in Glatt's case, a "score") in different ways containing that evidence, proof, or verification; (4) *accuracy* (objective verification, "very accurate" results in the case of Glatt); (5) *deterrence* (in Glatt's promise of "decrease," for example); (6) *speed and ease* (as discussed above in the cases of EVE and Plagiarism-Finder); and finally (7) *health screening* (at least metaphorically, e.g., Glatt's "drug testing," Plagiarism-Finder's "check up").

The fourth service under review, Turnitin.com, offers a similar suite of features. It also promises, in detecting plagiarism, to help educators and students "take full advantage of the Internet's educational potential." In the case of Turnitin, then, the Internet—cited by many (including Turnitin's founder) as the chief cause of the recent plagiarism epidemic—offers up its own remedy, salve, or cure in the fight against widespread digital pilfering. The Turnitin homepage makes this claim boldly by asking rhetorically: "What if the Internet could help students take more responsibility for learning and let teachers focus on teaching?" As discussed further in the next section, the Turnitin claim to "plagiarism prevention" relies extensively on this and other broader claims to educational reform premised, in turn, on the promise of the Internet's assumed "educational potential." Leading the charge in the fight against plagiarism, then, Turnitin.com thus rallies the troops (in this case, "teachers" who want to "focus on teaching") in defense of the very same "Internet" that purportedly caused the plagiarism problem in the first place.

TURNITIN.COM AND THE SCRIPTURAL ENTERPRISE OF PLAGIARISM DETECTION

Turnitin's founder John M. Barrie knows firsthand how the Internet can function as both friend and foe in the college classroom. As a teaching assistant at U.C. Berkeley in 1996, Barrie learned from a group of his students that another group was selling student papers posted to his class Web site (Larson). A firm believer in the Internet as "one of the biggest advancements in education," Barrie initially had wanted nothing more than to "add a web component" to his undergraduate classroom (qtd. in Larson), giving students the chance to "read and evaluate each other's term papers" (Loy). "[B]lindsided" by the news that some were trying to profit from this newly added component, Barrie set out to fight the "growing problem of 'digital cheating'" (Larson). In the end, with a team of Berkeley colleagues "familiar with database programming and pattern recognition" (McMasters), Barrie engineered one of the world's most utilized—and certainly most lucrative—plagiarism detection tools (McMasters).

In 1999, Barrie's Web-based solution to digital plagiarism drew the attention of *The Chronicle of Higher Education*, which set the tone for Turnitin's arrival using the now-familiar language of academic and technological combat:

> Just as the Internet has brought a proliferation of Web sites that help students plagiarize, professors can now fight back by turning to Web sites and computer programs that help detect whether students cheated on their papers. (Carnevale)

Fighting "online fire with online fire" (Loy), Turnitin thus entered the fray as a technological solution to a problem ostensibly caused by technology. Turnitin's mission from the outset was twofold: to combat Internet paper mills (the radical extreme, perhaps, of Barrie's own students' profiteering venture) and to ease the burden instructors have faced in conducting their own searches in an effort to ferret out instances of plagiarism. "Nobody has time to do it. Nobody's going to do it," Barrie suggested in the *Chronicle*. Thus, embarking on a "crusade" to make the job of plagiarism detection easier, Barrie, by the year 2000, had already earned the interest of thirty thousand site visitors anxious to outsource their labor to the Turnitin detection engine (Loy). This early "huge interest" in Turnitin.com can perhaps be explained, as Barrie opined in January 2000, by the "pent-up frustration out there" among professors and administrators (Loy). A month later, in a presentation concluding "Academic Integrity Week" at U.C. Davis, Barrie qualified this frustration by claiming (using statistics from a recent *Newsweek* article) that "[c]heating is the No. 1 problem of declining education" (qtd. in Larson). Digital cheating, Barrie added, "has ballooned because it is easy, and [students] get away with it without detection" (qtd. in Larson).

Ceding no ground to Glatt and EVE, Turnitin.com claims "100 percent" accuracy for its product (qtd. in Loy). Barrie defends "such a bold statement" (Loy) by pointing out the site's reluctance to use the "p" word too readily. The site "does not actually say whether the whole paper is plagiarized, just whether individual sections are identical to something from another document" (Loy). Thus, as Barrie is quick to emphasize, Turnitin never engages in direct accusations:

> We underline passages that are not properly cited and we never use the word "plagiarize". . . . We're just a technology that professors can use to make it easier to find out if a work is original. (qtd. in Larson)

The work of determining originality—if not the actual labor of highlighting unoriginal passages—falls to the instructor, for whom Turnitin's version of the plagiarism report acts as its own special kind of evidence in cases of digital misconduct.

In 2000 Barrie predicted that in the near future Turnitin would be "as common as the spell checker" (Loy). By the turn of the millennium, at least, Turnitin boasted a storehouse of more than one hundred thousand uploaded term papers and a client base of over three hundred universities (Loy). Since then, as thousands of schools, colleges, and universities have turned to the Internet for help with the fight against Internet plagiarism, many have adopted Turnitin.com as the preferred weapon of choice. Individual departments and instructors as well have elected to use the service in the absence of broader institutional mandates. Now used to various degrees in more than fifty countries and "licensed by over 2,500 institutions worldwide" (Turnitin's own figures), Turnitin.com has emerged as a key force in the prevention and detection of Internet plagiarism.

Hoping to avoid a knee-jerk indictment of this and other services as inherently restrictive or overtly punitive,[20] I offer an approach to Turnitin.com—and plagiarism detection software more generally—that takes into account the many historical, institutional, cultural, and pedagogical factors that continue to inform the plagiarism debate in higher education. Advertised as remedial pedagogy, the Turnitin service socializes student writers toward traditional notions of normality, docility, originality, and "uniqueness," and does so in ways reminiscent of many themes discussed in previous chapters. Moreover, as a corporate solution to a nagging pedagogical problem, the Turnitin phenomenon represents what I see as a continuing bureaucratization of writing and writing instruction consistent with past administrative practices and reflective of emerging corporate management alliances in higher education.

At the "heart" of Turnitin's plagiarism prevention system is its customized Originality Report. Like reports generated by EVE and Plagiarism-Finder, each Turnitin report derives from a paper submitted to the site reissued as an "exact" duplicate, except that "any text either copied or paraphrased appears underlined, color-coded, and linked to its original source." Whether matches turn up or not, the document returned to the client is not an "exact" duplicate, in fact, but rather a text repurposed to fit the Originality Report interface. I will address this software-driven conversion more fully below and in the conclusion. For now, I submit briefly that all papers sent up for Turnitin screening are reframed or remediated (Bolter and Grusin 55) to highlight the possible Internet-based origins of submitted texts. Following Bolter and Grusin, N. Katherine Hayles defines remediation as "robust interactions" between different media (5) resulting in significant and thus readable changes in material artifacts. Hayles suggests that "[t]o change the material artifact"—for example, by composing and producing literary documents on a screen rather than a page—"is to transform the context and circumstances for interacting with the words, which inevitably changes the meanings of the words as well" (23). In short, changes to the "material substrate" (39) of literary production require commensurate adjustments to the methods of critical analysis and reading in general.

Turnitin's Originality Report, I would argue, suggests one version of a remediated "material artifact" which, in recoding a submitted paper to reflect the presence or absence of borrowed materials, transforms "the context and circumstances" within which student writing will be read and assessed, whether as an instance of plagiarism per se or more broadly as a codified index of composition activity. To be clear, the report does not alter the words or structure of the submitted text in any explicit way (as Glatt arguably does) and is, in that sense, an "exact" duplicate. However, the Turnitin interface remediates submitted texts insofar as it changes the context of interaction while simultaneously modifying the actual surface of the submitted document. As a computer-specific detection service, Turnitin.com authorizes and initiates "material changes that can be read as marks" and thus qualifies as what Hayles would call an "inscription technology" (24). Inscribing submitted papers with the "marks" of plagiarism surveillance, Turnitin's Originality Report changes text into hypertext in order to index scriptural similarity and originality.

As noted in chapter 2, plagiarism often intersects with metaphors of weakness, disease, violence, rape, and other forms of sexual and textual violation. Sample Originality Reports from earlier versions of the Turnitin site suggest one way, albeit superficially, in which these metaphors take shape in the world of plagiarism detection. For example, one sample report appearing on the site until late 2002 featured a student essay written by "Jon Doe." The essay began:

> Serial killers have tested out a number of excuses for their behavior. Henry Lee Lucas blamed his upbringing; others like Jeffrey Dahmer say that they were born with a "part" of them missing. Ted Bundy claimed pornography made him do it. Herbert Mullin, Santa Cruz killer of thirteen, blamed the voices in his head that told him it was time to "sing the die song."

A companion "Jane Doe" report, derived from a student paper entitled "Mistaken Identity," began as follows:

> In Shakespeare's comedy, The Taming of the Shrew, one of the main ways that the theme is shown is by mistaken identity. The main theme of this play is that what a person is really like is more important than how they appear to be. . . . Most of the play's humor comes from the way in which characters create false realities by disguising themselves as other people. . . .

The serial killers of Jon Doe's plagiarized essay suggest the worst kind of bodily violation. In Jane's case, the borrowed topic pits genuine identity (true appearance) against identities mistaken or falsified.

My aim in citing these two now-defunct sample reports is not to suggest that Barrie or his team of architects at Turnitin intentionally selected these topics to underscore the moral and juridical crime of plagiarism. Even if such were the case, the overt alignment of plagiarism with serial murder and mistaken identity does not in and of itself suggest that the definitions, rules, and injunctions against plagiarism convey a similar narrative of moral and criminal reprehensibility. Nonetheless, these reports (now removed from the site)[21] do suggest the larger themes of destruction and dissimulation that often inform discussions of plagiarism. Adapting Roland Barthes's notion of "referential symbolism" (52), I would argue that the Jon and Jane Doe reports help flesh out a referential-symbolic field where seemingly nonessential allusions to murder and mistaken identity evoke an essential and essentializing equation of plagiarism with (masculine) brutality and (feminine) deception. As Randall has pointed out with regard to the latter:

> [T]he accusation of plagiarism presupposes not imitation, but copying; the existence of a copy presents the potential for a mistaken identity, the erroneous or unethical substitution of one discourse for another. And mistaken identity, in the realm of intellectual production, is a crime against the relation of authenticity subsisting between the author and the work. (31)

Moreover, the gendered division of sample reports into "Jon" and "Jane" suggests a second narrative layer whose nuances are hard to miss. Jon plagiarizes in the company of Dahmer and Bundy, while Jane plumbs the depths of "mistaken identity" via Shakespeare's clever shrew. As referential symbols, at least, these documents inherently brand plagiarists, to adapt Howard's and Groom's language, as pathological, deceitful, diseased, and/or violent.

As commonly described, the plagiarist makes either a deliberate or an uninformed choice between originality and duplication and is thus either pre-ethical or unethical. As Howard suggests, a student writer either does not know the "ethical issues" surrounding plagiarism or chooses to violate injunctions otherwise well understood ("Ethics" 85). In either case, the writer accused of missing or improper attribution assumes the identity of a plagiarist, and as suggested above and in previous chapters this identity intersects with, among other things, the several metaphors inherent to the category of plagiarism. Thus, one question remaining for this chapter is as follows: If plagiarism is a culturally laden category, and one for which student identity often serves as a site of categorical play and definition, then how do plagiarism detection services, such as those considered so far, deploy, extend, or challenge the identity constructs inherent to the plagiarism category? One immediate and simple answer is that plagiarism detection solutions in general—which build on the assumption that plagiarism by definition represents a kind of false or mistaken authorship—inherently cast plagiarists as significantly different from other categorically legitimate writers.

Turnitin's Originality Reports are in and of themselves symbolic markers of this difference. For example, one optional report interface available at the time of this writing reproduces the traditional side-by-side method for identifying textual similarities. Throughout the twentieth century, the technique of "comparison by conjunction," as Lindey describes it, was a "formidable weapon" in copyright disputes and other efforts to prove illicit appropriation (52–53). For plagiary-hunters bent on spotting suspicious matches, the technique made "a weak case look strong, and a good case look devastating" (Lindey 54). Lindey goes further in defining this "pursuit of parallels" as "a form of literary research" which, at various historical moments, has required the services of a large labor pool dedicated to "double column 'analysis'" (55). Barrie's conjecture (cited above) that few in academia have the time "to do" this kind of analysis bears out in Lindey's assessment of the intense labor traditionally required to perform this painstaking task (57). Furthermore, anticipating Barrie's remark in defense of Turnitin's purported neutrality, Lindey offers the compelling claim that "the use of parallels is neither good nor bad" (59). Their "value" depends, rather, on "the conclusions that are drawn from them" (Lindey 59).

Turnitin's "pursuit of parallels" ends in the production of a digital page split down the middle with the text of the submitted paper duplicated in the left window and the source content provided in the right. Color highlights (underlined text linking to source content) mark any borrowed content and index (by percentage and difference in hue) the degree of similarity in the submitted paper. The use of color, I should note in passing, underscores the symbolic power of material transmutation inherent to an arguably neo-alchemical Turnitin aesthetic. To revisit my discussion in chapter 4, medieval exoteric alchemists found in color change "the most important characteristic" of a metal undergoing alchemical transformation from "base" to finer form (Holmyard 24). Similarly, the Turnitin side-by-side interface conveys an implied insistence on "sequences" of color change (Holmyard 24) to mark one ostensibly "important characteristic" of a given composition—namely its originality or lack thereof. Color, in the case of Turnitin-style plagiarism detection, marks a particular degree of textual contamination, and conversely the absence of color (no matches, no highlighted links) suggests textual purity or the absence of linguistic similarity. Thus, the Turnitin version of conjunctive comparison recalibrates—or recodes—a submitted document to reflect the degree to which the writer, as literary alchemist, has transformed textual material submitted under the aegis of original production. In a manner akin to the alchemical measurement of transforming metals, "a standard sequence of colors is accepted as a check upon the success of transmutation" (Hopkins 121).

Furthermore, in performing this check, the Originality Report remediates a submitted paper insofar as it reproduces or refashions one material artifact in the form of another. In its ongoing effort to "remedy the disorder" (Illich, *Vineyard* 10) of student plagiarism, Turnitin outputs the information of student writing for purposes of surveillance, control, and classification. Pointing metaphorically to the submitted essay as the original, authentic locus of compositional activity, Turnitin's "new," "post," or "meta-media" report in fact reactivates student writing in the context of Web-specific plagiarism detection. This shift of orientation—from student composition to online, digital detection—marks a productive change or transformation otherwise overlooked in the language of "exact" duplication. Adapting Bolter and Grusin, I would thus argue that the Originality Report, as remediated material artifact, also "fills a lack or repairs a fault in its predecessor" (60) and is therefore remedial in the strict pedagogical, and perhaps religious, sense as well. To help remedy the disorder of student plagiarism, Turnitin sells a product that ostensibly orders all textual "lack" and "fault" in a language (code, convention) consistent with traditional forms of information control.

Some may object that in casting the Originality Report as a tool of technological repair or remedy, I too am relying too heavily on metaphor or, perhaps worse, misrepresenting or overstating the relevance of this or any other report interface as an assessment tool for instructors. However, I extend Howard's point in arguing that plagiarism, like authorship more broadly, makes sense only when charted against a broader set of signifying forms pertaining to literary, legal, pedagogical, and religious institutions. One of my aims throughout this book has been to suggest that antiplagiarism solutions derive from those same forms and therefore must be approached, so to speak, on their terms. The name of the product in this case—*Originality Report*—clearly capitalizes on the well-entrenched Romantic notion that real authors produce original works of art essentially free of undocumented source. In trying to understand the cultural work of Turnitin.com, therefore, I take these notions seriously as markers of broader cultural and educational traditions that also include, in this case, mechanisms of correction, remediation, and purification. In short, if the unoriginal or illegitimately copied student paper inherently signifies a kind of unhealthy, impure, or diseased alterity, then clearly the Originality Report—as both operational technology and signifying form—functions as a remedial device designed to index and recode in relation to standards of health and purity.

As an instance of ritual recoding, the Originality Report also appears in the guise of its contested domain, namely the World Wide Web. Color-coded, indexed, and, where appropriate, rife with hyperlinks, the report bears the likeness and functionality of a Web page and thus mirrors the very process and formal mode by which the hypothetical "new breed of appropriator" might go about cribbing written texts. Thus, as a literal transmutation of a submitted paper, the report is also real writing in the sense put forth by de Certeau: as a text in isolation, the Originality Report also faces off (albeit side-by-side) against its exteriorized other—the submitted paper—and assumes power over its surfaces. Moreover, in taking up its place in a contested Internet domain, Turnitin operates strategically in relation to the purported "epidemic" of Internet plagiarism. In other words, Turnitin's host Web site—www.turnitin.com—serves as a "base" from which the "targets or threats" of Internet plagiarism "can be managed" (de Certeau 35–36).

Turnitin.com manages the threats of student plagiarism, in part, by inverting traditional author positions and assuming ownership of a converted text product later sold back (as an "exact" duplicate) to the client. As the site acknowledges, papers submitted to the Turnitin service typically become part of a wider database of previously submitted texts. In this way, student writings sent up for source screening become, in a speed-of-light moment of digital reclassification, source or raw materials for future screenings. This process of reclassification has led some to wonder whether Turnitin.com is not itself in violation of copyright law. To counter this charge, Buerger offers a compelling defense of Turnitin on the grounds that students taking classes in colleges or universities typically receive academic "credit" in exchange for transferring rights (tacitly if not directly) to written work. No claim to copyright infringement can be made, Buerger argues, where rights to copy have already been ceded in exchange for academic credit:

> The submission of a paper in return for credit clearly demonstrates that any implicit intellectual-property interest vested in an accepted and credited assignment must belong to the institution, since an exchange has taken place: the student has received the equivalent of a fiduciary payment in return for his work. If legal theory must be applied, it should be that of the transfer of intellectual-property rights, rather than their violation. (329)

Buerger's argument has its merits but raises at least one potential caveat. A student submitting work for college credit receives "the equivalent of a fiduciary payment" only after the "work" has been evaluated and, in cases where online detection is used, after it has cleared the screening process. Granted, institutions may assume the "transfer of intellectual-property rights" after assigning credit for a given assignment. However, where an assignment is submitted for screening in advance of determining its mark (in the sense of either "grade" or "status" as plagiarized or not), an institution could be accused of transferring rights to the detection service before having "paid" the student with assignment credit. Certainly a paper could be submitted for screening after credit has been assigned, with credit rescinded, as it were, should evidence of plagiarism later be found. But this again begs the question regarding the timing of transfer: Does a crediting institution have the right to assume a "transfer" of property rights—and then to negotiate another transfer with Turnitin.com or another detection service—before any formal exchange of credit has taken place?

Clearly, the problem of copyright transfer raises a host of larger questions beyond the scope of this study. For the time being, I would argue in brief that Buerger's defense of Turnitin's stockpiling of student writing is grounded in the arguable notion that student writers function as Lockean "citizen-proprietors" (Shklar 35) whose primary responsibility to the texts they produce at school is to claim "self-ownership" via the free transfer of rights in exchange for credit.

Undoubtedly, in a twenty-first-century intellectual property climate, this system of transferable rights may indicate, for some, the preferred means of conducting the business of higher education. Student papers, in other words, may be valuable in ways beyond their status as material markers of credit-worthy "work." In fact, implicit to Turnitin's alchemical transmutation of student submissions into Originality Reports is the overt "rearticulation" (in a sense perhaps not imagined by Manovich) of scriptural raw material into a new documentary script made economically valuable in today's plagiarism detection market. Read literally, de Certeau thus anticipates the market appeal of Turnitin.com: "[W]hat comes in is something 'received,' what comes out is a 'product'" (135). However, once student writing begins to function as "product" or raw material for production, the question remains as to who, in the end, stands to profit most, and in what ways, from this particular kind of industrial inversion. Credit-based economies in higher education—as metaphors, really, for money-based exchange systems more broadly—do not account, in their current forms, for the complexities of intellectual property exchange otherwise assumed in Buerger's defense of Turnitin's use of student papers.

As noted above, I resist taking the moral high ground in accusing Turnitin.com and its many users—students, instructors, and institutions alike—of engaging in overtly constrictive or punitive practices in using this service. I claim only that Turnitin.com—as assessment gateway—does both old and new work in identifying submitted writing as either original or something else. The new work derives, obviously, from the storage and pattern recognition capacities inherent to today's networked computers and software systems. The old work, as suggested in previous chapters, did not start with Turnitin.com but rather in the legal codes, literary conventions, and cultural forms that for at least two centuries have structured intellectual property debates and, more recently, debates about the nature of student authorship in the information age.

Viewed as an industry that both authors new detection tools and capitalizes on detection conventions already in place, antiplagiarism services such as Turnitin serve a purpose arguably similar to that of the traditional writing program as described in chapter 3. The main function of the writing program, according to Strickland, has been to use writing as a "tool for surveillance and assessment" and "the enforcement of discipline" (461). Turnitin.com, as one agent of student identity formation, may indeed suggest a disciplinary effort to teach "normal" writing conduct as a core value within a standardized composition curriculum. However, as a "combatant," in de Certeau's sense, against wanton Internet plagiarism, Turnitin markets itself as a friendly and generous learning resource, positioning its detection service within a much broader array of educational products. The site offers, in addition to Plagiarism Prevention, the following three services: GradeMark (a "groundbreaking online tool" for marking papers "in a unique, paperless environment"); Peer Review ("bringing classroom collaboration into the Internet age"); and GradeBook (enabling instructors "to manage grades and assignments online" with a "computer-based grading interface").[22] Thus, as a suite of "facts, data, and events" relevant to computer-mediated education, Turnitin dons the "uniform" of the new education economy and advances toward the pedagogical "scene" of its law (de Certeau 185–86)—a law of research and citation rules and regulations accredited under the aegis of its own corporate banner.[23]

Still, Turnitin.com represents not so much a new or reformed pedagogy but rather a Web-based reformulation of rather old pedagogical formulae. An earlier version of the Turnitin homepage offered up the following declaration:

> Since 1996, Turnitin has been helping millions of faculty and students in 51 countries to improve writing and research skills, encourage collaborative online learning, ensure originality of student work, and save instructors' time—all at a very affordable price.

In the guise of helping faculty and students, improving skills, encouraging learning, and ensuring originality, Turnitin thus duplicates the textbook industry's promise of a time- and labor-saving complement to the educational experience. Like the generic textbook, though, Turnitin offers a prescriptive and normative educational agenda. As Bleich has noted, "Textbooks necessarily do not question the tradition" (28). In authoring Turnitin, Barrie and his team have likewise embraced a traditional educational paradigm encoded in, among other things, its use of vintage black-and-white photographs depicting well-dressed students and teachers engaged in various acts of reading, writing, and boisterous learning. Photos of predominantly white, short-haired men and boys betray an obvious appeal to a foregone age (mid-Fifties perhaps) of educational order and congeniality.[24] With regard to this "fetishism of the consumer rather than the commodity" (Appadurai 56), I would argue that Turnitin uses a rather quaint repertoire of images to invert the consumer relationship in such a way that what we come to buy (into) is not the "commodity" of antiplagiarism software itself but rather a pro-author, pro-originality mindset to counteract the taint of student plagiarism. Like its competitor Glatt, Turnitin inscribes its own case for consumer "uniqueness" in part by impressing the myth of educational prowess into the likeable faces of happy and healthy students and teachers.

I end my analysis of Turnitin by entertaining the point, raised briefly in chapter 3, that Turnitin.com—as self-proclaimed teaching resource and, for more students each day, a required component in the writing process—produces and distributes "an ethical technology of subjectivity that creates in students a healthy respect for the authority of the academy" (Crowley 217). Following Crowley, I submit that, like the "universal requirement" of composition itself, Turnitin "gets in between teachers and their students, in between students' writing and their teachers' reading" (217), but it does so in significantly different ways. Granted, texts submitted to the Turnitin service are not necessarily suspect going in but only deemed such after unacknowledged similarity has been detected. And again, it is certainly true that instructors, students, and other human agents get "in between" Turnitin.com, submitted texts, and the people who submit them. Nonetheless, in remediating submitted papers, Turnitin introduces, as "ethical technology," an ethical drug test (akin to Barbara Glatt's) to which participants must nonetheless submit. Whether guilty or innocent, writers who undergo the screening process see their writing "produced" in particular ways by the Turnitin remediation machine. In brief, all writers who participate fully in Turnitin.com's detection process provide raw material for the corporate detour known as plagiarism detection. In that sense, student writing functions as a kind of input—or base metal—for postindustrial and post-media corporate production. This production is an authoring: what comes in is something received, what comes out is a product. Moreover, as textual deviants, plagiarists provide material evidence that this detour is not only necessary but good for everyone, including students, educators, policy makers, and ardent defenders of literary tradition.

CONCLUSION: TURNITIN.COM IN THE "MANAGED" UNIVERSITY

Radical theories of education are replete with critiques of mechanized administrative solutions to nagging pedagogical problems. In 1970, Paulo Freire bemoaned the fact that in a "technological society" there is "always some manual" or set of "directional signals" hindering the learner's "capacity for critical thinking" (474–75). Likewise, Ivan Illich has described the "rules, codes or operators" by which modern institutions have commodified education in order to call up "a new type" of human being better suited to industrial life and labor (*Tools* 19–20). The new type produced by Turnitin.com is surely reminiscent of those that have come before, a point I return to in my last chapter. However, the plagiarism detection algorithm and its companion learning resources—as with textbooks, handbooks, standardized writing curricula, and perhaps the writing program more broadly—appear to provide yet another of the several "administrative therapies" Illich posited to explain industrial responses to social resistance.

Like a textbook or handbook, Turnitin capitalizes on potential authoring errors and misadventures, offering in this case an antidote to the ease, and disease, of downloading and copying materials off the Internet. As a remediation machine, the system serves as a form of scriptural remedy in an age, for some, of epidemic scriptural transgression. But Turnitin is not all etiology and antidote. The site also provides the equivalent of an online course book offering "preemptive education," as the site once noted, in the form of tips, guidelines, and suggestions for teachers and students trying to understand plagiarism in the information age. However, while promoted as educational resource, Turnitin nonetheless operates squarely within the realm of educational fix. While recoding plagiarism detection as prevention and deterrence, Turnitin still makes its money by pulling "unoriginal work" out of a sea of so-called originals. In short, Turnitin profits by battling those instances where learning goes wrong but nonetheless dresses its combative strategy in the uniform of preemptive educational reform. In this way, Turnitin writes itself "legible," in Foucault's sense, as a normative teaching and learning tool, even while its chief operation is to encode scriptural abnormality.

The Web, in fact, may offer the ideal platform on which the school of preemptive plagiarism education can write and rewrite its ongoing operations. For example, the belated removal of the early Jane and Jon Doe sample reports may mark not only a template revision to match a recent software update but also the intentional erasure of a scripted (and arguably sexist) past no longer suitable to today's "scriptural enterprise" (de Certeau 135). In any event, in educational settings especially, the Web has materialized in the last decade as the idealized technotopic solution to perennial administrative problems, the prevention and detection of plagiarism being just one of them. In this context, Bousquet's critique of the late-twentieth-century "managed university" is worth quoting at length:

> Understood as a humanly engineered historical emergence of the past three decades, the "managed university" names a global phenomenon: the forced privatization of public higher education; the erosion of faculty, student, and citizen participation in higher education policy, except through academic-capitalist and consumerist practices; the steady conversion of socially beneficial activities (cultivation of a knowledge commons, development of a democratic citizenry fit to govern itself) to the commodity form—the sale of information goods, such as patents and corporate-sponsored research, and the production of a job-ready workforce. . . . (510)

Bousquet's broad account of this "global phenomenon," I would argue, is clearly applicable to the Turnitin phenomenon. As a privatized (outsourced) educational elixir, the Turnitin service may not go so far as to erode "faculty, student, and citizen participation in higher education policy," but with regard to plagiarism and research writing in general it certainly suggests in its use a subtle transfer of pedagogical authority and responsibility to a "consumerist practice" and "commodity form" dressed in the camouflage of educational godsend. At a basic level, then, Turnitin and other services resemble the kind of "real training" that has always come, as Connors argued, from the "rules and tenets" found in the composition industry's earliest textbooks (qtd. in Austin 71). At the very least, as the new university historicized in chapter 3 arguably becomes "more and more of a corporate entity" (Micciche 432), Turnitin offers to intercept student-teacher participation in the writing process through its Originality Report and other scriptural operations serving as pedagogical support. In sum, the managed university finds in Turnitin.com an "academic-capitalist" partner in the collective fight against textual deviance.

To address the textual economies underwriting Turnitin.com and other plagiarism detection services is therefore to examine the politics of administrative remedy in higher education, particularly where such services function to write and rewrite student identity and experience to conform to a given set of normalized practices. While computer technology may certainly promise a new meta-media age of authorial experimentation, that experiment meets its corollary in reactionary interests exploiting the same technology to recode and reify traditional paradigms as progressive writing pedagogy. The student writer continues to serve not only as raw material for various forms of production but also as political scapegoat for broader problems of textual use and citation in the information age. Careful attention must therefore be paid to the ways in which plagiarism detection remedies socialize students under the aegis of preemptive education.

Conclusion

The Ghost of Plagiarism in the Post-Media Machine

It is not that students are *un*motivated, but motivated *askew*.

—Ted Nelson, *Computer Lib / Dream Machines*

DUE IN PART to the several perspectives on plagiarism represented in this book, I cannot now claim to know what motivates a student writer, or any writer for that matter, to plagiarize. In fact, my general aim has been to bracket issues of motivation—and general questions of individual responsibility and culpability—in favor of treating plagiarism more broadly as a socially significant category that means different things to different people at different moments. Nonetheless, while attending to the ever-changing historical and institutional variables of plagiarism, I endeavored to show that the plagiarism problem has continued to draw considerable interest over the years in part because it continues to serve larger debates about literary convention, social and technological progress, cultural difference, and human creativity, identity, and morality. Taking my lead from Howard, Randall, and Kewes in particular, I have tried to describe these multiple facets of plagiarism and plagiarism detection in the context of larger historical trajectories and traditional symbolic forms.

My aim in this conclusion, therefore, is to retrace my steps by considering some of the issues left lurking, as it were, in the shadows of this book. I will focus in particular on the use of today's post-media machines for purposes of conducting research, assembling material, and, for some, committing acts typically construed as plagiarism. Heralded in some circles as the latest instrument of artistic experimentation, the networked computer is also the new tool of choice for an ever-growing and ever-diversifying population of postmillennial readers and writers. As such, the new media "composer" brings with it a new set

147

of conventions and techniques that, while arguably new in particular ways, also revamp or remediate a range of authoring practices not altogether lost in our new media age. Thus, I will consider the ways in which post-media composition practices both reproduce and depart from earlier composition activities, considering issues of communication and literacy in this day (to adapt Nelson) of writing "askew." I want to argue, in brief, that the qualified *remedium* of the post-media writing machine invites a revised theory of reading and writing based in part in the respective tactics of plagiarism and plagiarism detection. In other words, recent mutations in text composing activities suggest a corollary transmutation of text reading practices in the digital age. These practices are currently—if not best—modeled in the pattern recognition engines of today's plagiarism detection services.

I begin by redressing an argument put forth by McCabe and Drinan concerning academic integrity and institutional reform. Writing for *The Chronicle of Higher Education* in late 1999, McCabe and Drinan advanced a series of suggestions intended to help higher learning institutions contend with "the problem of cheating." The authors recommended, for example, that colleges and universities provide more "guidance about how new technology raises new questions about cheating," particularly since students will tend to make "assumptions about appropriate use that are most convenient for them—assumptions that often differ substantially from the views of faculty members or the institution." More specifically, the authors argued, "some students seem to view almost anything that they discover on the Internet as general knowledge that does not require citation" (McCabe and Drinan). My aim here—rather than to challenge the strategic value of McCabe and Drinan's recommendation—is to consider the ways in which their statement invokes many if not all of the themes addressed in this book. Around the seemingly simple issue of Internet "cheating" swirls a constellation of implied claims regarding historic convention ("appropriate use," "views of faculty" or "institution," "general knowledge," rules of "citation"), social and technological novelty ("new technology," "new questions"), cultural difference (student "assumptions" differing "substantially" from those of faculty), and human activity ("guidance," "disover[y]").

I wish to suggest, in brief, that really no discussion of plagiarism, or cheating more broadly, can avoid this constellation of issues. McCabe and Drinan are right, in fact, that the emergence of the Internet or any other new technology introduces a number of "new questions" for higher education and contemporary education generally. I would argue further, however, that the challenge facing educators—and writing instructors in particular—is to think carefully and critically about what questions to ask in the first place. For example, McCabe and Drinan address student assumptions without considering just why, and to what end, students hold those assumptions while surfing the Web. More specifically, if some students find it more "convenient" to regard what they find online as "general knowledge," then what factors inform that sense of convenience, and whose interests are at stake in stipulating that such knowledge, by default, requires citation? To be fair, the authors have introduced this and other strategies in part because far too many educators, in their words, have been "silent" with their students on the "proper use" of the Internet as a "research tool." Indeed, if educators choose to ignore (or hope to bypass) the several questions surrounding the Internet and other new technologies, then clearly it would serve them well to consider McCabe and Drinan's advice. I wonder, however, if many remain silent on these issues precisely because the rules for "proper use" remain tethered to tired intellectual property laws and outmoded institutional policies controlling academic conduct.

I therefore resist these and other actions leaning, as McCabe and Drinan's title suggests, "toward a culture of academic integrity" because the call for institutional reform, while granting that new technologies invite new questions, nonetheless relies on rather staid moral and pedagogical conveniences. If the Internet indeed raises "new questions," then perhaps those questions should target the traditions of proper use themselves, as well as—perhaps in lieu of—targeting student "assumptions" about what does and does not pass for general knowledge. Moreover, I would argue provisionally that much could be learned by studying what today's technology users—including today's Internet plagiarists—consider convenient and appropriate when using their preferred compositional tool. In other words, I do not dismiss the larger claim that student cheating is a problem wherever and however it occurs. Nonetheless, in my view one of the new questions for higher education in the early twenty-first century should be not how do educators best guide student researchers away from those "assumptions that differ" (alas, a very old question) but rather what can educators learn about technology, and about their students, by attending to those differences?

To be sure, antiplagiarism remedies—from the research paper assignment to institutional plagiarism policies to Web-based detection services—have worked through the years to channel or discipline student assumptions regarding the use and incorporation of source materials. Indeed, for the most part the remedies described in this book have been designed not only to police plagiarism but also to shore up, under the aegis of plagiarism prevention, certain time-honored claims to authorial authenticity and originality. Glatt's "cloze" reading program, for example, assumes overtly the search for authorial "uniqueness" in the pall of potential plagiarism. Likewise, Turnitin's Originality Report indexes not plagiarism really but rather those traces of originality, scored in base-metal black, that punctuate the new post-media page made "visible" (Illich, *Vineyard* 99) in the search for similarity.

Thus, while arguing generally that these and other remedies have functioned as particular solutions to the plagiarism problem, I have also made the corollary claim that the real value of plagiarism detection lies not just in the antiplagiarism remedies themselves but also in the ways such remedies shine a warm light on the modern authoring subject. It is, after all, the authorized individual (teacher, professor, or perhaps student) who determines whether or not another individual (as potential plagiarist) has broken the codes of literary conduct. Like the formidable weapon of parallel hunting in an earlier age, the originality report, or plagiarism score, or similarity index—the technology, that is—simply codes and compiles the evidence for later human-judicial review. Buerger, echoing Barrie and the Turnitin Web site, follows this line of reasoning in claiming that "[a]nti-plagiarism software is a tool, not a solution" (326). Barrie said as much in describing his service as simply a "technology" useful to educators trying to determine whether or not a given work "is original" (qtd. in Larson).

Indeed, on the surface at least, Turnitin.com, Glatt, EVE, Plagiarism-Finder, and even the traditional research paper and the 1913 University of Minnesota antiplagiarism "Instructions" do not promise to solve the plagiarism problem outright. More subtly, each mechanism offers only to provide educators with an appropriate "tool" for managing the problem toward an appropriate, local outcome. I have tried to argue, however, that services such as Turnitin do, in fact, solve the plagiarism problem not by eradicating the scourge outright, nor even by mitigating the damage done, but rather by offering to reframe, or reinscribe, the plagiarism debate in the service of larger social and pedagogical mandates. Disciplinary mechanisms of this order—an order whose chief domain is that of disorder—reconvene at various historical moments over the conventions of good practice and proper use and put forth, as scriptural enterprise, a scriptural solution to a problem that otherwise will not go away. The tool of plagiarism prevention and detection is thus a perennial solution insofar as it writes legal right over the illegitimate (perhaps illegible) marks of errant scriptural practice.

I argued in chapter 7 that Turnitin.com operates strategically in setting up its "base" in the same domain where nefarious Internet users—paper mills most obviously but also the "new breed" of student appropriators—go about their business. Against the planned strategy of Turnitin, therefore, should be posited the improvised tactics of Internet users who set out—intentionally if not maliciously—to test or practice some of the assumptions McCabe and Drinan postulated on behalf of today's post-media researchers. A "tactic," I should note, is arguably "an art of the weak," a kind of "trickery" or activity of "last resort" (de Certeau 36) for those targets or threats who, unable or unwilling to build (or pay for) the kind of strategic strongholds enjoyed by "the strong," must engage in a different set of "ruses and surprises" (de Certeau 40). In some cases, the ruses of the weak, as argued by Randall, suggest a potential counter-script in the form of "guerrilla plagiarism" and other seditious attacks against established modes of knowing and doing (see chapter 2).

I submit further that—for both student plagiarists and plagiary-hunters (those instructors, for example, who Google their way to evidence in support of a plagiarism claim)—the tactical game of searching the Web for either bits to copy or bits inappropriately copied amounts to a particular kind of "art of putting one over" on the respective other (de Certeau 40). This "art," to press the point, deploys a series of "maneuverable, polymorph mobilities, jubilant, poetic, and warlike discoveries" (de Certeau 40). And yet, in maneuvering toward either plagiarism or antiplagiarism evidence, the "weak" in both cases suffer the fallout of conflicting assumptions. In brief, human bodies—belonging to plagiarists and plagiary-hunters alike—tool the machine of plagiarism detection even as antiplagiarism technology performs the dirty work of hunting down errant similarities. Hence, the game of combat that saturates centuries of plagiarism rhetoric—materializing for example in the "plagiarism racket" of the early twentieth century—continues unabated in the task of maneuvering tactically through digital information in search of one's preferred "warlike discoveries."

I also made the claim in chapter 7 that Turnitin and other services, in performing a pseudo-alchemical transmutation of student texts, also write or author students and their writings in significant ways. In fact, to avoid the appearance of overt copying (or plagiarism, or copyright infringement), such services must perform an authoring operation in order to make students' texts, in effect, their own. However, in the case of EVE, Plagiarism-Finder, and Turnitin.com in particular, this fictional authoring (borrowing-transmuting) of textual materials is camouflaged in a secondary fiction of simple duplication: as rehearsed several times already, each service produces and returns a copy of the submitted text, albeit annotated (changed, remediated) for purposes of providing evidence. The mere copy of scholastic technique gets reproduced here as the "mirror copy" of plagiarism detection technology. The mirroring of textual materials for purposes of detection, as I argued, also suggests an industrial inversion of student writing in the interest of preserving a preferred set of authoring conventions.

The writing or scripting of originality/plagiarism reportage also models a set of rules and rituals for reading, but reading in the technical sense of ordering or valuing information for purposes of gathering evidence. In his 2000 Academic Integrity Week presentation at U.C. Davis, the founder of Turnitin.com explained the "basic idea" behind his service: "The basic strategy is to take a sea of information, go to the website, and read and review the paper" (qtd. in Larson). Barrie's exact emphasis here is unclear, but in general he posits a "strategy" for Turnitin that places the activity of reading and reviewing a paper in a Web context, where the evidence needed to support plagiarism claims can be compiled and assessed. The ways in which Turnitin and users of Turnitin go about reading student writing is clarified in Barrie's subsequent description of the "two steps" by which the service determines a "possibly plagiarized piece of work" (Larson). As Larson summarizes, "Step one involves determining the value of words in an essay" using a "program that gives every word in the English language a value from one to 10." Barrie explains further that "common" words such as "the" would generate a "low value of one," whereas a less common word such as "Shakespeare" "would have a value of 10" (qtd. in Larson). After valuing all the words in a submitted essay, the program "finds high-value words in the paper and extracts 12 word phrases around each high-value word" (Larson). Then, having coded each submission for "high-value" text strings, the program performs the next step in the plagiarism-hunting process. As Larson puts it, the phrases identified for "high-value" content are "sent out to search engines all over the Internet" in order "to check for any Web sites that may contain the particular high-value phrase." In other words, the kind of literacy programmed into the Turnitin search algorithm requires, first, reading for high-value English and, second, skimming or scanning the Internet for high-value text similarity.

Thus, as a text reading technology, the Turnitin service, much like its competitors, offers a new "technique of ordering" (Illich, *Vineyard* 45) information in the guise of policing textual disorder. For the twelfth-century monastic, the ultimate remedy for the disorder of medieval life was the search for "God as wisdom." More to the point, as Illich suggests, the concept of *remedium* provides twenty-first-century thinkers with "a unique way to address the issue of technique or technology" (11). In teaching the art of reading to his pupils, Hugh taught an "ontologically remedial technique" (11) that Illich believed might shed some light on today's reading techniques in the age of "new reference tools" and other devices of textual ordering. Adapting Illich, I propose that Turnitin and other plagiarism detection services go far to educate a post-media, post-Internet audience in the benefits and hazards of "remedial," computer-mediated reading. However, in this particular case the search for plagiarism begins and ends not with God or wisdom (nor even with an avant-garde "rearticulation" of material content) but rather with the attribution of linguistic "value" in the hunt for textual similarity and authorial uniqueness. For Web-based detection services, in other words, the new technology of the Internet affords a new methodology for determining (reading for) authorial originality. This new methodology breeds, in its own way, a new ritualized technique of ordering information whose purpose is nonetheless the healthy ordering of human subjects.

The technique of reading with and among computers implies a potentially new set of literacy conventions for twenty-first-century computer users. As Hawisher et al. have argued, "people's adoption of computers as literacy tools and environments" can shape and be shaped by a wide range of factors, including "social contexts," "education practices," "cultural and ideological formations," "family practices and experiences," and so on (644). To understand how people make use of the new post-media machines, that is, one must attend to the "*cultural ecology* of literacy," which, for Hawisher et al., implies a "complex web within which both humans and computer technologies coexist" (644).

Echoing Illich, Hawisher et al. theorize a recent turn in human reading techniques away from a "conventional, alphabetic, and print literacy" (671) and toward more "visual" or "multimodal" literacies. One question emerging at the
end of this book, therefore, is how do today's educators perceive and respond to
the problem of plagiarism in a manner sensitive to the changing "cultural ecology" of literate activity in today's computer-mediated, multimodal writing environments? In other words, if the applied techniques of ordering information
have changed or are changing in accordance with new "literacy tools and environments," then how do we manage human-computer "coexistence" in the
realm of Internet plagiarism and plagiarism detection?

For Illich, at least, the story of Hugh of St. Victor—whose *Didascalicon*
reinvented reading for twelfth-century French monks—helps us negotiate "another epochal turn in the social history of the alphabet that is happening within
our lifetime: the dissolution of alphabetic technique into the miasma of communication" (117). Clearly, this "miasma" may account for the kind of reticence
McCabe and Drinan record among educators anxious to guide student assumptions but hesitant or cautious before the "new questions" inherent to Internet research. And to be sure, Illich does not celebrate but rather bemoans the
slow suspension of "alphabetic technique" due to his apparent suspicion that as-
cendant modes and methods of communication (e.g., on screens, over networks, through "media") may not order the disorder as well or as healthfully as
those alphabetic techniques now fast on the wane.

Illich's worry is perhaps unfounded, however, given the urgency with
which many leap to the defense of conventional literacies seemingly threatened
by new technologies (the Internet) and new techniques of ordering (Internet
plagiarism). In this book, in fact, I have endeavored to map the trajectory of one
such defense materializing in the form of antiplagiarism remedies in higher education. In the spreading fog of post-media communication, that is, one can
still spy the "reified visions of information" that Boyle, for one, situates squarely
within the ever-renewed and renewable "ideology of a liberal society" (109).
Despite the epochal changes theorized by Illich and others, traditional values
pertaining to authorship, for instance, remain well-entrenched bastions of an
ideologically "liberal" intellectual property regime. Turnitin.com, for its part,
presents a vision arguably "reified" in accordance with a liberal epistemology
whose central values—including those pertaining to literate, reading and writing humans—have not changed, by and large, for nearly three centuries.

Still, if Hawisher and company are correct in arguing that, for more and
more students each day, "literacies that are primarily alphabetic are fading"
(665), then perhaps the historic battle underway between plagiarists and plagiary-hunters marks a radical conflict between not only authors and nonauthors
but also between two or more differing views of literacy. The common student
view of general knowledge described by McCabe and Drinan may simply fail to

match up—side-by-side or otherwise—with prevailing "visions" of information
and old-school assessments of "communication ability" among today's largely
print-age educators (Hawisher et al. 671). In other words, in the realm of communication and composition instruction, and perhaps in the realm of plagiarism
detection, today's professionals may not know enough about the kinds of reading, writing, research, and compiling expertise that today's students bring to the
college classroom:

> Our professional radar is tuned so narrowly to the bandwidth of print
> and the alphabetic—to school-based and workplace writing—that we
> miss a great deal of the more interesting and engaging self-sponsored
> reading and composing students do on their own time. (Hawisher
> et al. 676)

I enthusiastically endorse this important call for teachers to adjust their professional vision to account for new "multimodal" strategies imported, by students as
well as instructors, into today's classrooms. However, I wonder at the same time
how certain varieties of "self-sponsored reading and composing" activities—in
particular those techniques of ordering that lead some to accuse students of plagiarism—would show up on the "radar" of today's twenty-first-century educators,
even those sensitive to newly emergent multimodal literacies. My concluding
question, therefore, is this: Does Internet plagiarism in the age of post-media
composition represent one of many laudable literacies students with a new "communication ability" bring to the classroom, or is it, as it always has been, a fraudulent or failed venture in the realm of compositional technique, multimodal
or otherwise?

This question, like most questions about plagiarism, invites a range of
potential concerns. For example, in using the "p" word to label what likely
amounts to several distinct student activities, I nonetheless resort to singular-
ity in asking whether Internet plagiarism (as one problem? as many disparate
activities?) belongs in the lofty realm of post-media literacy or in the dungeon
of literacy gone wrong. I concede this contradiction in part because the jury by
and large is still out with regard to the best way to imagine plagiarism—and
imagining plagiarism has always been central to the game of knowing plagiarism—in the age of networked writing machines. I therefore end by proposing,
by way of Hawisher et al., that what passes (or rather does not pass) as plagiarism on the Internet or elsewhere is best understood as operating within a wide
"range" of "semiotic practices and channels" in education (677). Just how plagiarists operate, of course, remains one of the more relevant questions for historians of new and old writing technologies. Nonetheless, in the realm of the
new, I urge more focused attention to the semiotic import of practices (such as

Internet plagiarism, or even Internet plagiarism detection) commonly coded as subversive or reactionary in relation to dominant modes and practices.

For example, the Web-based antiplagiarism remedies discussed in this book suggest a rough model for how to envision reading and research practices in the post-media age. Reading—as an information age technique of ordering, organizing, and composing data—generates in the plagiarism detection world a kind of hard evidence (as score, as report) often used to bolster charges of plagiarism. For the student researcher, similar techniques of ordering, organizing, and composing may provide a way to explore the "channels" of post-media knowledge domains without either raising the hackles of plagiary-hunters or submitting, in all senses, to the range of assumptions that continue to inform attempts to define and disclose instances of plagiarism. Such explorations could take the form of revamped research essays or note-taking or patchwriting techniques, as described in chapter 6, or they could assume the look and feel of Turnitin's Originality Report—indexing, that is, textual similarities toward the articulation of textual or thematic affinities across a wide range of documents discovered on the Web and elsewhere.[25] The exact nature of the practice (as formal mode, as assignment) is not as important as the broader recognition that the computer, considered as a post-media composing machine, is, by definition, designed for material exchange and, by extension, appropriation and manipulation of material content. Hawisher et al.'s defense of multimodal literacies thus helps frame a theory of reading and research that emphasizes, in this way, not only the particular communicative techniques emerging in the age of computers and the Internet, but also the ways in which such techniques might be put to use by today's educators still enmeshed, arguably, in the world of print production.

To choreograph a poetics of post-media research techniques requires a complementary commitment to studying the plagiarism question—and questions of research writing more broadly—under the light of the new "visible page" of plagiarism detection. The Hugh of Illich's *Vineyard*, therefore, is perhaps the model educator for any who now stand "silent" over the visibly original or plagiarized pages of today's student writers. In making this claim, I do not mean to resort to a nostalgic, premodern search for *remedium* in order to lift an ailing postmodern epistemology into the rosy health of a more authentic reading or writing experience. Rather, taking my lead from Illich, I find in the prescholastic methodologies a helpful way to address issues of technique or technology, particularly with regard to real or imagined student assumptions about how to use text materials found on the Internet or elsewhere.

Clearly, more could be done to chart these methodologies in pre- and postscholastic domains, with Illich's foray into the world of St. Victor representing just one such attempt. Meanwhile, I propose that an adequate methodology of writing—and teaching writing—in the post-media college or university should begin by approaching research as remedial technique, in the many senses articulated throughout this book. To read and write on the computer is, following Hayles, to change or transform the circumstances under which readers and writers interact with words and other media objects. Techniques of textual remediation thereby change the discursive and productive relationships between readers and writers, writers and computers, and computers and readers, not to mention the larger cultural relationships between those who, in various ways, do either the right or the wrong work of textual production. Today's Web-based plagiarism detection machines already use remediation techniques to produce student texts toward the formulation of safe, healthy, and legitimate writing subjects. In today's institutions of higher learning, the time may have come to turn those techniques around—literally and figuratively—to better serve today's post-media, multimodal learners.

Notes

1. Marshall McLuhan most famously (*Understanding Media*, 1964), and more recently Paul Virilio (*Open Sky*, 1997 [1995]), Pierre Lévy (*Collective Intelligence*, 1997; *Cyberculture*, 2001 [1997]), Steven Johnson (*Interface Culture*, 1997), Jay David Bolter and Richard Grusin (*Remediation*, 1999), and Lev Manovich (*The Language of New Media*, 2001).

2. See Peter Charles Hoffer's book, *Past Imperfect: Facts, Fictions, Frauds—American History From Bancroft And Parkman To Ambrose, Bellisles, Ellis, And Goodwin*, for a more detailed critique of the Ambrose and Goodwin stories in the context of other misdeeds in the subdiscipline of U.S. history.

3. In fact, Ambrose's actual children, particularly his son Hugh, factor significantly in this story and are indeed used by Ambrose as agents of literary production.

4. The *MLA Handbook for Writers of Research Papers* (Gibaldi) characterizes the research paper assignment as an opportunity to learn how "to investigate, review, and productively use information, ideas, and opinions of other researchers" in formal academic writing. See pp. 3–6, in particular.

5. Connors is quoting Manly and Rickert's (1919) *The Writing of English*. See Zemliansky (chapter 8 in particular) for more on this textbook as an early-twentieth-century example of what Connors has called "current-traditional" rhetoric.

6. In this section, all page references to Illich refer to this text.

7. Elena Esposito makes a similar point in her recent article, "The Arts of Contingency," in which she describes "a foment of active experimentation" in textual production which predates the printing press by several centuries.

8. All page references refer to Screech, *The Essays of Michel de Montaigne*. York: Penguin, 1991.

9. The *Concise Oxford Dictionary* defines "cento" as a composition made up of quotations from other authors. Significantly, the term derives from the Latin word for "patchwork garment."

10. The relationship between writing and memory is well rehearsed in French poststructuralist theory as well. In "Linguistics and Grammatology" Derrida describes writing as a "mnemotechnic means" which, "supplanting good memory, spontaneous

memory, signifies forgetfulness" (*Grammatology* 37). He then traces this notion to the *Phaedrus*, in which Plato described writing, in Derrida's terms, as "the auxiliary aide-mémoire to the living memory" (37).

11. Most critical editions, including the one used here, record Montaigne's editorial changes over time in accordance with the following notation: A=1580, B=1588, and C=Bordeaux manuscript usually used for modern editions (see Brush 266).

12. Pavel Zemliansky provides multiple examples of other "nontraditional" research writing assignments. Here I focus on Ballenger's version in order to foreground the implicit if not explicit use of Montaigne and Renaissance rhetoric in twentieth-century composition pedagogy.

13. And Pierre Lévy. See in particular *Collective Intelligence* (1997), 71. Here Lévy uses the term *post-media* in discussing the particular mechanisms useful to a technologically enhanced "real-time democracy."

14. Teachers College at Columbia University and the City University of New York, respectively.

15. In May 2003, I conducted a database search for news articles addressing the issue of "Internet plagiarism" in higher education. Using ERIC (Educational Resources Information Center) and LexisNexis University News, and focusing on articles published since 1990 (ERIC) and since 1998 (LexisNexis), I found a total of forty-two records posted to Eric and 153 records (excluding duplicates) posted to LexisNexis University News (*The Chronicle of Higher Education* and University News Wire). The following discussion of Internet plagiarism and other cheating practices among college and university students derives largely from this research.

16. Donald McCabe is the center's founding president. Patrick Drinan, dean of arts and sciences at the University of San Diego, also served for a time as president.

17. For example, using specific rather than general writing topics, working more actively with students during the writing process (outlines, drafts), and using more in-class and fewer take-home exams.

18. Unless otherwise noted, all quoted material comes directly from the service's respective Web site as it appeared between July 2003 and November 2004. URLs: Glatt (http://plagiarism.com); EVE2 (http://www.canexus.com/eve/); Plagiarism-Finder (http://www.m4-software.de/); Turnitin (http://www.turnitin.com or http://www.plagiarism.org). For an earlier, more general analysis of these and other services, including the now-defunct Integriguard, see Buerger, 326–29.

19. For more on Taylor, the cloze procedure, and information theory more broadly, see chapter 4 in Griffin's *A First Look at Communication Theory* (McGraw-Hill, Inc.).

20. Rebecca Howard's article in the November 16, 2001, *Chronicle of Higher Education* ("Forget About Policing") is exemplary. Howard claims that in using sites such as Turnitin.com, teachers "risk becoming the enemies rather than the mentors" of their students and likewise risk "replacing the student-teacher relationship with the criminal-police relationship." While I agree generally with Howard's later claim that "our own pedagogy needs reform" in the area of plagiarism education, not to mention research

writing education more broadly, I balk at the suggestion that the "risk" factor goes up, as it were, with the use of plagiarism detection software in and of itself. I pursue this objection in greater detail in my conclusion.

21. Significantly, a third sample report, posted without the "Jon Doe" or "Jane Doe" bylines, derived from a submitted paper on the topic of schizophrenia. That report has also (since July 2003) been removed from the site.

22. A fourth service, Digital Portfolio (an "online archiving system" providing for "an authentic assessment of the learning experience"), has since folded.

23. The "about us" section of the site offers the following description of the corporate "team" and its mission: "The iParadigms team is a group of dedicated professionals that includes award-winning teachers, graphic designers, computer scientists, and business professionals working together to stop the spread of Internet plagiarism and promote new technologies in education."

24. As this book goes to press, the Turnitin site now reflects yet another transformation in its corporate appearance. The photographs are different (and now in full color), but the controlling theme, fetishizing educators and learners as consumers of well-ordered educational products, remains the same.

25. Some writing teachers have used Turnitin.com in a manner close to what I'm proposing broadly here, deploying student originality reports to demonstrate the explicit ways in which source-based writing enters into dialogic relation with sources quoted and cited.

Works Cited

Adams, Charles Francis, Edwin Lawrence Godkin, and George R. Nutter. "Report of the Committee on Composition and Rhetoric." 1897. *The Origins of Composition Studies in the American College, 1875–1925*. Ed. John C. Brereton. Pittsburgh: U of Pittsburgh P, 1995. 101–27.

Adams, Charles Francis, Edwin Lawrence Godkin, and Josiah Quincy. "Report of the Committee on Composition and Rhetoric." 1892. *The Origins of Composition Studies in the American College, 1875–1925*. Ed. John C. Brereton. Pittsburgh: U of Pittsburgh P, 1995. 73–100.

Adams, W. H. D. "Imitators and Plagiarists." *The Gentleman's Magazine* 272 (1892): 502–16, 613–28.

Ancekewicz, Elaine M. *The Critical Connection: The Question of History and the Essays of Michel de Montaigne*. New Orleans: UP of the South, 2002.

Appadurai, Arjun. "Introduction: Commodities and the Politics of Value." *The Social Life of Things: Commodities in Cultural Perspective*. Ed. Arjun Appadurai. Cambridge: Cambridge UP, 1986. 3–63.

Austin, Wendy Warren. "The Research Paper in Cyberspace: Source-Based Writing in the Composition Classroom." Diss. Indiana University of Pennsylvania, 2000.

Babbitt, Irving. *Literature and the American College: Essays in Defense of the Humanities*. 1908. Clifton: August M. Kelley, 1972.

Bakhtin, M. M. *The Dialogic Imagination*. Ed. Michael Holquist. Trans. Caryl Emerson and Michael Holquist. Austin: U of Texas P, 1982.

Baldwin, Charles Sears. *A College Manual of Rhetoric*. London: Longmans, Green, and Co., 1902.

Ballenger, Bruce. *Beyond Note Cards: Rethinking the Freshman Research Paper*. Portsmouth, NH: Boynton/Cook, 1999.

Barthes, Roland. *Image—Music—Text*. Trans. Stephen Heath. New York: Hill and Wang, 1977.

Becker, Howard S. *Art Worlds*. Berkeley: U of California P, 1982.

Beninger, James R. *The Control Revolution: Technological and Economic Origins of the Information Society.* Cambridge: Harvard UP, 1986.

Benson, E. F. "Plagiarism." *The Nineteenth Century* 46 (1899): 974–81.

Berkenkotter, Carol, and Thomas N. Huckin. *Genre Knowledge in Disciplinary Communication.* Hillsdale, NJ: Lawrence Erlbaum Associates, 1995.

Bizzell, Patricia. *Academic Discourse and Critical Consciousness.* Pittsburgh: U of Pittsburgh P, 1992.

Bledsoe, Biz. "Plagiarists Pay for Cheating." *Arizona Daily Wildcat* 19 Nov. 2002. Lexis-Nexis. U.C. San Diego Central Library. 8 Mar. 2003 <http://web.lexis-nexis.com>.

Bleich, David. "In Case of Fire, Throw In (What To Do With Textbooks Once You Switch to Sourcebooks)." *(Re)visioning Composition Textbooks.* Ed. Xin Liu Gale and Fredric G. Gale. Albany: State U of New York P, 1999. 15–42.

Bolter, Jay David, and Richard Grusin. *Remediation: Understanding New Media.* Cambridge: MIT Press, 1999.

Bousquet, Marc. "Composition As Management Science: Toward a University Without a WPA." *Journal of Advanced Composition* 22:3 (2002): 493–526.

Boyle, James. *Shamans, Software, and Spleens: Law and the Construction of the Information Society.* Cambridge: Harvard UP, 1996.

Brereton, John C., ed. *The Origins of Composition Studies in the American College, 1875–1925.* Pittsburgh: U of Pittsburgh P, 1995.

Brodkey, Linda. *Writing Permitted in Designated Areas Only.* Minneapolis: U of Minnesota P, 1996.

Brush, Craig B. *From the Perspective of the Self: Montaigne's Self-Portrait.* New York: Fordham UP, 1994.

Buerger, Geoffrey E. "The Owl and the Plagiarist: Academic Misrepresentation in Contemporary Education." Diss. Dalhousie University, 2002.

Buranen, Lise, and Alice M. Roy, eds. *Perspectives on Plagiarism and Intellectual Property in a Postmodern World.* Albany: State U of New York P, 1999.

Carbone, Nick. "Diving Into the Text: Rediscovering the Myths of Our Books." *New Worlds, New Words.* Ed. John F. Barber and Dene Grigar. Cresskill, NJ: Hampton Press, 2001. 233–50.

Carnevale, Dan. "Web Services Help Professors Detect Plagiarism." *The Chronicle of Higher Education* 12 Nov. 1999. Lexis-Nexis. U.C. San Diego Central Library. 6 Mar. 2003 <http://web.lexis-nexis.com>.

Catts, Tim. "Plagiarism on the Rise at Binghamton U." *Pipe Dream* 8 Sept.1998. Lexis-Nexis. U.C. San Diego Central Library. 8 Mar. 2003 <http://web.lexis-nexis.com>.

Cave, Terence. "Problems of Reading in the *Essais.*" *Michel de Montaigne.* Ed. Harold Bloom. New York: Chelsea House, 1987. 79–116.

Certeau, Michel de. *The Practice of Everyday Life.* Berkeley: U of California P, 1984.

Chouliaraki, Lilie, and Norman Fairclough. *Discourse in Late Modernity: Rethinking Critical Discourse.* Edinburgh: Edinburgh UP, 1999.

Connors, Robert. *Composition-Rhetoric: Backgrounds, Theory, and Pedagogy.* Pittsburgh: U of Pittsburgh P, 1997.

Coombe, Rosemary J. *The Cultural Life of Intellectual Properties: Authorship, Appropriation, and the Law.* Durham: Duke UP, 1998.

Cremin, Lawrence A. *The Transformation of the Schools: Progressivism in American Education, 1876–1957.* New York: Vintage, 1964.

Critical Art Ensemble. "Utopian Plagiarism, Hypertextuality, and Electronic Cultural Production." *Critical Issues in Electronic Media.* Ed. S. Penny. Albany: State U of New York P. 105–118.

Crowley, Sharon. *Composition in the University: Historical and Polemical Essays.* Pittsburgh: U of Pittsburgh P, 1998.

Derrida, Jacques. *Of Grammatology.* Trans. Gayatri Chakravorty Spivak. Baltimore: Johns Hopkins UP, 1976.

Desruisseaux, Paul. "Cheating Is Reaching Epidemic Proportions Worldwide, Researchers Say." *The Chronicle of Higher Education* 30 Apr. 1999. Lexis-Nexis. U.C. San Diego Central Library. 6 Mar. 2003 <http://web.lexis-nexis.com>.

Dewey, John. *The Child and the Curriculum.* 1902. Chicago: U of Chicago P, 1956.

———. *Democracy and Education.* New York: Macmillan, 1916.

———. *The School and Society.* 1900. Chicago: U of Chicago P, 1956.

Donaldson, Ian. "'The Fripperie of Wit': Jonson and Plagiarism." *Plagiarism in Early Modern England.* Ed. Paulina Kewes. Houndmills: Palgrave MacMillan, 2003. 119–33.

Eakin, Emily. "Stop, Historians! Don't Copy That Passage! Computers Are Watching." *New York Times.* 26 Jan 2002. Lexis-Nexis. U.C. San Diego Central Library. 9 Oct. 2002 <http://web.lexis-nexis.com>.

Eisenstein, Elizabeth. *The Printing Press as an Agent of Change: Communications and Cultural Transformations in Early-modern Europe.* Cambridge: Cambridge UP, 1979.

Eschbacher, Karen. "Internet Has Little Effect on Plagiarism, Experts Say." *The Daily Free Press* 10 Dec. 1998. Lexis-Nexis. U.C. San Diego Central Library. 8 Mar. 2003 <http://web.lexis-nexis.com>.

Esposito, Elena. "The Arts of Contingency." *Critical Inquiry* 31 (2004): 7–25.

Faigley, Lester. *Fragments of Rationality.* Pittsburgh: U of Pittsburgh P, 1992.

Fairclough, Norman, and Ruth Wodak. "Critical Discourse Analysis." *Discourse as Structure and Process.* Vol 1. Ed. Teun A. van Dijk. London: Sage, 1997. 258–84.

Foucault, Michel. *Discipline & Punish: The Birth of the Prison.* Trans. A. Sheridan. New York: Vintage, 1979.

————. *Power/Knowledge*. Ed. Colin Gordon. Trans. Colin Gordon, Leo Marshall, John Mephan, and Kate Soper. New York: Pantheon, 1980.

Fox Special Report With Brit Hume. Fox News Network. 23 Jan 2002. Transcript #012304cb.254. Lexis-Nexis. U.C. San Diego Central Library. 9 Oct. 2002 <http://web.lexis-nexis.com>.

Fresh Air. WHYY. 25 Feb 2002. Transcript. Lexis-Nexis. U.C. San Diego Central Library. 9 Oct. 2002 <http://web.lexis-nexis.com>.

Freire, Paulo. "Cultural Action and Conscientization." *Harvard Education Review* 40:3 (1970): 452–76.

Gale, Xin Liu, and Fredric G. Gale, eds. *(Re)Visioning Composition Textbooks*. Albany: State U of New York P, 1999.

Gee, James Paul. *An Introduction to Discourse Analysis: Theory and Method*. London: Routledge, 1999.

Gibaldi, Joseph. *MLA Handbook for Writers of Research Papers*. 6th ed. New York: The Modern Language Association of America, 2003.

Giovannetti, Chris. "Many Profs Don't Use Plagiarism Foil Available at San Jose State U." *Spartan Daily* 23 Oct. 2001. Lexis-Nexis. U.C. San Diego Central Library. 8 Mar. 2003 <http://web.lexis-nexis.com>.

Grazia, Margreta de. "Sanctioning Voice: Quotation Marks, the Abolition of Torture, and the Fifth Amendment." *The Construction of Authorship: Textual Appropriation in Law and Literature*. Ed. Martha Woodmansee and Peter Jaszi. Durham: Duke UP, 1994. 281–302.

Green, Stuart P. "Commentary; Historian Broke the Rules, but Is That So Bad?." *Los Angeles Times*. 13 Jan 2002. Lexis-Nexis. U.C. San Diego Central Library. 9 Oct. 2002 <http://web.lexis-nexis.com>.

Groom, Nick. *The Forger's Shadow*. London: Picador, 2002.

————. "Forgery, Plagiarism, Imitation, Pegleggery." *Plagiarism in Early Modern England*. Ed. Paulina Kewes. Houndmills: Palgrave MacMillan, 2003. 74–89.

Halbert, Debora. "Poaching and Plagiarizing: Property, Plagiarism, and Feminist Futures." *Perspectives on Plagiarism and Intellectual Property in a Postmodern World*. Ed. Lise Buranen and Alice M. Roy. Albany: State U of New York P, 1999. 111–20.

Hall, Michael L. "Montaigne's Uses of Classical Learning." *Journal of Education* 179:1 (1997): 61–97.

Hall, Stuart. "The Problem of Ideology: Marxism Without Guarantees." *Critical Dialogues in Cultural Studies*. Ed. David Morley and Kuan-Hsing Chen. London: Routledge, 1996. 25–46.

Hammond, Brean S. "Plagiarism: Hammond Versus Ricks." *Plagiarism in Early Modern England*. Ed. Paulina Kewes. Houndmills: Palgrave MacMillan, 2003. 41–55.

Harris, Joseph. *A Teaching Subject*. Upper Saddle River, NJ: Prentice-Hall, 1997.

Hart, John S. *A Manual of Composition and Rhetoric: A Text-book for Schools and Colleges.* Philadelphia: Eldredge and Brother, 1874.

Hauptman, Karen. "Improved Detection Cited in Rise of Plagiarism Cases." *The Chronicle* 5 Mar. 2003. Lexis-Nexis. U.C. San Diego Central Library. 6 Mar. 2003 <http://web.lexis-nexis.com>.

Hawhee, Debra. "Composition History and the *Harbrace College Handbook.*" *College Composition and Communication* 50:3 (1999): 504–23.

Hawisher, Gail E., and Cynthia L. Selfe, with Brittney Moraski and Melissa Pearson. "Becoming Literate in the Information Age: Cultural Ecologies and the Literacies of Technology." *College Composition and Communication* 55:4 (2004): 642–92.

Hawisher, Gail E., and Cynthia L. Selfe. *Critical Perspectives on Computers and Composition Instruction.* Columbia: Teachers College Press, 1989.

Hayles, N. Katherine. *Writing Machines.* Cambridge: MIT Press, 2002.

Hegel, G. W. F. *Elements of the Philosophy of Right.* Ed. Allen W. Wood. Trans. H. B. Nisbet. Cambridge: Cambridge UP, 1991.

"Historian Paid Off Angry Author." *Chicago Sun-Times.* 23 Jan. Lexis-Nexis. U.C. San Diego Central Library. 9 Oct. 2002 <http://web.lexis-nexis.com>.

Holmyard, E. J. *Alchemy.* Baltimore: Penguin, 1957.

Hopkins, Arthur John. *Alchemy Child of Greek Philosophy.* New York: AMS Press, 1967.

Howard, Rebecca Moore. "The Ethics of Plagiarism." *The Ethics of Writing Instruction: Issues in Theory and Practice.* Ed. Michael A. Pemberton. Stamford, CT: Ablex Publishing, 2000. 79–89.

———. "Forget About Policing Plagiarism. Just Teach." *The Chronicle Review* 16 Nov. 2001. Lexis-Nexis. U.C. San Diego Central Library. 6 Mar. 2003.

———. "The New Abolitionism Comes to Plagiarism." *Perspectives on Plagiarism and Intellectual Property in a Postmodern World.* Ed. Lise Buranen and Alice M. Roy. Albany: State U of New York P, 1999. 87–95.

———. "Plagiarisms, Authorships, and the Academic Death Penalty." *College English* 57 (1995): 788–805.

———. "Sexuality, Textuality: The Cultural Work of Plagiarism." *College English* 62:4 (2000): 473–91.

———. *Standing in the Shadow of Giants: Plagiarists, Authors, Collaborators.* Stamford, CT: Ablex Publishing, 1999.

Illich, Ivan. *In the Vineyard of the Text.* Chicago: U of Chicago P, 1993.

———. *Tools for Conviviality.* New York: Harper and Row, 1973.

James, William. *The Writings of William James.* Ed. John J. McDermott. New York: The Modern Library, 1967.

Jameson, Fredric. "Symptoms of Theory or Symptoms for Theory?" *Critical Inquiry* 30 (2004): 403–408.

Johnson, Steven. *Interface Culture: How New Technology Transforms the Way We Create and Communicate.* New York: Basic Books, 1997.

Kaplan, Nancy. "Literacy Beyond Books: Reading When All the World's a Web." *The World Wide Web and Contemporary Cultural Theory.* Ed. Andrew Herman and Thomas Swiss. New York: Routledge, 2000. 207–34.

Kaufer, David, and Cheryl Geisler. "Novelty in Academic Writing." *Written Communication* 6:3 (1989): 286–311.

Kellogg, Alex. P. "Students Plagiarize Online Less Than Many Think, a New Study Finds." *The Chronicle of Higher Education* 15 Feb. 2002. Lexis-Nexis. U.C. San Diego Central Library. 6 Mar. 2003.

Kewes, Paulina. *Plagiarism in Early Modern England.* Houndmills: Palgrave MacMillan, 2003.

Kirkpatrick, David. "2 Say Stephen Ambrose, Popular Historian, Copied Passages." *New York Times.* 5 Jan 2002. Lexis-Nexis. U.C. San Diego Central Library. 9 Oct. 2002 <http://web.lexis-nexis.com>.

———. "Author Admits He Lifted Lines from '95 Book." *New York Times.* 6 Jan 2002. Lexis-Nexis. U.C. San Diego Central Library. 9 Oct. 2002 <http://web.lexis-nexis.com>.

———. "Historian Says Publisher Quickly Settled Copying Dispute." *New York Times.* 23 Jan. 2002. Lexis-Nexis. U.C. San Diego Central Library. 9 Oct. 2002 <http://web.lexis-nexis.com>.

Kleine, Michael W. "Teaching from a Single Textbook 'Rhetoric': The Potential Heaviness of the Book." *(Re)Visioning Composition Textbooks.* Ed. Xin Liu Gale and Fredric G. Gale. Albany: State U of New York P, 1999. 137–61.

Lamb, Robyn. "High-Tech Plagiarism a Problem at U. Maryland." *The Diamondback* 11 Dec. 2000. Lexis-Nexis. U.C. San Diego Central Library. 8 Mar. 2003 <http://web.lexis-nexis.com>.

Larson, Andy. "Plagiarism.Org Web Site Deals With Growing Issue of Digital Cheating." *The California Aggie* 23 Feb. 2000. Lexis-Nexis. U.C. San Diego Central Library. 8 Mar. 2003 <http://web.lexis-nexis.com>.

Lévy, Pierre. *Collective Intelligence.* Trans. Robert Bononno. New York: Plenum Trade, 1977.

———. *Cyberculture.* Trans. Robert Bononno. Minneapolis: U of Minnesota P, 2001.

Lindey, Alexander. *Plagiarism and Originality.* Westport, CT: Greenwood Press, 1952.

Long, Pamela O. *Openness, Secrecy, Authorship: Technical Arts and the Culture of Knowledge From Antiquity to the Renaissance.* Baltimore: Johns Hopkins UP, 2001.

Love, Harold. "Originality and the Puritan Sermon." *Plagiarism in Early Modern England.* Ed. Paulina Kewes. Houndmills: Palgrave MacMillan, 2003. 149–65.

Loy, Brendan. "Web Site Attracts U. Southern California in Quest to Eradicate Plagiarism." *Daily Trojan* 21 Jan. 2000. Lexis-Nexis. U.C. San Diego Central Library. 8 Mar. 2003 <http://web.lexis-nexis.com>.

Lunsford, Andrea. "Foreword: Who Owns Language?" *Perspectives on Plagiarism and Intellectual Property in a Postmodern World.* Ed. Lise Buranen and Alice M. Roy. Albany: State U of New York P, 1999. ix–xii.

Lunsford, Andrea A. "Refiguring Classroom Authority." *The Ethics of Writing Instruction: Issues in Theory and Practice.* Ed. M. A. Pemberton. Stamford, CT: Ablex Publishing, 2000. 65–78.

Lüthy, Herbert. "Montaigne, or the Art of Being Truthful." *Michel de Montaigne.* Ed. Harold Bloom. New York: Chelsea House, 1987. 11–28.

Mallon, Thomas. *Stolen Words: Forays Into the Origins and Ravages of Plagiarism.* New York: Penguin, 1989.

Manovich, Lev. *The Language of New Media.* Cambridge: MIT Press, 2002.

———. "New Media from Borges to HTML." *The New Media Reader.* Ed. Noah Wardrip-Fruin and Nick Montfort. Cambridge: MIT Press, 2003. 13–25.

Marchi, Dudley M. *Montaigne Among the Moderns: Receptions of the Essais.* Providence: Berghahn Books, 1994.

Marsden, George M. *Fundamentalism and American Culture.* Oxford: Oxford UP, 1980.

McCabe, Donald L., and Patrick Drinan. "Toward a Culture of Academic Integrity." *The Chronicle of Higher Education* 15 Oct. 1999. Lexis-Nexis. U.C. San Diego Central Library. 6 Mar. 2003.

McLuhan, Marshall. *Understanding Media: The Extensions of Man.* New York: Signet, 1964.

McMasters, Joy. "Web Service Aims to Prevent Use of Internet for Plagiarizing Papers." *Daily Bruin* 16 Feb. 2000. Lexis-Nexis. U.C. San Diego Central Library. 8 Mar. 2003 <http://web.lexis-nexis.com>.

Mead, George Herbert. *On Social Psychology.* Ed. Anselm Strauss. Chicago and London: U of Chicago P, 1934.

Micciche, Laura R. "More Than a Feeling; Disappointment and WPA Work." *College English* 64:4 (2002): 432–58.

Miller, Susan. *Textual Carnivals: The Politics of Composition.* Carbondale, IL: Southern Illinois UP, 1991.

Montaigne, Michel. *The Essays of Michel de Montaigne.* Trans. and Ed. M. A. Screech. New York: Penguin, 1991.

"More Questions Raised Over Ambrose's Books." *Los Angeles Times.* 10 Jan 2002. Lexis-Nexis. U.C. San Diego Central Library. 9 Oct. 2002 <http://web.lexis-nexis.com>.

Mueller, Nick. "U. Iowa Tests Online Plagiarism Police." *The Daily Iowan* 9 Oct. 2002. Lexis-Nexis. U.C. San Diego Central Library. 8 Mar. 2003 <http://web.lexis-nexis.com>.

Mulhern, James. *A History of Education: A Social Interpretation.* New York: The Ronald Press Company, 1959.

Nelson, Theodor H. "From *Computer Lib / Dream Machines.*" In *The New Media Reader.* Ed. Noah Wardrip-Fruin and Nick Montfort. Cambridge: MIT Press, 2003 (1974). 301–38.

The NewsHour with Jim Lehrer. PBS. 28 Jan 2002. Transcript #7254. Lexis-Nexis. U.C. San Diego Central Library. 9 Oct. 2002 <http://web.lexis-nexis.com>.

Nowakowski, Xan. "Columbia U. Declines Plagiarism-Catching Technology." *Columbia Daily Spectator* 9 Nov. 2001. Lexis-Nexis. U.C. San Diego Central Library. 8 Mar. 2003.

Oliphant, David J. "No Justification for Plagiarism (Letter to the Editor)." *Los Angeles Times.* 17 Jan 2002. Lexis-Nexis. U.C. San Diego Central Library. 9 Oct. 2002 <http://web.lexis-nexis.com>.

Orgel, Stephen. "Plagiarism and Original Sin." *Plagiarism in Early Modern England.* Ed. Paulina Kewes. Houndmills: Palgrave MacMillan, 2003. 56–73.

Owens, Derek. "Essay." *Keywords in Composition Studies.* Ed. Paul Heilker and Peter Vandenberg. Portsmouth, NH: Boynton/Cook, 1996. 85–88.

Palumbo, Roberta M. "Montaigne in the Composition Class." *College Composition and Communication* 24 (1978): 382–84.

Papert, Seymour. "From *Mindstorms: Children, Computers, and Powerful Ideas.*" *The New Media Reader.* Ed. Noah Wardrip-Fruin and Nick Montfort. Cambridge: MIT Press, 2003 (1980). 413–32.

Perrin, Robert. *Handbook for College Research.* Second Edition. Boston: Houghton Mifflin, 2002.

"The Plagiarism Racket." *The Nation* 129 (1929). N. pag.

Price, Margaret. "Beyond 'Gotcha!': Situating Plagiarism in Policy and Pedagogy." *College Composition and Communication* 54:1 (2002): 88–115.

Randall, Marilyn. *Pragmatic Plagiarism: Authorship, Profit, and Power.* Toronto: U of Toronto P, 2001.

Readings, Bill. *The University in Ruins.* Cambridge: Harvard UP, 1996.

Richardson, Eudora Ramsay. "The Ubiquitous Plagiarist." *Readings in Present-Day Writers.* Ed. Raymond Woodbury Pence. New York: MacMillan, 1933 (1931). 323–30.

Richardson, Lisa. "Plagiarism and Imitation in Renaissance Historiography." *Plagiarism in Early Modern England.* Ed. Paulina Kewes. Houndmills: Palgrave MacMillan, 2003. 106–18.

Ricks, Christopher. "Plagiarism." *Plagiarism in Early Modern England.* Ed. Paulina Kewes. Houndmills: Palgrave MacMillan, 2003 (1998). 21–40.

Schemo, Diana Jean. "Many on Campuses Disdain Historian's Practice." *New York Times.* 15 Jan 2002. Lexis-Nexis. U.C. San Diego Central Library. 9 Oct. 2002 <http://web.lexis-nexis.com>.

Shklar, Judith N. *American Citizenship: The Quest for Inclusion.* Cambridge: Harvard UP, 1991.

Simmons, Sue Carter. "Competing Notions of Authorship: A Historical Look at Students and Textbooks on Plagiarism and Cheating." *Perspectives on Plagiarism and Intellectual Property in a Postmodern World*. Ed. Lise Buranen and Alice M. Roy. Albany: State U of New York P, 1999. 41–51.

Spellmeyer, Kurt. "A Common Ground: The Essay in the Academy." *College English* 51:3 (1989): 262–76.

Spellmeyer, Kurt. "The Great Way: Reading and Writing in Freedom." *(Re)Visioning Composition Textbooks*. Ed. Xin Liu Gale and Fredric G. Gale. Albany: State University of New York Press, 1999. 45–68.

Stearns, Laurie. "Copy Wrong: Plagiarism, Process, Property, and the Law." *Perspectives on Plagiarism and Intellectual Property in a Postmodern World*. Ed. Lise Buranen and Alice M. Roy. Albany: State U of New York P, 1999. 5–17.

Strickland, Donna. "Taking Dictation: The Emergence of Writing Programs and the Cultural Contradictions of Composition Teaching. *College English* 63:4 (2001): 457–79.

Taylor, Warner. "A National Survey of Conditions in Freshman English." *The Origins of Composition Studies in the American College, 1875–1925*. Ed. John C. Brereton. Pittsburgh: U of Pittsburgh P, 1995 (1929). 545–62.

Trupe, Alice L. "Academic Literacy in a Wired World: Redefining Genres for College Writing Courses." *Kairos: A Journal for Teachers of Writing* 7:2 (2002). 15 Nov. 2002 <http://english.ttu.edu/kairos/7.2/binder.html?/sectionone/trupe/ WiredWorld.htm>.

Virilio, Paul. *Open Sky*. Trans. Julie Rose. London: Verso, 1997.

Williams, Raymond. "Base and Superstructure in Marxist Cultural Theory." *Rethinking Popular Culture: Perspectives in Cultural Studies*. Ed. Chandra Mukerji and Michael Schudson. Berkeley: U of California P, 1991 (1980). 407–23.

Williamson, Rachael. "Study Shows 25 Percent of Students Plagiarize." *Cornell Daily Sun*. 18 Feb. 2003. Lexis-Nexis. U.C. San Diego Central Library. 8 Mar. 2003 <http://web.lexis-nexis.com>.

Woodmansee, Martha, and Peter Jaszi, eds. *The Construction of Authorship: Textual Appropriation in Law and Literature*. Durham: Duke UP, 1994.

Woodmansee, Martha. "On the Author Effect: Recovering Collectivity." *The Construction of Authorship: Textual Appropriation in Law and Literature*. Ed. Martha Woodmansee and Peter Jaszi. Durham: Duke UP, 1994. 16–28.

Yood, Jessica. "Writing the Discipline: A Generic History of English Studies. *College English*, 65:5 (2003): 526–40.

Zemliansky, Pavel. "Genuine Training in Academic Discourse or an Artificial Construct?: Reconsidering the Past, Present, and Future of the College Research Paper." Diss. Florida State University, 2002.

Index

171